Social Stratification

SOCIOLOGICAL STUDIES 1

Social Stratification

EDITED BY

J. A. JACKSON

Senior Lecturer in Sociology
University of East Anglia

CAMBRIDGE
AT THE UNIVERSITY PRESS
1968

Published by the Syndics of the Cambridge University Press
Bentley House, 200 Euston Road, London N.W.1
American Branch: 32 East 57th Street, New York, N.Y.10022

Library of Congress Catalogue Card Number: 68 26986
Standard Book Number: 521 07338 3

Printed in Great Britain
at the University Printing House, Cambridge
(Brooke Crutchley, University Printer)

EDITOR'S PREFACE

Sociological Studies is a new international annual which is intended to review a number of different aspects of contemporary sociology. Contributors will be particularly concerned to consider the present state of the theoretical concepts and the research methods available in the study of different topics of sociological interest. Each volume will be devoted to a specific theme. The next two volumes will be on 'Migration' (1969) and 'Professions and Professionalization' (1970).

Norwich　　　　　　　　　　　　　　　J. A. J.
January 1968

CONTENTS

CONTRIBUTORS

M. ABRAMS
Director, Research Services Ltd., London

E. ALLARDT
Professor of Sociology, University of Helsinki

L. BROOM
Professor of Sociology, Australian National University, Canberra

S. N. EISENSTADT
Professor of Sociology, Hebrew University, Jerusalem

F. FÜRSTENBERG
Professor of Sociology, Institute for Sociology, Linz

F. LANCASTER JONES
Fellow in Sociology, Australian National University, Canberra

W. G. RUNCIMAN

E. SHILS
Professor of Social Thought, University of Chicago, and Fellow of King's College, Cambridge

K. SŁOMCZYŃSKI
Lecturer in Sociology, University of Łódź

W. WESOŁOWSKI
Professor of Sociology, University of Łódź

J. ZUBRZYCKI
Professorial Fellow in Sociology, Australian National University, Canberra

I

EDITORIAL INTRODUCTION—
SOCIAL STRATIFICATION

JOHN A. JACKSON

This volume is devoted to the broad, but central, theme of social stratification. That all societies and, indeed, all social groupings are in some measure stratified is not in question. The strata are, at one level, maintained as the result of individual recognitions and responses, acts of deference and superiority, by which social position is tenuously preserved. The crystallization of the different elements of stratification may, as has been exemplified by Weber and his successors, be considered in relation to at least three areas or arenas—power, status and class. These in turn reveal complex problems of identification, access, consolidation, participation and demonstration of the attributes considered appropriate to each area—quite apart from the inter-relationship between them. The establishment of these dimensions of stratification may themselves give rise to further considerations of relative advantage and disadvantage, 'relative deprivation' as Runciman[1] has described it, and differential attainment of those elements of 'power and privilege' which may be prized in any particular society.

The lack of uniformity in society, the existence of 'all sorts and conditions of men' has provided a central thread in the development of thinking about society. The distinctions between citizen and slave, between seigneur and serf, between master and servant, between those fit to govern and those fit to be governed, between king and commoner, between bourgeois and proletarian have been essential components of both conservative and radical social thought. These divisions are just as necessary a part of the structural analysis of society by St Thomas Aquinas as they are to that of Marx. The argument turns round their form and function.

The study of social stratification has produced an extensive theoretical discussion as well as a rich variety of empirical evidence. It is clear, however, that the description of particular stratification systems is an immensely complex task in which a variety of overlapping and subtly interwoven factors must be considered. Both the conceptual framework and the empirical tools employed need continual development and

[1] W. G. Runciman, *Relative Deprivation and Social Justice* (London 1966).

assessment. The investigator in this field must not merely measure and analyse the characteristic pattern of stratification within a given society. He must also endeavour to assess its meaning within the broad social processes of the society. As he breaks down the varieties and components of the stratification system and the different conceptualizations of it that are held he must attempt to disentangle precise terminological meanings. Having established indices of stratification he must validate their utility as measures of real or imagined 'situation' more or less crystallized and more or less related to other sets of 'situations' in terms of the extent to which they attract deference, give similar or different life-chances, have differential access to, or differentially utilize, power.

Three main areas may be distinguished in the attempt to describe social stratification. The first is the delineation and description of the forms and elements of stratification. Here the tradition which has developed through the work of Marx and Weber has contributed most to both the definition of class and the distinctions between class, status and power structures.

The second concerns the way in which the different strata, as well as the components of the different elements of stratification systems, are arranged and articulated with each other. It is here that the analysis of the function of stratification and its relation to the division of labour has made its most valuable contribution, whether from the more static analysis of 'functionalist' sociology or the more dynamic analysis of social change implied in Marxist, and other, 'conflict' theories.

The third area involves the question of access to and participation in the various strata. This in turn opens up numerous avenues of inquiry into social mobility and life chances as well as the broader questions of the degree of 'openness' or 'closedness' which exists within any particular social system.

These three areas can rarely be explored in isolation. It is, indeed, one of the consequences of the centrality of social stratification that it relates to every aspect of social analysis and research. In almost every study it will appear as a variable which is considered significant by the investigator although the range of definitions which it is given tend all too often to mean that the concept of 'class' becomes a rag-bag, the contents of which are often jumbled together indiscriminately. The measures used by investigators to assess 'class position' are now considerably refined and it is possible to indicate the effects of variables such as occupational position and class position with considerable accuracy. These methods, however, must remain only so good as the conceptual assumptions which lie behind them and it is here that the uncertainties of definition and delineation appear much greater. The difficulties, even in a relatively static analysis, of securing a base which is not itself subject to unknown shifts, appear to be great even if one takes a fairly objective and verifiable factor such as occupation.[1] The more ephemeral factors such as those subjectively evaluated in terms of social position, status or power are clearly far more difficult to define sufficiently exactly to allow precise measurements to be made. Nevertheless the attempt must be made in order to arrive at an adequate means of describing the web of relationships and their stratified patterning in society.

If these matters are difficult within any particular social system they, of course, become immeasurably more so when attempts are made to compare stratification patterns in different societies with different economic structures. Even within any particular society difficulties arise, particularly when an attempt is made at clarifying primary producers such as farmers in a stratification system based on industrial occupational categories. This is quite apart from the problems involved in categorizing dependent sectors of the population such as the old, the young, and married women (who may or may not continue working during marriage). Even in Britain, which has the highest proportion of its economically active males earning wages and salaries (90 % in 1950), there are difficulties in classifying those who lie outside this work force. With significantly lower percentages of wage and salary earners in countries such as Egypt (44 %) or Pakistan (16 %) the problem is clearly much greater.[2]

Occupation is only one of the criteria of social stratification, however. Its significance is clearly twofold because it relates to an economic relationship with the means of production but also defines a work-situation which will in turn have consequences on both the consciousness of class identity and also will help to define patterns of status estimation and attitude to the stratification system both within and outside the work-situation. It serves to demonstrate the kind of problems which must be faced if some more adequate framework for discussion is to be found for the dynamic and comparative treatment of stratification in society.

The changes which have been taking place in industrialized societies suggest that both the Marxian and the functionalist theories are inappropriate for the analysis of the competing interests of power élites in a situation where access to power is not necessarily dependent upon either the ownership of property or the 'value' of the performance of needed tasks to the society. The managerial component in industry, in

[1] For two valuable discussions of the question of change in occupational structure see Otis Dudley Duncan, 'Methodological issues in the analysis of social mobility', pp. 51–97 and Wilbert E. Moore, 'Changes in occupational structure', pp. 194–212, both in Neil Smelser and Seymour Martin Lipset (eds.), *Social Structure and Mobility in Economic Development* (London, 1966).

[2] Moore, 'Changes in occupational structure', p. 211. These figures are taken from the table compiled by Moore from the United Nations *Statistical Yearbook* (New York, 1955).

particular, introduces new criteria for social differentiation and the manipulation of power which are not readily defined by either of these theories. The borderlines between working class and middle class have already been explored by Lockwood and his colleagues.[1] Their work raises important questions about the character of the divisions them- selves and the extent to which contemporary 'privatization' among the so-called 'affluent workers' represents not so much *embourgeoisment* which these authors discount, as emancipation, or perhaps withdrawal, from the traditional divisions by which class position and identity have been defined. A similar disassociation from traditional patterns is also observ- able in the apparent shifts of political commitment and patterns of voting in this group.

However, Lockwood[2] has, himself, provided a very necessary correc- tive to the assumption that these phenomena, among a small proportion of workers who are well paid, represents, in any real way, 'the working class'. 'The comparison between the "new" and the "old" must guard against the mistake of comparing the most prosperous and least socially distinctive sections of the working class of today with the least prosperous and most socially distinctive sections of the working class yesterday.'[3]

In the same paper Lockwood refers to the different dimensions of class crystallization that must be taken into account to gain a clear picture of what is happening. Apart from work, life in the family and participation in community social activities are likely to provide the main arenas where a man can see how he is treated by others. On the basis of the treatment he receives he is likely to define not only his aspirations but also his attitudes and expectations.

A refreshing approach to this problem of individual participation in social stratification processes is suggested by Berger and Luckmann.[4] They comment on the consequences for personal identity of what they call a 'relatively fluid' stratification system in which some divorce has occurred between the traditionally associated components of class, status and power. The consequences for the individual actor are to be measured in the attempts made by individuals to assess their own position *vis-à-vis* that of others in a like, but different status. Such subjective evaluations as these may operate in relation to aspects of class or status or power independently or in varying degrees of association. The evaluation of these 'dislocations' and new crystallizations may be one of the most fruit- ful means of explaining the dynamics of social stratification in the future.

---

[1] D. Lockwood, *The Blackcoated Worker* (London, 1958); J. H. Goldthorpe, *et al.* 'The affluent worker', *Sociology*, I (January 1967), 11–39.

[2] D. Lockwood, 'The new working class', *European Journal of Sociology* (1960), pp. 248–59.

[3] *Ibid.* p. 251.

[4] P. Berger and T. Luckmann, 'Social mobility and personal identity', *European Journal of Sociology*, v, 2 (1964), 331–44.

II

In his 1953–54 trend report on 'Social Stratification', Donald MacRae cited T. H. Marshall's dictum that sociology was in danger of turning too much to either the stars (vast generalization) or to the sand (minute empiricism) and expressed the fear that in the field of stratification studies had all too often wallowed in the quicksand.[1] The intervening period since 1954 has certainly added enormously to the wealth of detailed empirical study but it has also, and particularly in the last few years, yielded a number of important contributions that lie at least 'in orbit' somewhere between stars and sand.

In both the 'conflict' and the 'functionalist' traditions there has been a discernible move away from ideological presuppositions and a consequent emphasis, not merely on the minutiae of empirical analysis but on the fundamental components of stratification systems themselves. Some important signposts of this shift should be mentioned here. The debate initiated in the United States by Kingsley Davis and Wilbert E. Moore's paper 'Some Principles of Stratification'[2] which appeared in 1945 has continued and has been sustained and developed both by its proponents and its critics. A recent book which appeared at the end of 1967 by Tumin, one of the original critics, continued the debate, although not, I believe, introducing any new elements to it.[3] Tumin argues persuasively against those defences of the functionalist stratification model which have been established on the basis of differential sacrifices deserving differential rewards. He claims that this argument does not hold up since 'prolonged training periods (are) important and gratifying advantages enjoyed by a small élite: chances to have their minds and sensibilities trained, their tastes refined and their perspectives enlarged.'[4] It is less easy, on the other hand, to go along with his main conclusion that since the results of unequal evaluating and rewarding are mixed it is desirable to abandon it in favour of some undefined alternative. One suspects that what is needed to give greater force to his model is a classification of the distinction between objective stratification—distribution of prestige, rewards, power and status in society and the framework of values (evaluation)—within which it is operated.

It may be presumptuous and even unfair to make the suggestion that the debate itself may prove ultimately more interesting to the historian of social thought for its characteristics as a measure of development

[1] D. G. MacRae, 'Social stratification: a trend report and bibliography', *Current Sociology*, No. 1 (1953–4), p. 13.
[2] Kingsley Davis and Wilbert E. Moore, 'Some principles of stratification', *American Sociological Review*, 10 (April 1945), pp. 242–9.
[3] Melvin M. Tumin, *Social Stratification: the Forms and Functions of Inequality*, New Jersey: Englewood Cliffs, 1967.   [4] *Ibid.* p. 110.

within American sociology as a whole than for any fresh contributions that it has made to the study of stratification as such. One can see in the papers of Davis,[1] Moore,[2] and their critics Tumin,[3] Wrong,[4] Buckley,[5] Simpson,[6] Wesołowski,[7] and Parsons[8] the modification of the earlier functionalist position as increasingly both structural and comparative factors necessitated changing the context in which the debate was continued. I believe that one has here one of those examples of ideological commitment already referred to in which the particular blinkers worn by a group of sociologists prevented them from looking squarely at the myths by which their position was supported and to which it has given weight. Much of the demythologization has been carried out by those who have examined some of the factors on which assumptions about the 'efficient division of labour' principle of functionalist theory was based. In particular, Lipset and Bendix's *Social Mobility in Industrial Society*[9] and Smelser and Lipset's *Social Structure and Mobility in Economic Development*[10] do much to break down the rather static idea of an 'open society' functionally arranging itself in convenient and ordered ranks.

In the case of the 'conflict' approach new dimensions have been developed in the important work of Dahrendorf, *Class and Class Conflict in Industrial Society*,[11] and this has influenced writers concerned with aspects of class awareness and class consciousness. Ossowski,[12] Wesołowski[13] and others in Poland have continued a discussion carried further by Wesołowski's paper in this volume of the relevance of either Marxist or Western 'free enterprise' stratification models to socialist societies.

[1] Kingsley Davis, 'The abominable heresy: a reply to Dr Buckley', *American Sociological Review*, 24 (February 1959), pp. 82–3. See also Kingsley Davis, *Human Society* (New York, 1949), especially pp. 366–78, which is a considerably revised version of the theory.

[2] Wilbert E. Moore, 'But some are more equal than others', *American Sociological Review*, 28 (1 February 1963), pp. 13–18.

[3] Melvin M. Tumin, 'Some principles of stratification: a critical analysis,' *American Sociological Review*, 18 (August 1953), pp. 378–94.

[4] Dennis H. Wrong, 'The functional theory of stratification: some neglected considerations', *American Sociological Review*, 24 (December 1959), pp. 772–82.

[5] William Buckley, 'Social stratification and the functional theory of social differentiation', *American Sociological Review*, 23, 3 (1959), pp. 369–75.

[6] Richard L. Simpson, 'A modification of the functional theory of social stratification', *Social Forces*, 35 (December 1956), pp. 132–7.

[7] Włodzimierz Wesołowski, 'Some notes on the functional theory of stratification' in R. Bendix and S. M. Lipset (eds.), *Class, Status and Power*, 2nd edition (New York, 1966), pp. 64–8.

[8] Talcott Parsons, 'A revised analytical approach to the theory of social stratification' in R. Bendix and S. M. Lipset, *op. cit.* pp. 92–128.

[9] S. M. Lipset and R. Bendix, *Social Mobility in Industrial Society* (Berkeley, 1959).

[10] N. J. Smelser and S. M. Lipset, *Social Structure and Mobility in Economic Development* (London, 1966).

[11] Ralf Dahrendorf, *Class and Class Conflict in Industrial Society* (Stanford, 1959).

[12] S. Ossowski, *Class Structure in the Social Consciousness* (London, 1963).

[13] W. Wesołwski, 'Changes in the class structure in Poland', in J. Wiatr (ed.), *Studies in Polish Political System* (Warsaw, 1967), pp. 33–80.

The emphasis of both traditions has increasingly turned toward the problem of meaning and definition of the stratification model employed and the relationship between its parts. The idea of plural stratification consisting of overlapping stratification systems within any given society has become increasingly accepted in both the analysis of less developed and 'modern' societies. Hoselitz[1] has discussed the interaction between 'pre-industrial' and 'industrial' stratification systems and a somewhat similar theme is developed in the community study by Stacey where status evaluation took place in two dimensions, one 'total' and one 'local'.[2] Lockwood in developing this argument has underlined the generality of these localized systems of status evaluation in industrial groupings such as mining communities.[3] One would also expect this to apply to ethnic differences. All of these arguments are concerned to demonstrate the failure of 'holistic' stratification models to act as an adequate analytical tool for the analysis of stratification within complex societies.

Doubt has also been thrown on the extent to which traditional stratification models can be made to apply to new and rapidly changing social situations. It has been suggested by a number of writers that there is a tendency for society to increasingly merge into one great middle class. Porter[4] in his important book on Canada, for instance, considers this view in some detail and it is also taken up under the general heading of 'embourgeoisment'. That this view is not supported by the facts is the main case of those concerned to stress the continuation of deprived classes of poor within apparently prosperous and 'aggregated' societies. Harrington in his work on the poor in the United States,[5] Matza[6] and in England writers such as Wedderburn,[7] Townsend,[8] Abel-Smith[9] and Titmuss,[10] have all been concerned to show how little inequalities have been diminished or wealth distributed as the result of apparently egalitarian 'Welfare State' measures, let alone the process of industrialization itself.

Stimulated largely by David Lockwood's *The Blackcoated Worker*, attention has been increasingly paid to the transitional processes of

[1] Bert F. Hoselitz, 'Interaction between industrial and pre-industrial stratification systems', in Neil J. Smelser and Seymour M. Lipset, *op. cit.* pp. 177–93.
[2] Margaret Stacey, *Tradition and Change* (London, 1960).
[3] David Lockwood, 'Sources of variation in working class images of society', *Sociological Review* (November 1966), pp. 249–67. Fürstenburg adds support to this in his paper in the present volume.
[4] John Porter, *The Vertical Mosaic* (Toronto, 1965).
[5] Michael Harrington, *The Other America* (London, 1963).
[6] David Matza, 'The disreputable poor', in N. Smelser and S. M. Lipset, *op. cit.* pp. 310–39.
[7] Dorothy Cole Wedderburn, 'Poverty in Britain today—the evidence', *Sociological Review*, x, 3 (November 1962), pp. 257–82.
[8] Peter Townsend, 'The meaning of poverty', *British Journal of Sociology*, xiii, 3, pp. 210–27.
[9] B. Abel-Smith and Peter Townsend, *The Poor and the Poorest* (London, 1965).
[10] R. M. Titmuss, *Income Distribution and Social Change* (London, 1962).

social mobility and in particular the question of the move from the working class to the middle class. The theme of 'embourgeoisment' defended by writers such as Zweig[1] who argued for a process of increasing 'assimilation' of workers into an expanded middle class has been attacked by Lockwood and Goldthorpe, whose own research has done much to substantiate their view. Their work has placed increasing emphasis on the concept of 'work situation' and its influence on the attitudes of workers. They have introduced the concept of 'privatization' to describe the apparent effects of what one might call 'deproletarianization' among workers.[2]

Such studies of the working class and its redefinition and demarcation have been matched by a number of important contributions on the middle class. Both Odaka[3] and Vogel[4] as well as Dore[5] have provided a valuable analysis of a rapidly changing middle class pattern in Japan. In Britain and the U.S.A. such studies have tended to concentrate more on what has come to be considered the core determinant of middle class position—professionalization. There have been a number of papers in the American journals of which Wilensky's 'The Professionalization of Everyone?'[6] provides a valuable guide and raises in a new form the question of the possibility of the merging of society into one large 'professionally qualified' middle class.

Similar themes have been pursued in Britain by Halmos,[7] Young[8] and in a number of studies of professional organization such as those of Prandy,[9] Millerson,[10] Abel Smith and Stevens[11] among others.

Increasingly the role of the middle class and élitist groups in developing societies are claiming attention both in terms of recruitment to their number and their consolidation within the social structure. Of a number of studies that have appeared in the last few years that edited by Lipset and Solari[12] on Latin America and that edited by P. C. Lloyd[13] on Africa give an indication of the range of this material.

[1] F. Zweig, *The Worker in an Affluent Society* (London, 1961).
[2] The first two substantive reports on this research are: J. Goldthorpe *et al. The Affluent Worker: Industrial Attitudes and Behaviour* (Cambridge, 1968); and D. Lockwood *et al. The Affluent Worker: Political Attitudes and Behaviour* (Cambridge, 1968).
[3] Kunio Odaka, *The Middle Class in Japan*, Contribution to the meetings of the Stratification and Social Mobility Research Committee, Sixth World Congress of Sociology (Evian, 1966).
[4] Ezra Vogel, *Japan's New Middle Class* (Berkeley, 1963).
[5] R. P. Dore, *Social Change in Modern Japan* (Princeton, 1966).
[6] Harold L. Wilensky, 'The Professionalization of Everyone?', *American Journal of Sociology*, LXX, 2 (September 1964), pp. 137–58.
[7] Paul Halmos, *The Personal Service Society* (London, 1967).
[8] Michael Young, *The Rise of the Meritocracy* (London, 1961).
[9] Kenneth Prandy, *Professional Employees* (London, 1965).
[10] G. Millerson, *The Qualifying Associations* (London, 1964).
[11] B. Abel-Smith and R. Stevens, *Lawyers and the Courts* (London, 1966).
[12] S. M. Lipset and Aldo Solari, *Elites in Latin America* (London, 1967).
[13] P. C. Lloyd (ed.), *New Elites in Tropical Africa* (London, 1966).

Another related aspect of the study of stratification has been its effects on the structure of politics and political action. Here again Lipset[1] has made an important contribution in relation to the congruence of political attitudes and behaviour to class position and the theme has been developed more recently by Lipset in a paper on the 'Changing Class Structure and Contemporary European Politics'.[2]

It is only possible here in a short introduction to the theme of social stratification to indicate some of the more important 'growth points' which suggest both the basis on which future research can be based and also suggest some of the themes which are taken up and developed in the present volume. Before we turn to the present set of papers, however, two further important developments must be noted.

The first is the development, especially in the United States, of the study of status congruence and status crystallization. This theme developed in terms of the extent to which particular status determinants such as 'occupation' define patterns of social relations in other spheres of social activity is discussed fully in the paper by Wesołowski and Słomczynski. It is also very relevant to Fürstenberg's paper and to the paper by Broom, Lancaster Jones and Zubrzycki. Broadly expressed this approach involves the relationship between objective factors such as occupation or income and subjective assessments of status and the distribution of attitudes. Employing social distance measures of prestige a recent study by Laumann[3] along these lines both summarizes previous American material and suggests useful features of subjective social distance in an urban setting.

The second development is pointed up by the extent to which common ground can be found between many of these studies in Western 'post-capitalist' societies and the socialist societies of Eastern Europe. When viewed from the point of view of the effect of the stratification system on the pattern of social relations it is clear that the ideological overtones of concepts such as 'classlessness' or 'egalitarianism' can usefully give way to studies of the extent of status congruence in a comparative context. Increasingly in both old and new states the growth of the 'organized section of the work-force'—e.g. that in a socialized sector or in a similar large-scale enterprise—may influence the extent to which status attributes in different sectors are related to occupational skills and income levels. These 'social values', as Wesołowski and Słomczynski define them, are increasingly the determining factors of a stratified pattern of social relationships. Although the effects of restratification

---

[1] S. M. Lipset, *Political Man* (New York, 1960)—especially Chapter IV: 'Working-class authoritarianism.'
[2] *Daedalus* (Winter 1964), pp. 271–303.
[3] Edward O. Laumann, *Prestige and Association in an Urban Community* (New York, 1966).

along these lines, associated with a process of destratification in the private sectors, may be more obvious in a society undergoing a planned social revolution as well as industrialization, the process is matched to a considerable degree in other industrialized or industrializing societies in which the 'social values' already referred to and their distribution have increasing relevance to both national interest and development. The studies presently being undertaken in Eastern Europe can provide important evidence of the ways in which established patterns of social stratification may be modified and the effects which such modification is likely to have. Although it is the work of Polish sociologists which is most widely known outside the socialist countries themselves—and a recent comprehensive volume, *Studies in Polish Political System*,[1] suggests the different dimensions in which their work has developed—there are also a considerable number of valuable studies in different areas of stratification in a number of other socialist countries. A recent bibliography prepared at the Institut für Wirtschaftswissenschaften der Deutschen Akademie der Wissenschaften zu Berlin (D.D.R.) of works on the theme 'Die Sozialstruktur in den sozialistischen Ländern' includes 190 titles published between 1960 and 1967 and this appears to be only a partial list. It excludes, for instance, a number of important works published toward the end of 1967 such as Helmut Steiner's study (based on secondary sources) of social classes in West Germany[2] which is to be followed by a comprehensive analysis of social stratification in the D.D.R.

In spite of the diversity of approaches and aspects of the subject of social stratification which have been the subject of recent sociological investigation (and it has only been possible to comment on a few of them here) it would appear that in this area of sociology both methods of investigation and analysis and the development of theoretical models from which hypotheses can be developed is reaching an encouraging stage of maturity in which many of the rifts which have in the past limited comparability have been bridged over. Whether these rifts are seen in terms of micro- or macro-analysis functionalist or consensus versus conflict models or varieties of egalitarian ideology they are seen to pale in significance before the real complexities and fascination of the persistent and subtle features of social stratification itself. Allardt in his paper in this volume asks again the question posed by Lenski's[3] recent book—'Is a synthesis possible?' To a much greater degree than we realize when working within particular national contexts it may already have occurred.

[1] Jerzy J. Wiatr (ed.), Warsaw (1967). For an earlier account of the development of sociology in Eastern Europe see: Jerzy J. Wiatr, 'Political sociology in Eastern Europe', *Current Sociology*, XIII, 2 (1964).
[2] Helmut Steiner, *Soziale Strukturveränderungen im modernen Kapitalismus* (Berlin, 1967).
[3] Gerhard Lenski, *Power and Privilege. A Theory of Social Stratification* (New York, 1966).

III

The papers in this first volume of *Sociological Studies* represent many of the different aspects of social stratification. Each of them is concerned in a particular dimension to devise and refine adequate theoretical and empirical equipment to describe what the implications of the process of social stratification is in the societies to which they refer. It is clear that the dynamic character of modern societies, together with an increasing dissatisfaction with monolithic theoretical models, makes it essential to approach the conceptual apparatus of stratification in terms of its ability to describe both the subtle and infinitely complex process of social differentiation and also the large mass aggregates which themselves undergo shifts of both collective and individual mobility.

There is a tendency especially in the way in which sociological definitions of class have become part of conventional usage—a point to which Abrams refers in his paper—for it to be assumed that the hierarchical and tripartite arrangement of social classes into some variation of upper, middle and lower was something 'given'. A model, in other words, having the sanctity of Natural, if not Divine, Law. In the case of social stratification one has had, as has happened so often elsewhere in the social sciences, a situation where the fit has for some time been less than good between the actual societies which were being described and the conceptual apparatus which was being used to describe them. It is to be hoped that these papers will play some part in assisting our escape from the stranglehold of outdated or irrelevant theoretical assumptions while stimulating us to devise constructs as pliable and varied as the social process we are trying to describe. It would, however, be equally foolish to dispense out of hand with concepts which, though less than perfect, still represent appropriate and necessary dimensions of a framework of analysis. Runciman, for instance, in his discussion of the validity of class, status and power makes a strong case for the retention of these variables on both conceptual and empirical grounds in spite of the difficulties involved in their use. If class, status and power are, as he argues, empirically as well as conceptually distinct, then any general theory of stratification must be expressed in terms of them.

Eisenstadt in his paper on 'Prestige, Participation and Strata Formation' considers the basic problem of the ways in which the differential evaluation of roles and tasks in a society gives rise to both a hierarchy of roles and a hierarchy of strata. The relationship between social differentiation and the division of labour in the Imperial societies of India, China and Western Europe is examined with particular reference to the distribution of prestige and participation in and access to the centres of the social structure.

The emphasis on prestige as an aspect of status in Eisenstadt's paper is matched by the emphasis on deference in that of Shils. Deference is the fundamental factor in relationships between those having different roles and different positions within a status hierarchy. Thus, it may be advantageous to reinterpret 'status' as 'deference-position' in order to give it both more precision and a more dynamic conceptual quality.

The paper by Abrams turns somewhat from the theoretical discussion of the conceptual apparatus to consider the ways in which the defining concepts of stratification and their empirical variables have been used and abused in sociological investigation as well as in market research and public opinion polls.

Fürstenburg's study of chemical workers in West Germany considers one of the important features of occupational status—the work-situation—and discusses its influence on the perception of the stratification system. His study has interesting parallels with the study of chemical workers in Britain by Goldthorpe and Lockwood. As Fürstenburg points out, 'work and occupational behaviour still maintain fundamental importance for determining individual and group life chances'. The technological and social changes in the work-situation are seen to have profound effects diminishing on the one hand working class solidarity and, on the other, emphasizing individualistic (privatized) responses to situational pressures.

The paper by Wesołowski and Słomczynski takes a broader view of situational factors and includes both education and income as well as occupation and power as defining social values in a three-tier analysis of stratification. The social values in the first tier determine the consumption of cultural and technical values in the second tier and these in turn have effects on the third tier of differentiation in group consciousness or what they refer to as 'the crystallization of social consciousness'. The study of three Polish cities on which their paper is based provides an opportunity to assess the participation of groups differentiated by the first tier of factors in second- and third-tier values.

In the final paper in this volume an attempt is made by Broom, Lancaster Jones and Zubrzycki to use nation-wide data to assemble the components of social stratification in a society popularly assumed to be essentially egalitarian in character. Five measures of social rank are used to identify the major strata in the society and the location of individuals in them. Three of these measures are the objective attributes of income, education and occupation and the remaining two are subjective measures on the one hand by the respondent of his own class identification and on the other by the interviewer who must assess the economic class of the respondent. One of the findings of the subjective ranking suggests that compared to Britain and the United States the middle class component of Australian society seems very high. They suggest that the apparent proneness of Australians to subjectively assess themselves as middle class may reflect real differences in the perception of social stratification in different countries which wider use of such a scale as they have developed may demonstrate.

2

THEORIES ABOUT SOCIAL STRATIFICATION

ERIK ALLARDT

INTEGRATION AND CONFLICT THEORIES: IS A SYNTHESIS POSSIBLE?

For about a decade it has been popular to distinguish between two master theories of social stratification, the integration theory and the conflict theory of society. Important contributions toward the specification of this distinction have been made for example by Dahrendorf,[1] Ossowski,[2] and van Den Berghe.[3] Recently the same theme has been developed by Gerhard Lenski in his book, *Power and Privilege. A Theory of Social Stratification*.[4] Lenski speaks about the integration theory as the conservative and about the conflict theory as the radical perspective.

In the main two things seem to differentiate these two theories. On the most general level in integration theory it is assumed that the basic factor in maintaining social order and a sufficient level of social integration in a society is a value consensus, whereas conflict theory holds that the social order is based on force and constraint. More specifically integration theorists regard the causes of social stratification as the outcome of the functional specialization needed in any society, whereas conflict theories consider social stratification as a result of the struggle for power.

There are, however, different interpretations of the implications of the distinction between the two theories. Dahrendorf in particular regards the two theories as complementary perspectives which cannot be combined into an integrated theory of conflict and integration. Society is Janus-headed, he says, and the two faces have to be described by different theories. From the point of view of the development of a unified macrosociological theory Dahrendorf is pessimistic. In comparison with Dahrendorf it seems reasonable to say that Gerhard Lenski is overly optimistic. Lenski does not look at the two theories as two clearly com-

---

[1] Ralf Dahrendorf, *Class and Class Conflict in Industrial Society* (Stanford, 1959), pp. 157–70.
[2] Stanislaw Ossowski, *Class Structure in the Social Consciousness* (London, 1963), pp. 19–68.
[3] Peter van Den Berghe, 'Dialectic and functionalism: toward a theoretical synthesis', *American Sociological Review*, vol. 28, no. 5, pp. 695–705.
[4] Gerhard Lenski, *Power and Privilege. A Theory of Social Stratification* (New York, 1966).

peting and irreconcilable perspectives. Both theories are right in some respects and wrong in some others and elements from both theories can be combined into a new and useful theory of social stratification. Lenski stresses that this kind of theoretical integration cannot only be accomplished but that such a synthesis is already under way.

The above-mentioned authors use the word 'theory' in a very general and broad way. Nevertheless different interpretations of what a theory is seem to account for Dahrendorf's pessimism and Lenski's optimism. Lenski's suggestions for remedying the lack of integration between the two theoretical approaches are in this respect revealing. According to him the new synthesis can mainly be accomplished in two ways. The first is to transform categorical concepts into variable concepts, and the second is to break down compound concepts into their constituent elements. Lenski aims mainly at some sort of a *propositional theory* concerned with the formulation of the most parsimonious statements and propositions about the results from different researches. Dahrendorf's approach is definitely more *dimensionalistic* than propositional.[1] It is more an effort to point to concepts and dimensions that should or could be used than to relate them to propositions and hypotheses. It is symptomatic that Dahrendorf's main target among the integration theorists is Talcott Parsons, who has also been for some decades the leading dimensionist in modern sociological theory.

There are probably also some other epistemological differences between propositional and dimensionistic theories than just their logical form. Explanations derived from or included in propositional theories are generally causal explanations. In a causal explanation the phenomena regarded as cause and effect are defined so that they are clearly logically independent from each other. Thus causal explanations are empirical. In sociological dimensionistic theories the explanations usually contain finalistic or teleological elements. In finalistic explanations phenomena regarded as causes are not logically independent from the effects or results. Most explanations given in terms of motives or intentions are finalistic since the motives or intentions are usually inferred from the observed and resulting behaviour. The Parsonian theory seems to contain finalistic elements. At least this is very clearly indicated by the Parsonian point of departure. Parsons defines social action as a behaviour which is characterized by intentions, goals, etc. On the other hand, social action is also explained in terms of intentions and goals.

Strong positivists are inclined to condemn finalistic explanations as

---

[1] For the difference between these two approaches see Hans L. Zetterberg, 'Review of modern sociological theory in continuity and change', *American Sociological Review*, vol. 23, no. 1, pp. 95–6.

unscientific. This is not at all the intention here. It seems reasonable to say that finalistic or teleological explanations have a legitimate place in social science. Otherwise a very large body of theory and explanations in present-day sociology would have to be thrown into the waste basket. The point here, however, is that those who make the most of the distinction between integration and conflict theories in the field of social stratification seem to have a predilection for finalistic explanations. For example, conflict theorists such as Dahrendorf use power—or rather authority—both as the cause and as an effect of social stratification. It is well known that the so-called integration theories contain explanations of a similar kind. Societies are defined as based on some kind of value consensus. On the other hand, value consensus is also used as an explanation of the fact that a society can maintain itself.

Accordingly, the whole dilemma of whether integration and conflict theories can be combined or are irreconcilable seems to depend on what kind of theories and explanations are preferred. Dahrendorf's pessimism is probably unfounded as long as the aim is propositional theories and causal explanations. At least it does seem to be interesting to pose such a dilemma if the aim is propositional theory. On the other hand, Lenski's optimism seems unfounded if the interest is focused on dimensionistic theories and finalistic explanations. There is, of course, no necessity for a dimensionist to see the integration and conflict theories as opposites, but this is a very likely outcome. The dimensionists develop orderly schemata of anything social and conduct empirical studies by identifying subjects along these dimensions. These schemata are the more orderly the more they can be restricted to one set of intentions or goals.

IS THERE A MASTER TREND?

According to Lenski there are two principles which determine how goods and services are distributed in society. These two principles are *need* and *power*. In the simplest societies or in those which are technologically most primitive the available goods and services are distributed on the basis of need. Privilege is defined by Lenski as possession or control of a portion of the surplus of goods and services produced by the society, and accordingly privileges will not emerge until there is surplus in the society. The distribution of the surplus and hence privileges, is, however, determined on the basis of power, defined by Lenski as the probability of a person or a group to carry out his or its will even when opposed by others. In any case, according to Lenski, privilege is largely a function of power.

Lenski's point of departure implies primarily that there is a high amount of equality in technologically primitive societies. Since he assumes that privilege is determined by power, and that men are basically self-seeking, it can also be deduced that the degree of inequality increases with the amount of surplus produced by the society. By and large these two propositions follow logically from Lenski's definitions and basic assumptions. However, on the basis of inductive reasoning or other kinds of evidence he also states that at some point in the course of history there occurs a reversal of the basic trend toward ever increasing inequality. In order to describe these two basic trends, the trend toward increasing inequality and its subsequent reversal, he develops a typology of societies. The typology is based on an assumption of a continuum defined by the overall technological efficiency, and it contains the following types of societies: hunting and gathering societies, simple horticultural societies, advanced horticultural societies, agrarian societies, and industrial societies. The main portion of the text consists in a description of the system of social stratification in these different types of societies. As far as I can judge the typology is well grounded and skilfully applied by Lenski. However, from a theoretical point of view the most crucial theme is the reversal of the basic trend, which occurs in the industrial societies. Lenski lists several causes of the reversal. The most important of these, according to Lenski, is the increasing complexity of society. Society has become so complex that those who govern are unable to control the whole distributive process. There are, however, many secondary factors, such as the rapidity and magnitude of the increase in productivity. By increasing the share of the lower classes the governing élite is able to raise productivity higher and higher. The reversal is reflected in the new democratic ideology and in the increasing demands for equality.

Lenski's main propositions are suggestive in their simplicity. One can, however, doubt whether it is reasonable to describe primitive societies as those in which goods and services are distributed mainly on the basis of need. In technologically very primitive societies some have the privilege of staying alive while others will die because their needs are not met. It seems hard to explain these differences otherwise than on the basis of differential power. Of course, Lenski's analysis can be saved by restricting the analysis to those who stay alive. If we focus our attention on the opposite end of Lenski's typology, it seems easy to point out industrial societies with an exceptional concentration of power and privilege in the élite. Lenski's propositions can perhaps again be saved by saying that such societies are unlikely to last very long.

In any case, it is reasonable to ask whether it is fruitful logically to connect the amount of surplus and the amount of power via the concept of privilege in the way Lenski does it. It would probably be more fruitful to regard the amount of surplus and the amount of power as logically independent variables that can exist in various combinations in the real world. If Lenski really aims at a propositional theory about social stratification and a theory which combines both hypotheses about integration and conflict, his theory contains a difficult logical dilemma. Privilege is a function of power, and differences in power explain differences in privileges. On the other hand, the privileges themselves concern in most cases privilege to exert some kind of power. As long as the theory contains circular reasoning of this type it can hardly be regarded as a propositional theory but rather as a dimensionistic scheme useful in classifying and labelling phenomena.

One might put forward the demand that a theory about social stratification should explain stratification by factors and variables which are as such logically independent from the stratification variables. The distribution of power and privilege are both stratification variables that have to be explained by other independent factors. One such variable, which is logically independent and so to say lies outside the system of social stratification, is the amount of surplus of goods and services produced in the society. The surplus can be defined without any reference to differentials in power and privileges and in all likelihood it could be used as a very fruitful concept in a theory about social stratification.

It does not appear impossible to develop theories about social stratification which use factors outside the stratification system as explanatory or independent variables and which can nevertheless account for Lenski's main propositions. A very simple model as an outline of such a theory may be suggested here. One crucial explanatory factor may be the *surplus of goods and services*. Another explanatory factor may be labelled as the *strength of social constraints* existing in a society. Even if the strength of social constraints is a variable hard to operationalize we may say that the social constraints can be considered strong when repressive sanctions are very severe. One could perhaps argue that strong social constraints always require a very uneven distribution of power. However, this is not necessarily the case. In technologically very primitive and thereby often also very small societies everyone is to some extent able to control everyone else by the force of custom. This is the Durkheimian case of mechanically solidary societies: solidarity is induced by strong collective consciousness in the form of social norms imposing uniformity under the threat of strongly repressive sanctions.

If for the sake of simplicity we dichotomize the two variables, the amount of surplus, and the strength of social constraints, and then crosstabulate them, the following fourfold table is obtained:[1]

---

[1] A similar kind of model has been more fully described in Erik Allardt, 'Reactions to social and political change in a developing society', in K. Ishwaran (ed.), *Politics and Social Change* (Leiden, 1966), pp. 1–10.

		The amount of surplus in goods and services	
		Small or no surplus	Great surplus
Social constraints	Strong	1. Mechanically solidary societies: a high amount of equality	3. Situation of coercion: high amount of inequality
	Weak	2. Situation of uprootedness: high amount of inequality	4. Organically solidary societies: a high amount of equality

The predictions about the amount of equality in the four cells representing different types of societies can be described as follows:

In case 1, mechanically solidary societies, everyone is to some extent able to control everyone else, and equality is imposed in the fulfilment of needs.

In case 2, societies of uprootedness, the weak social constraints will enable some individuals to gain privileges. Most individuals will feel alienated, but in this situation some individuals will be able to pursue their own interests more easily than in mechanically solidary societies.

In case 3, societies of coercion, the strong social constraints will hinder interaction and social exchange. In a technologically advanced society these constraints have to be imposed by powerful élites. Case 3 typifies societies which are either dictatorships or rigid class societies.

In case 4 the lack of constraints will enable a high amount of interaction and exchange. Satisfaction and solidarity will occur when people's exchange activities are hindered as little as possible. Equality will result at least in the sense that ascriptive rules will lose their meaning. Hereditary élitism weakens, and at least equality on the basis of achievement will result.

The model suggested here can, of course, be elaborated. It seems to account for Lenski's main propositions about the societal master trends, but it also accounts for deviations from the trend. A developmental sequence is built into the model. Despite the deviant cases (cells 2 and 3) there is an assumption of a development from mechanically to organically solidary societies, and it is also assumed that the mechanically and the organically solidary societies are those in which inequality has been most reduced. This hypothesis or assumption is already found in classical sociological theory as the references to the Durkheimian concepts, mechanical and organic solidarity, suggest. This has also been a rather common assumption in modern political sociology. Statements about 'end of ideology' are, for example, usually built on such an assumption.[1]

The assumption of increasing equality when proceeding from agrarian to industrial societies has also been questioned. It is well to remember that Marx and the Marxists assume that inequality will reach its peak in capitalist, industrial societies but it is probably more important to note that many non-Marxist authors also have doubted the assumption of increased equality in industrial society. The different positions concerning increases and decreases in equality depend very much on what is meant by equality, and a brief scrutiny of the concept itself seems to be in order.

THE CONCEPT OF EQUALITY

Lenski clearly distinguishes between different types of equality (pp. 84–5, 104–5) but nevertheless he seems to stress different criteria when speaking about equality in technologically primitive and in advanced societies. When speaking about primitive societies he clearly speaks about equality according to need, but in describing the increasing equality in industrial societies the stress is clearly on such things as the absence of élitism, the increasing importance of achievement over ascription, and political equality.

Lenski gives a telling formulation when he says that the field of social stratification is the study of the distributive process in society, and that the crucial question is 'Who gets what and why'. In speaking about the distributive process it is important to note that this process can concern different things, such as the distribution of goods, services, rank and power. Equality-inequality can concern different things, and we might say that equality is spoken about in terms of different criteria. This corresponds to the first part of Lenski's question, namely, 'who gets what'. Apparently, however, the question 'why' is also important in any analysis of equality-inequality. Those who participate in the distributive process will somehow always have to justify their claims. Equality in the distribution of goods, services, rank and power means also that the distribution is somehow justified or considered just. Thereby the process of justification enters into discussions about equality-inequality. By equality it is seldom meant that everybody involved should get exactly the same amount of everything distributed.

Accordingly, as a point of departure it is useful to apply a distinction between *absolute* or *relative equality*, or if we want to use Aristotle's terminology, between *arithmetical* and *proportionate equality*. We may speak about absolute or arithmetical equality when everyone involved

---

[1] See, for example, Seymour Martin Lipset, 'The changing class structure and contemporary European politics', *Daedalus* (Winter 1964), pp. 271–303.

gets the same amount of rewards or goods distributed. Absolute equality may be said to prevail at a children's party if every child gets an equally large slice of the cake, or within an occupational group if it is demanded that everybody should get exactly the same pay. However, even in these cases it is assumed that everybody should get an equal slice of the cake because all are equally qualified. At a children's party adults may get smaller slices, and other occupational groups get a different pay. In practice, and particularly when a whole society is concerned, the debate over equality always focuses on relative or proportionate equality. The question is that everybody should be equal relative to or in proportion to some specific criterion. Aristotle's criterion is merit: everybody should be equal in proportion to his merits. There are, however, other and in many circumstances more salient criteria. One such criterion is need: everybody should get rewards and goods in proportion to his needs. In any case, the debate about equality is a debate about what criteria should be applied in the distributive process.

The idea of relative and proportionate equality also implies that there is no universally valid and detailed answer to the question how equality should be implemented in practice. The problem of equality is a problem of justification in terms of specific criteria, and justifications will always depend on existing social conditions. In a discussion about the rights and duties of states this view has been very clearly expressed by Morris Ginsberg, who writes 'equality does not mean that states are in fact equal, nor that they ought to be treated as though they were. It asserts that they are all entitled to equal consideration and that differential treatment requires justification in terms of relevant differences between them or in the circumstances.'[1] Another English sociologist, W. G. Runciman, assumes in his work on a theory of social justice that problems of equality are problems of fairness.[2] Accordingly, what the problem of equality in practice amounts to is that all inequalities require to be justified. This is to say, the debate about social justice and equality centres around what criteria should be selected and how they should be applied in moving from arithmetical to proportionate equality.

It can also be shown empirically that particular solutions of the problem of equality actually work as justifications for other kinds of inequalities. The aim of equality of opportunity is to eliminate hereditary privileges. It actually works this way but it also gives rise to new inequality. Under a system of equal opportunity the capable individuals will be of course favoured in the process of selection, and once they have started their career with every step they will be further removed from

---

[1] Morris Ginsberg, *On Justice in Society* (Baltimore, 1965), p. 13.
[2] W. G. Runciman, *Relative Deprivation and Social Justice. A Study of Attitudes to Social Inequality in Twentieth Century England* (Berkeley, 1965), pp. 258–64.

the less fortunate ones. This has been very seminally described by T. H. Marshall, who in his famous essays writes that equal rights to opportunity in essence is the equal right to display and develop differences, the equal right to be recognized as unequal. This system gives, as Marshall points out, the poor boy an equal chance to show that he is as good as the rich boy but the final outcome is a structure of unequal status.[1] Equality of opportunity will no doubt increase social mobility, but social mobility will, if anything, produce a tendency to inequality unless provisions are made for sheltering the less fortunate ones. One such provision is to organize the lower classes and in such a fashion enable them to fight for their rights. To a large extent this is also what has happened in the European welfare states. Increased educational opportunities have enabled people to move from the working class into other classes, but at the same time working-class parties and trade unions have emerged to protect the rights of the workers. In any case, equality of opportunity is a principle on the basis of which certain kinds of inequalities are justified. The criterion applied in instigating equality of opportunity is merit.

In the United States equality is often explicitly equated with the more specific term of equality of opportunity. Equality and achievement are often described as dominant values in the American society, and the role of these values in the evolution of American society is also the key theme of Lipset's famous book about the United States as the first new nation. Another way of formulating the same observation would be to state that in the United States the criterion for equality is achievement. The use of achievement as a criterion for equality means elimination of élitism and denial of ascriptive rights, but it also means that many forms of inequalities can be justified in terms of differences in achievement. Lipset, of course, is aware of the fact that equality of opportunity can lead to strong inequalities in other respects. In discussing the fate of the American Negro he states 'that equality is not enough to assure his movement in larger society'.[2] A more precise way of formulating this dilemma would be to say specifically that equality of opportunity is not enough to make the Negroes full citizens. Securing the Negroes the same rights as other Americans apparently also requires an implementation of equality according to need.

In Communist states the main criterion for equality and for the distribution of goods and services is, at least in principle, need. However, unless there are precise and agreed-upon methods for measuring needs they have to be imposed by a politically very powerful élite, as no

---

[1] T. H. Marshall, *Class, Citizenship and Social Development* (Garden City, N.Y., 1964), pp.120–1.
[2] Seymour Martin Lipset, *The First New Nation. The United States in Historical and Comparative Perspective* (New York, 1963), pp. 1–2, 331.

market-mechanisms will tell us how to solve the distributive problem. More than other nations today, both the capitalistic United States and Communist Soviet Union seem to be systems strongly stressing a singular principle of equality which also functions as a justification of inequalities in other respects. In practice, of course, both the United States and the Soviet Union also implement provisions which diminish the inherent strains towards inequality.

Despite the diversity of the criteria applied, there seems to be some agreement about the most important criteria for equality. Runciman assumes that there is some consensus on three broad criteria or principles in the light of which inequalities are justified. These are *need, merit,* and *contribution to the common welfare.*[1] As Lenski does not very clearly distinguish between different criteria of equality, his propositions about the trend towards equality when proceeding from agrarian to industrial societies have a clear mark of tentativeness and uncertainty.

Even granted that the discussants of the trends concerning equality and inequality are aware of the fact that equality may be defined in terms of different criteria, statements, or perhaps rather denials, of the increasing equality may take at least three different forms:

(1) One of the aims of social welfare measures is to further equalization but it is, of course, possible that some measures have actually increased the inequality instead. If the discussion focuses on only one criterion or principle of justification this would mean that the ordering of individuals has been reversed in such a fashion that the welfare measures favour those who already have high positions against those with low positions. This might have happened in individual instances. In general, however, it is likely that most welfare measures in today's societies have an equalizing effect.

(2) It could be stated by someone that altogether wrong criteria have been used in furthering equality. The argument is certainly rare in this very crude form. A more common form of the argument is to say that some criteria have been applied at the expense of others. Some pay-scales may be adjusted so that merit or achievement will be accounted for in a better way than has been the case. However, this may mean that inequality in terms of need has increased.

(3) The criteria for equality can be applied in a stronger and weaker degree. The criteria are applied in a very weak degree if only a minimum of welfare, equality of opportunity and political participation is guaranteed. All so-called welfare states strive to provide a modicum of welfare for their citizens but this may be done to a greater or lesser degree. If the criteria have been set at a very low point on the scale from inequality to equality, relative deprivation, or rather relative misery,

---

[1] W. G. Runciman, *op. cit.* pp. 263–4.

may increase. If what is considered a minimum standard of living is set very low but the surplus in the society has greatly increased then the relative misery will increase. One of the core ideas in groups which are subsumed under the common denominator of the New Left is that there has occurred an increase in relative deprivation in the political sphere. In liberal democracies political equality has been enforced by securing everybody's right to political participation in both the sense of the franchise and in the right to run for political office. On the other hand, the elected are equipped with power in order to ensure a stable government. The justification for this kind of inequality is, of course, that the elected have been entrusted by the electors as the most competent to further the common welfare. However, as the members of the society have grown in social competence and social awareness many individuals feel an increasing discontent with not being able to make decisions, particularly in matters concerning themselves. This is in any case the background and argument behind the New Left's demand for participatory democracy.

No answers to the question of whether equality has increased or decreased, and in what respects, will be provided here. It seems, however, that Lenski, in his otherwise comprehensive text, has not discussed all crucial possibilities. As it was said before, it also appears that in discussing technologically primitive and technologically advanced societies Lenski uses different criteria for equality.

SOME CONCLUDING REMARKS

From the point of view of a sociology of sociology Lenski's book is in many respects an interesting phenomenon. At least as far as general American texts on stratification are concerned it means a departure from the functionalist tradition that has been strongly dominating American sociology for the last decades. Lenski has really been able to combine elements from both the integration and conflict theories mentioned in the beginning. In this respect Lenski has forerunners among European sociologists, such as Dahrendorf and Ossowski. It is interesting to note that in this new departure in the field of social stratification European sociology has actually been more at the giving whereas American sociology has been more at the receiving end.

Lenski's book signifies a new departure also in another respect. The book is clearly comparative. This is perhaps not in itself very remarkable; the interesting feature, however, is that Lenski as an American sociologist only starts from the American society as a model for his comparisons to a very limited degree. He starts from very broad historical, international material and his intentions are truly comparative.

3

CLASS, STATUS AND POWER?

W. G. RUNCIMAN

The notion that societies are stratified in the three separate 'dimensions' of 'class', 'status' and 'power' is thoroughly familiar in the academic literature. But it cannot be said to have established itself as orthodoxy. From time to time it is openly questioned; more often it is tacitly ignored in favour of some other chosen variant; only occasionally is it explicitly adopted as the framework for empirical research. This lack of agreement one way or the other is surprising not only because so much has been written on social stratification but because the question is in any case not one whose answer must necessarily await the results of empirical research still to be carried out. Whatever subsequent research may reveal about either present or past societies, it should be possible to settle already whether or not 'class', 'status' and 'power' can furnish an adequate framework for the classification and analysis of systems of stratification. In this paper I shall not try to review the recent theoretical or empirical literature, but merely to set out and criticize the kinds of argument which require to be established in order to settle whether the three-dimensional framework is or is not, after all, appropriate to its task.

I

Discussion of the problem generally begins by reference to the ideas of Max Weber. But influential though these have been, it can be argued that they have sometimes hindered the progress of the discussion as much as they have helped it. Weber, like Marx, died leaving his work on stratification incomplete, and (again like Marx) it is unlikely that any one interpretation of it will ever satisfy all his readers. A strong, but not conclusive, case can be made for the view that Weber did not regard class, status and power as separate dimensions of social structure; he may rather have thought that, as one of his commentators has put it, 'whatever its form, stratification was a manifestation of the unequal distribution of power'.[1] But at the same time he was at pains to make clear that power is not a direct concomitant of either class or status, and at the end of his life he was increasingly concerned with the origins and

---

[1] Leonard Reissman, *Class in American Society* (London, 1960), p. 58.

effects of political parties and industrial or governmental bureaucracies considered independently from their relation to the market, with whose influence he had been preoccupied in his earlier studies. It is evident that he regarded power as different in kind from either market-situation on the one hand or prestige-ranking on the other. But this much would be accepted by everybody. Beyond this, any attempt to arrive at a definitive summary of Weber's views merely leads to controversies which in the nature of the case are incapable of settlement. The merits of a three-dimensional framework should, and can, be settled irrespective of how far Weber either foreshadowed or would have been disposed to agree with the verdict given.

On similar grounds, it might be argued that the terms 'class', 'status' and 'power' are better dispensed with, since 'class', in particular, is associated with a long history of sterile verbal disputes which should if possible be bypassed altogether. But this ought not to be necessary. The restriction of 'class' and 'status' to the traditional distinction between wealth and prestige is sufficiently familiar that it can be adopted without risk of misunderstanding. These things are matters of convenience, and although 'class' and 'status' should be qualified or abandoned as becomes necessary, there is no warrant for departing from them unless they prove even more unsatisfactory than they have done in the past. It is only necessary to make it clear from the outset that 'class' and 'status' are not being used in the quite different sense whereby 'Class is differentiated from status in that the latter suggests a range and continuum, while class connotes a degree of unity and some form of homogeneity among its members'.[1] In any case, this paper is not concerned to try to settle what terms are most appropriate, but what it means to claim that social stratification is three-dimensional and by what means such a claim might be invalidated.

If social stratification is three-dimensional, it must follow that the position of every person within a society is in principle capable of being designated as a vector in three-dimensional space. Accordingly, society itself will have to be seen as a sort of box, in which the lowest position is the bottom left-hand corner and the highest position the top right-hand one. To make the metaphor of top and bottom more vivid, we could say that society is a box balanced upright on one corner so that that corner is the bottom in all three dimensions and the further end of the diagonal the top. Or if the highest position in one or more of the dimensions is indeterminate, then it would be better to describe society not as a box but as an up-ended pyramid with an apex but no base. We could further say that 'social mobility' is a path from any one point to any other point

---

[1] Walter Goldschmidt, 'Social class in America—a critical review', *American Anthropologist*, LII (1950), 491.

within the space enclosed by the three co-ordinates; and if it were to be found that there is an exact coincidence between the hierarchies of class, status and power then every member of society would be located somewhere along the diagonal (and the society in question would in effect be one-dimensional). It will not follow from this that it is easy or even possible to assign a place to every member of every society even in terms of ordinal rankings. But if we are to say that stratification is three-dimensional, then this is what we must mean by it.

It should be clear, however, that to say this implies nothing about where the dividing lines should be drawn within any given social space between one 'stratum' and another. Once every person, or simply every role, has been assigned a place, it will still be an open question how they should be categorized in terms of 'classes', 'castes', 'estates' or any other concrete collective term used to designate those sharing an approximate common location. An enormous volume of argument has been devoted to this problem. But there is no one answer to it, and the appropriate classification will vary according to the questions which the investigator has in mind and the distinguishing features of the particular society or societies under study. Indeed, it can be argued that in some societies it is wrong to speak of 'strata' at all, if the term is so used as to presuppose a strictly demarcated differentiation of roles. The appropriate criterion may be purely statistical, expressed in terms of percentiles, or standard deviations, or whatever measure is most suitable to the particular distribution found in each dimension; or the distribution in the three dimensions may be such that all, or nearly all, the members of the society seem to fall into one of a small number of clearly separated clusters; or there may be designated points where mobility is drastically restricted; or it may be more useful to distinguish between strata on the basis of some qualitative criterion, such as mode of entry, or ideological rationale, or legal or historical origin. The principle chosen must not, of course, do violence to the actual location of the individual members of the designated category. But for many purposes, it may well be important to classify society in terms of very different dividing-lines. Even if cardinal rankings could be assigned in the three dimensions, different observers would be free to draw different distinctions in terms of 'proletariat' and 'bourgeoisie', 'élite' and 'mass', 'nobility' and 'commoners', 'honestiores' and 'humiliores', 'citizens', 'metics' and 'slaves', 'Brahmans', 'Kshatriya', 'Vaishya' and 'Shudra', and so forth. But nothing follows from this one way or the other about the validity of the claim that where we are concerned with stratification and not simply differentiation, there are only three dimensions in which it can operate.

In the same way, it should be clear that a three-dimensional framework is compatible with any view either of 'subjective' class or of the 'dynamics', as opposed to the 'statics', of stratification. It in no way rules out what is implied in such views as that 'class' is a phenomenon which only arises when 'some men, as a result of common experiences (inherited or shared), feel and articulate the identity of their interests as between themselves';[1] or that '*class* is always a category for purposes of the analysis of the dynamics of social conflict at its structural roots, and as such it has to be separated strictly from *stratum* as a category for purposes of describing hierarchical systems at a given point of time'.[2] The term 'class' can quite well be used in some such sense as these if it is found useful, and if it is, it can be perfectly well accommodated within the three-dimensional framework. Further, 'class consciousness', defined as 'implying consciousness of the special interests of the class and actions directed towards preserving those interests' may be marked off from simple 'class awareness'.[3] Nor is there any reason to deny that the 'dynamic' or 'subjective' aspect of stratification is indispensable to the explanation of how and why any system of stratification came to be as it is and either changes or fails to change. The temptation to use 'class' in a general and subjective as well as a limited and objective sense is unfortunate, since it makes it still more likely that disputes about terminology will be mistaken for disputes about fact. But a theory of how people see their situation and interests, and how this affects in turn the structure and workings of the system within which those interests are perceived or neglected, is in no sense a rival to the claim that societies are stratified in three and only three dimensions. On the contrary, it is an essential complement to it.

II

What, then, are the theoretical objections which can be made to the three-dimensional framework? First of all, it will have to be clear that we are indeed dealing with stratification and not merely with differentiation; or in other words, the metaphor of high and low must be appropriate. This question too has sometimes led to confusion. But it should be self-evident that when speaking of either wealth, prestige or power we are speaking of something which by definition admits of the notion of ranking. Of course, there are other human attributes which admit of ranking, such as physical height, but from a sociological standpoint, these are individual, not institutional, differentiations. What needs to be clear at the outset is that economic class, status and power both

---

[1] E. P. Thompson, *The Making of the English Working Class* (London, 1963), p. 9.
[2] Ralf Dahrendorf, *Class and Class Conflict in an Industrial Society* (London, 1958), p. 76.
[3] P. C. Lloyd, 'Introduction', in P. C. Lloyd (ed.), *The New Elites of Tropical Africa* (London, 1966), p. 57.

admit of ranking and that these rankings, however they are measured or described, are institutionalized or, in Rousseau's distinction, 'conventional' as opposed to 'natural'.

That inequalities of wealth are institutionalized is obvious, since they are in themselves the outcome of a system of regulated co-operation and competition between interrelated individuals or economic groups. Similarly, inequalities of power must to some degree be institutionalized in any society where conduct is at all regulated by sanctions, whether or not overtly coercive; indeed, without some such sanctions it would be debatable whether we should speak of the existence of a society at all. Only with inequalities of status is it possible to conceive of a society where, although they might exist, they were not institutionalized—where, that is, although some people might be looked up to by some other people, the distribution of admiration or deference was either so nearly random, or else so fluid and unpredictable, that it could not be said to constitute a status-system at all. But even here, it has to be allowed that no society has yet been found which does not have a status-system of some rudimentary kind. Explorers and anthropologists have in the past claimed to have found such societies: Captain Cook, to take only one example, thought he had found one in Tierra del Fuego. But more careful investigation has shown that it is a mistake to suppose that even in the most egalitarian societies there are no attributes, whether age, or strength, or skill in hunting or battle which are not more highly regarded than others to a more general extent than would fit a hypothesis of randomness. Accordingly, it seems that it can be said of status with as much validity as of power or class that it is one of the ways in which all societies are at once vertically and 'conventionally' differentiated.

[If this is so, then a theoretical objection to the three-dimensional framework can only take one or other of two forms. It will have to be shown either that societies can be regarded as stratified in other ways which are not reducible to one or more of class, status and power, or else that one or more of the three is not really, although it may appear to be, a separate dimension.]

III

It is evident that we do not mean the same thing by 'class' (in the economic sense), 'status' and 'power'. But it does not follow from this alone that the three are in fact conceptually distinct in the way that is required if we are to talk of separate dimensions, for if one of them is no more than a kind of one of the others, then to talk of dimensions is illegitimate. In order, however, to establish this criticism it becomes necessary to show that any statement about economic class entails some statement about either status or power (or that any statement about status entails some statement about class or power, or that any statement about power entails some statement about class or status). Furthermore, it would not be enough to show that there always is some connection in any known instance; if we are talking about a conceptual and not an empirical relation, any counter-example whatever will be enough to show that the three are distinct after all. For example, it might be an accurate prediction that in any society where the institution of slavery is in operation slaves will be found to enjoy lower status than slaveholders. But this is a contingent relationship only; it is not a logical one. As it happens, there are examples in the anthropological literature of relationships where servitude is claimed not to be accompanied by loss of prestige: Boas, for example, said of the Central Eskimo that where men unable to provide for themselves are adopted by the able-bodied as dependent servants, they 'are not less esteemed than the self-dependent providers',[1] and in Korea during one period in its history slaves, who could be manumitted by purchase, were forbidden by law from associating with members of the hereditary pariah caste. But even if this were never so, it would not follow that the statement that a person is a slave *logically* entails anything about his location in the dimensions of either class or status. Similarly, to say that a man is a pauper does not *logically* entail anything about his power or his status; and to say that he is a pariah does not *logically* entail anything about his power or his economic class. Whatever relation there may be between the three, it does not follow simply from the meaning which we attach to these terms.

It would be truer to say that there are three separate families of related terms, such that there are conceptual links within each family but not between one family and another. Thus to the notion of economic class are linked such terms as: wealth, income, price, capital, market. To the notion of status are linked such terms as: esteem, gentility, exclusiveness, deference, condescension. To the notion of power are linked such terms as: command, obedience, autonomy, tyranny, rebellion. But there is not in the same way a logical link between the members of the three sets. There are, it is true, many terms which span the barriers in a way that these do not; perhaps the most obvious are the general words like 'subordination', 'hierarchy', 'dominance' and so forth. But it is only if such other terms cannot be broken down among the three families that they constitute a challenge to the three-dimensional framework; and they then imply not so much that class, status and power are logically linked to each other as that they are not between them all-embracing.

---

[1] F. Boas, 'Central Eskimo', in *Smithsonian Reports VI*, p. 581, quoted by Gunnar Landtman, *The Origin of the Inequality of the Social Classes* (London, 1938), p. 11.

To bring the point out still more clearly, the three may be distinguished in terms of the kind of aspiration which they represent. To want wealth is not necessarily to want prestige or power; to want prestige is not necessarily to want power or wealth; to want power is not necessarily to want wealth or prestige. It can even be said that 'The difference between a rich man, a celebrity and a ruler is something like this: A rich man collects cattle and hoards of grain, or the money which stands for them. . . . A ruler collects men. Grain and cattle, or money, mean nothing to him except insofar as he needs them to get hold of men. . . . A celebrity collects a chorus of voices. All he wants is to hear them repeat his name.'[1] This imagery is perhaps a little fanciful, but the point which it serves to make is clear. Whether in terms of position or aspiration, there is a self-evident conceptual distinction between the three.

The confusions which arise, accordingly, are due more to the long-standing imprecision of the terminology of stratification than to a genuine conceptual overlap between power, wealth and prestige. This is due not simply to the conflicting uses of 'class' and 'status', which I need not review further here. In addition, not only 'power' but also 'rank' have been responsible for a good deal of unnecessary difficulty. 'Rank' causes difficulty for two reasons. First, it is sometimes used in such a way that to 'rank' one person above another in any respect is by definition to accord him prestige. This is plausible enough when approval or deference is involved—to 'accord someone high rank' is then by definition incompatible with according him low status. But to see that this will not hold in general, it is necessary only to go back to such examples as height and weight where 'ranking' is quite independent of any overtones of prestige. Secondly, 'rank' is sometimes used for particular hierarchies (such, for example, as military hierarchies) where there is a direct link between power and prestige. This, again, is perfectly plausible in the appropriate contexts. But it can be seriously misleading if it is allowed to imply that it is logically impossible, which it certainly is not, for a man to be the superior in status of those whom he is compelled to obey.

'Power', however, raises yet a further difficulty. Not only does it have to be made clear that its relation to status is a contingent and not a necessary one, but the same must also apply to economic class if we are to talk about three separate dimensions. 'Purchasing power', after all, is presumably power of a sort, and the notion of wealth carries with it the notion of power in at any rate the sense that wealth is by definition the capacity to acquire socially valued things. But the important distinction becomes clear as soon as we move from power over things, in this sense,

[1] Elias Canetti, *Crowds and Power* (tr. Stewart) (London, 1962), p. 397.

to power over people. It is sometimes said that economic class is necessarily linked to power because, for example, all employers have, simply by virtue of being employers, some measure of power over their employees. But the link is not, in fact, a necessary one. To say 'Jones has £5' means (assuming that the money is not counterfeit, the economy has not broken down, there is not a total shortage of goods on the market, and so forth) that Jones has the 'power' to acquire £5 worth of goods; or if it does not, then the possession of £5 ceases to constitute wealth by definition. But to say 'Jones pays Smith £5 a week for laying bricks' means that Smith chooses, as it happens and for whatever reasons, to take £5 for the work rather than not to. Even if he is compelled to, because in the society in question employers are allowed powers of physical coercion, the power of Jones over him is still not the necessary consequence of Jones's capacity to pay him £5. In other words, what can be called 'reward power'[1] is conditional; it does not logically follow from the possession of wealth. Of course, the notion of power does still raise notorious difficulties of definition, to which I shall return in a later section of the paper. But I hope enough has been said to make clear that conceptually, at least, economic class, status and power are genuinely distinct, however easy it may be in particular contexts to ignore or disguise the distinction.

IV

But are we entitled to say that there are *only* these three dimensions in which societies can be said to be stratified? Or are there other ways in which their members are institutionally ranked above and below each other which cannot be conceptually reduced to one or other of the three? A question of this form is always difficult to answer conclusively, since it is impossible to go through an exhaustive list of all conceivable candidates. But there are at any rate a few possible contenders about which something should be said before it can be assumed that the three-dimensional framework is valid on purely conceptual grounds.

First of all, it might be argued that in some cultures the most important term in the vocabulary of stratification is one which ties wealth, status and power together so tightly as to be impossible to disentangle. Indeed, it may even be that the language used does not contain the concepts in which such a disentanglement could be expressed. What, for example, are we to say about the Polynesian *mana*, of which Mauss says in his essay on *The Gift* that it 'symbolizes not only the magical power of

¹ John R. P. French Jr. and Bertram Raven, 'The bases of social power', in Dorwin Cartwright (ed.), *Studies in Social Power* (Ann Arbor, 1959), pp. 156–7.

the person but also his honour, and one of the best translations of the word is "authority" or "wealth"'?[1] But the answer to this is that the distinctions which are not made in a language are not therefore invalid even for the society or culture whose language it is. Where a distinction is made, then we are indeed bound to take it seriously whether or not it is one which our own language is able to accommodate. But the reverse does not hold. The investigator of Polynesian society is entitled to place its members within a three-dimensional framework whether or not they can grasp what he is up to. It may be, of course, that there is a good reason for their lack of the distinction since it may be that the correlation between the three dimensions in Polynesian society is so close that the positions to be described are all located along the diagonal. But again, this is not evidence one way or the other for the validity of a threefold distinction. If valid, it can meaningfully be applied to Polynesian society just as much as to any other, whatever may be the ideas about stratification entertained by the Polynesians themselves.

A different kind of candidate for a fourth dimension of stratification is what has been called 'informational status'—that is, the 'amount of skill or knowledge possessed'.[2] But it is not difficult to demonstrate that where knowledge and skill do constitute an advantage which 'conventionally' ranks their possessor above his fellows, this is precisely because it constitutes an advantage in the hierarchies of either class, status or power. Education does not by definition stratify society, it only differentiates it. Polymaths do not constitute a high-ranking stratum in the way that the rich, or the social aristocracy, or the holders of governmental office do. Where education does stratify rather than differentiate, this is because of its contingent association with economic *Lebenschancen*, or social prestige, or influence and authority, or possibly all three. Without such an association, the distinction between the educated and the uneducated is not stratification any more than is the distinction between the tall and the short or the fat and the thin. It is perfectly true that education, knowledge and skill do as a rule secure advantages for their possessors in a way that physical height does not. But this is merely to say that education is a significant determinant of social location. It is not thereby a separate dimension. On the contrary, the educated man might in some conceivable societies be lower in all three dimensions than the uneducated. The millionaire, the celebrity and the ruler enjoy a high social position by definition; it is one or other of these three kinds of things that having a 'high' social position means. The same cannot be said to be true by definition even of the most talented or knowledgeable members of a social system.

---

[1] Marcel Mauss, *The Gift* (tr. Cunnison) (London, 1954), p. 36.
[2] Kaare Svalastoga, *Social Differentiation* (New York, 1965), p. 16.

A third candidate might be the so-called 'leader-follower' relationship which is clearly unequal but which cannot be unequivocally assigned to the dimension of power. It is a kind of power to the extent that the leader is able to influence his followers in such a way that they carry out his will. But it is also a kind of prestige, since the relationship is not a coercive one and the superiority of the leader to the led consists precisely in his ability to elicit from them a willing and even eager obedience. As it is described, for example, by Freud (summarizing Le Bon), the 'prestige' of the leader is a 'mysterious and irresistible power', a 'sort of domination' which 'entirely paralyses our critical faculty, and fills us with wonderment and respect'.[1] Stated in these terms, the relationship may seem one which belongs to the study of individual psychopathology more than of social inequality. But in its institutionalized aspect, it is one which might be argued to be impossible to break down within the simple dichotomy of status and power.

Certainly, leadership is complex and often difficult to explain. But it does not follow from this that the sense in which leaders must be ranked higher than followers is a sense over and above status and power (however these may be intertwined in leader-follower relationships). To say that a man is a leader is to say (by definition) that he enjoys both status and power. It is not to say that he enjoys something else which ranks above his fellows. A leader is different from a ruler because of the element of willing obedience—a ruler's power may be entirely coercive whereas a leader's is not. But this does not mean that if we were to be able to rank leaders themselves in order —that is, to treat leadership as though it *were* a separate dimension—their ranking could not at once be translated into a ranking in the hierarchies (however measured) of status and power. This, in turn, is not to say that the identification of leaders and the explanation of their influence and its consequences may not be of importance in analysing the dynamics of stratification. But as I have already emphasized, the importance of such categories within the three-dimensional framework is not evidence against its validity. Before saying that the phenomenon of leadership invalidates it, it would be necessary to show not that some kinds of power are directly tied to status (or, for that matter, vice versa) but that some kinds of leadership rank leaders above non-leaders in yet a further way. But this is not a conclusion to which the study of leadership in its social context has so far been held by anyone to lead.

An altogether different line of attack might be by way of the notion of 'rights'. The rights of citizenship can, perhaps, be directly contrasted with the system of 'social class', and the resulting distinction between

---

[1] Sigmund Freud, *Group Psychology and the Analysis of the Ego* (ed. Strachey) (London, 1959), p. 13.

'civil', political' and 'social' rights on the one hand and inequalities of 'social class' on the other might be a more valid one than the simple addition of 'power' as a third dimension to class and status. This is the argument of T. H. Marshall's *Citizenship and Social Class*, in which the rise of the 'Welfare State' is described in terms of 'the impact of a rapidly developing concept of the rights of citizenship on the structure of social inequality'.[1] On this view, equality of citizenship is not only distinct from economic equality or equality of social esteem, but is itself very much more complicated than simple equality of 'power'. As Marshall points out, the trend towards equality of citizenship covers a progressive transition from liberty of the person, equality before the law, and the rights of property and contract, to the franchise, the right to membership in elective assemblies, and the eligibility to membership in any body invested with authority, and thence to the right 'to share to the full in the social heritage and to live the life of a civilised being according to the standards prevailing in the society'.[2] The historical importance of the difference between these three stages is unquestionable; so might it not be argued on the strength of it that the three-dimensional view of stratification falls down?

The answer, however, is the same as in the previous case. To invalidate the three-dimensional framework, it would be necessary to show that one or more of the rights of citizenship enumerated by Marshall ranks a man relatively to his fellows in some way which cannot be classified as an inequality of economic class, status, or power. This might have some force if the definition of economic class were to be restricted purely and simply to wealth instead of to what are generally called 'life-chances', or if the definition of 'power' were to cover only powers of direct physical coercion over other men and not the capacity of a more general kind to determine the actions of oneself as well as other people. But there is no warrant for imposing such restrictions; and without them, it is easy to show that where the possession of rights of citizenship does constitute a ranking in the system of social stratification it is a ranking in one or other of the three dimensions. Thus, liberty of the person and the right to vote are both aspects of inequality of power; the right to own property and the right to draw national assistance are both aspects of equality of economic *Lebenschancen*; and the right to 'live the life of a civilised being', if so vague a term can be more precisely specified, presumably covers equalities in all three dimensions, including the right not to be debarred from social relations with other members of the same society on such grounds of status as colour or race. Once again,

---

[1] T. H. Marshall, 'Citizenship and social class', in *Citizenship and Social Class and Other Essays* (Cambridge, 1950), p. 85.
[2] *Ibid.* p. 11.

it would have to be demonstrated that 'citizenship' denotes an equality with the other members of the same society which cannot be assigned to any one of the three dimensions; and although the several kinds of citizenship may for some purposes be more important than the three fundamental kinds of social equality, there does not seem to be any one aspect of citizenship which constitutes an equality or inequality in some fourth dimension of stratification.

Finally, we should perhaps briefly consider whether any of the evidence furnished by the study of animal societies serves to invalidate the three-dimensional framework on conceptual grounds. Much more is now known about the social life of animals than even a few decades ago, and it is perhaps significant that stratification in animal societies is generally discussed in terms not of 'class', 'status' and 'power' but of 'dominance', 'hierarchy', 'peck-order', 'supersedence' and so forth. Should we therefore conclude that animal societies are stratified in terms of relations of superiority and inferiority which fall outside the three-dimensional classification?

It may be rash for the non-specialist to give too confident an answer to this without detailed knowledge of the present state of ethological research. But the best-known evidence does not seem to suggest that the stratification of animal societies in any way invalidates the three-dimensional framework. The vocabulary in which animal hierarchies are described is guided by a proper caution against the dangers of anthropomorphism, and where the terms taken from human behaviour seem out of place this is more because of the greater simplicity of the 'peck-order' or 'dominance hierarchy' studied than because there is some further dimension in which it would make sense to speak of animal societies as stratified. Animal hierarchies may be of many different kinds, and may be described in many different ways. But they have not (as far as I know) supported the existence of an additional dimension of stratification beyond those in which human societies are stratified. Animal hierarchies often rest on force, or the threat of force, and in this sense are relationships of power, even where the threats have been highly ritualized and thus serve the function of inhibiting fights to the death. But given ritualization, there can be an additional element of what it is perhaps legitimate to call 'status' in the relationship, as is seen in the gestures of positive and respectful submission shown, for example, by wolves and some monkeys towards their superiors, or in the non-coercive leader-follower relationships observed among ducks, sheep and deer. Similarly, property rights and hence 'economic' advantages may be established and maintained not only by fighting but also by custom as, for example, among rooks. Or again, status may be established not merely by force or threat but by display, as in 'leks' in which low-ranking birds are ignored altogether and from which they seem to accept their exclusion with acquiescence and even humility. In general, the biological function of animal hierarchies in apportioning territory, inhibiting intra-group aggression and restricting indiscriminate breeding leads to composite rank-orders for which a general term signifying an unspecified dominance is likely to be the most appropriate. But it does not follow from this that animal hierarchies are ever of a kind to suggest that the threefold distinction between 'class', 'status' and 'power' is conceptually invalid. On the contrary, the more sophisticated societies can even be argued to illustrate it, provided that it is not applied in terms which presuppose the existence of specifically human institutions.

V

It would seem, then, that there is no convincing argument for rejecting the three-dimensional framework on conceptual grounds. But it could still be claimed that it is not empirically valid, for it might be either that one of the three is strictly reducible to another or that one is a consistent function (even if a lagged function) of another. Both these, however, are strong claims, and to substantiate them would require a more convincing demonstration than has yet been offered.

If the first is to be substantiated, it will have to be shown not merely that there is an isomorphism between the relations holding for the two classes of phenomena but that there is a strict interchangeability between the respective terms. Now this possibility cannot be ruled out entirely, since it is always possible that further research will show that a reduction can be made, however unlikely this may have seemed at one time. In the way that, for example, it has been suggested that rules of marriage are reducible to rules of information exchange (although there is not, of course, an identity of meaning between the two), so it might be suggested that the laws governing inequalities of status, say, are reducible to the laws governing inequalities of class, that the constants in both are identical, and that 'status' and 'class' are interchangeable throughout. But nobody has yet claimed this; and indeed it would be easy to assemble much evidence against it.

Perhaps some examples can be cited which show how a reduction of this kind might operate: thus, the 'potlatch' can perhaps be interpreted as an instance of an ostensible status phenomenon which is reducible to a phenomenon of economic class in the sense that status is here a purchasable commodity acquired by the surrender of an amount of material goods equivalent in value. The same could be said to be true of all instances of 'conspicuous consumption'. Indeed, if in all known communities status in the eyes of a man's fellows could only be acquired in this way, and in strict accordance with the rules of the market, then the case for treating status as a separate dimension of stratification might disappear. But it is enough to show that there are, at any rate, some status phenomena where this does not hold, and where the explanation of the status order cannot be plausibly fitted to what is thought the best explanation of the order of economic class, for the reductionist claim to be very implausible at best.

In the same way, it is perfectly possible that a model for the distribution of power might be found to fit closely in a large number of instances with the distribution of wealth. But it would not follow from this fact by itself that the reductionist case had been established. Once again, a single example where an inequality of power could not be explained by direct reference to the laws of economic class, or where the empirical terms in the two relationships were not interchangeable, would be enough to show the reductionist case to be untenable. In any case, the more obvious inference from a close fit to a common model would be not that power 'is' wealth in the sense that, to take a classic example from the physical sciences, electromagnetic waves 'are' light waves, but simply that for a number of well-known reasons there is in practice a close correlation between the two.

The different claim that one or other of the three kinds of inequality has a general causal priority is more familiar. It has never, as far as I know, been seriously advanced on behalf of status (although status has, of course, often been treated as an independent variable in the analysis of social structure, notably by Weber and Tocqueville). But priority has often been claimed both for class, in the sense of relation to the mode of production or, as Marx himself sometimes puts it, 'the property question', and for power. For the present argument, it does not matter which of these is more convincing than the other, since if either can be vindicated this will furnish sufficient grounds for rejecting the three-dimensional approach. But conversely, the claim of economic class will fall down if even a single instance of autonomous inequality of power or status can be put up against it, and the claim of power will similarly fall down if confronted with an autonomous inequality of status or class.

In a sense, the rival claims of class over power and power over class serve to cancel each other out. If there is the least plausibility in both of them, then the claim by either to universal priority becomes to that degree impossible to sustain. Indeed, it may well be that there is nowhere in the contemporary literature on stratification a claim to priority for either of them which is as extreme as it needs to be to undermine the validity of the three-dimensional scheme. Nobody is now likely to deny the importance of relations to the mode of production; but at the same time nobody is now likely to claim that every possible inequality of status or power is a function of them. Similarly, many inequalities of wealth or access to it can be argued to result from some initial superiority in the means of coercion; but this is very different from claiming that the distribution of wealth in any and all societies can be traced back exclusively to violence and conquest or (as some versions of the power theory have maintained) to the legal controls which the dominant group first laid down and which then governed the subsequent allocation of property. There is no unified doctrine of the primacy of power in the way that there is, or has been, of the primacy of class, and it is often difficult to tell how far statements such as 'The type of stratified society that develops in a situation of contact depends largely on the relative power of the contending groups'[1] or 'because sanctions are necessary to enforce conformity of human conduct, there has to be inequality of rank among men'[2] are compatible with a three-dimensional framework. It is probably true that among contemporary writers, at least, even those most anxious to emphasize the causal importance of relations of power, capacities for physical force, and the strength of legal and therefore ultimately coercive sanctions would not want to argue that absolutely all institutional inequalities are functions of them. But in any case, if we want to refute the claim that either power or economic class is the sole determinant of all other inequalities, it will already be enough to show that inequalities of status can arise, however rarely, on their own.

The examples most commonly cited to show that prestige can be independent of either wealth or power are those of priests, shamans, teachers and intellectuals in general. In the case of priests or shamans, the complete independence of their status may be debatable since their status may well derive from the imputation to them of supernatural powers. But the point can be readily demonstrated by reference to secular activities, despite such blanket assertions as are sometimes made to the effect that 'prestige is essentially determined by power'[3] or that status 'derives from the attempt of those with power to legitimize their position'.[4] Public entertainers furnish the most obvious example. How is the prestige accorded them to be shown to be either synonymous with or derived from one of the other dimensions? When Wright Mills says that 'the "power" of the celebrity is the power of distraction'[5] his own use of inverted commas shows that he is merely playing with words. In some cultures, artists and musicians are highly esteemed and well-rewarded:

---

[1] Tamotsu Shibutani and Kian M. Kwan, *Ethnic Stratification* (New York, 1965), p. 250.
[2] Ralf Dahrendorf, 'On the origin of social inequality', in Peter Laslett and W. G. Runciman (ed.), *Philosophy, Politics and Society*, second series (Oxford, 1962), p. 104.
[3] Stanislaw Andrzejewski, *Military Organisation and Society* (London, 1954), p. 21.
[4] Kenneth Prandy, *Professional Employees* (London, 1965), p. 174.
[5] C. Wright Mills, *The Power Elite* (New York, 1959), p. 360.

in others, they are recruited only from an inferior caste. But the cases where their status is curiously low cannot be traced to variations in power or wealth any better than the cases where their status is curiously high.

More generally still, the autonomy of status can be demonstrated from the study of play itself, and particularly agonistic play. This point is well made by Huizinga when he describes the 'honour and esteem' which accrues to the 'winner' and thence by extension to the group to which he belongs. There are, of course, many instances where a competitive game, even if carefully regulated, is a competition for power or wealth and not merely for status. But equally, there are many instances where status and only status is what it is the purpose of the game to determine. As Huizinga says, 'the competitive "instinct" is not in the first place a desire for power or a will to dominate. The primary thing is the desire to excel others, to be the first and to be honoured for that. The question whether, in the result, the power of the individual or the group will be increased takes only a second place. The main thing is to have won.'[1] Indeed, the point hardly needs to be laboured. Rousseau, for all his emphasis on the institution of private property as the root of 'conventional' inequality, is also very much aware of what he calls 'cette ardeur de faire parler de soi, cette fureur de se distinguer'. This ardour is at least somewhere present in all societies, and in some it is absolutely overriding: it has been said of the Mestizos of Aritama, in Colombia, that to be 'respected' is 'the ultimate goal of life, and all human activities are essentially oriented toward achieving this end'.[2] It is only necessary to reassert its existence when it is being denied that *any* institutionalized difference of status can arise except as a function of inequality of either class or power.

To be sure, it is always possible that (as with a reductionist argument) further research will vindicate a claim which does not at the moment look plausible. If, for example, the historical evidence were adequate—which it is not—to show how the Indian system of caste came into being, it might turn out that causal priority should, after all, be assigned either to property and the division of labour or to political and military dominance or to status derived from religious conceptions of purity and pollution. But it would still be necessary to prove that the primary dimension in this instance was also the primary dimension over the whole range of systems of stratification. If there is any general conclusion to be drawn from the mass of heterogeneous and often conflicting evidence with which the student of stratification is confronted, it is surely that inequalities of all three kinds can under at least some circum-

[1] Johan Huizinga, *Homo Ludens* (Boston, 1955), p. 50.
[2] Gerardo and Alicia Reichel-Dolmatoff, *The People of Aritama* (London, 1961), p. 441.

stances arise autonomously, and that the causal relations between the three are sometimes in one direction and sometimes in another. Thus the relation between wealth and power may be directly reversed depending on the stage of economic or political development reached by the society in question. For example, it has been said both that 'in pre-market societies wealth tends to follow power; not until the market society will power tend to follow wealth'[1] and, conversely, that 'in the emergent countries, the Party, rather than being the expression of the economic interests of a class, is itself the opening to economic opportunity. Wealth derives *from* political power; it docs not create it.'[2] It is only under limited conditions that a simple one-way model giving primacy to class or power is likely to fit the facts. To say this is not to decry the importance of theories which assert that under given conditions of, say, industrialization, or expansion of population, or military conquest, or cultural diffusion the resulting system of stratification will be determined by the relations holding between the respective groups in one dimension rather than another. But it is, I think, safe to say that no claim for the consistent and universal primacy of one dimension over the others has yet been successfully put forward. If, therefore, the three-dimensional framework is invalid as such, it is not on empirical any more than on conceptual grounds.

VI

To have established, however, that the three dimensions are both conceptually and empirically distinct does not mean that it is therefore possible to assign a precise location to each member even of a small organization, let alone a large and complex society. It might seem plausible to regard class, at least, as lending itself to straightforward measurement and analysis (and in fact I shall say less about it than either status or power). But although it is easy to say that by economic 'class' is meant every aspect of a person's relation to the commodity and labour markets expressed in terms of money or the probability of obtaining money or its equivalents, it is by no means easy to define and list these aspects in such a way as to yield a cardinal ordering.

In principle, it should be possible to ascertain the distribution of income, or wealth, and then to fit it to the Pareto or lognormal or whatever is the most appropriate curve. But there are still serious difficulties. There is not merely the technical difficulty that there may be societies in which the units of money are not such as to furnish an adequate measure of utility and therefore of wealth. More important, there are

[1] Robert Heilbroner, *The Making of Economic Society* (Englewood Cliffs, 1962), p. 27, quoted by Gerhard E. Lenski, *Power and Privilege* (New York, 1966), p. 229.
[2] Peter Worsley, *The Third World* (London, 1964), pp. 192–3.

aspects of class-situation which do not lend themselves to satisfactory quantification even in societies with a sophisticated market economy.

The first difficulty can, perhaps, be dismissed as of increasingly little importance. There do exist societies where there is not a stable and reciprocal unit of currency, or where 'wealth' consists in the possession or accumulation of objects which have no exchange value, like the famous 'stone money' of the Yap Islanders, so that it becomes impossible to draw comparisons even in terms of a basic unit of goods or the work-time required for its acquisition. The same could be said, indeed, of Europe in the early middle ages, when the coinage was limited in supply and locally variable in value, or of any society where the development of currency has not reached the point at which a 'market-situation' can properly be said to exist. But even where a fully developed money economy is in operation, it is impossible to express all the various aspects of 'class'-situation precisely in terms of it. In practice, significant economic inequalities can be calculated well enough to furnish many useful comparisons both within societies and between them. But a full assessment of class-situation will have to include not merely earnings and possessions but net real reward related to labour time, all gifts, receipts, benefits in kind or remissions of expenditure, allowance for any expenses regarded as mandatory, such as the maintenance of dependants, and allowance for all potential or expected benefits which are a function of present position in relation to the market. Further, in any economy in which public funds are held in some sense on behalf of the population at large, these should be somehow credited to the presumed beneficiaries; but this is as problematic in sophisticated societies, where costly social services (including national defence) are centrally financed, as in simpler societies where there is no clear line between the public funds and the ruler's private purse. Finally, the definition of 'class-situation' may need to be broadened to include what has been called 'work-situation',[1] or in Weber's words the 'allgemeinen typischen Lebensbedingungen' consequential on market-situation, such as the need to submit to the discipline of the workplace.[2] Perhaps it can be assumed that any aspects of 'work-situation' which do not fall under either status or power can be expressed in monetary terms. But even so, it is as well to remember how far we are, even in the dimension of economic class, from the cardinal rankings which the monetary yardstick and the market mechanism would appear to make possible.

[1] David Lockwood, *The Blackcoated Worker* (London, 1958), p. 15.
[2] Max Weber, 'Die Wirtschaftsethik der Weltreligungen', in *Gesammelte Aufsätze zur Religionssoziologie*, I (Tübingen, 1922), 274.

VII

The difficulties raised by the notion of status, however, are (as is well known) more formidable still. Not only does status rest by definition on subjective attitudes which may not be susceptible to precise description and measurement; but even if these attitudes can be unambiguously expressed, there will remain the problem of deriving an ordering from them. It may be that for some purposes a cardinal ranking will not be called for. To establish, for example, the existence in the status hierarchy of post-medieval Europe of a middle stratum of 'bourgeoisie' with its own life style, ideology and pattern of social contacts between the aristocracy on one side and the proletariat on the other, it is not necessary to measure by just how much it is either below the one or above the other. Further, it is perhaps only in ordinal terms that some distinctions of status can be said to have meaning at all. But inequalities of status can take many forms, and if we are to assign to each member of a society a place in the dimension of status, let alone to compare one society with another, then it will be necessary somehow to decide the relative weight to be assigned to one distinction as against another and to measure the social distance by which individuals or strata are accordingly separated.

The investigator of a status-system needs in principle to know only the criteria by which its members rank each other and the scores which they assign. He can then plot the distribution of the population studied, and if he is satisfied that the scorings are capable of being related to a common scale he can compare one population with another. Moreover, he can make comparisons in terms not only of the height and scatter of the several distributions, but also the number and consistency of criteria used, the degree of unanimity underlying the composite scores, and the changeability both of the criteria themselves and the rankings assigned by reference to them. It is sometimes said in criticism of the analysis of status in terms of reciprocal rankings that it presupposes a face-to-face community in which the antecedents and attributes of every member are known to every other member. But although this is a self-imposed limitation in studies in which status is deliberately defined in terms of actual relations between designated individuals, it is hard to see why it should be necessary in principle to speak of inequalities of status only in face-to-face terms. If we wish to speak of the distribution of status in a large community or even a nation, then what we mean is presumably the different prestige rankings which people would accord to each other on the basis of their possession or lack of the attributes which merit prestige in the scorer's eyes.

The difficulties arise when it comes to constructing a status distribution in practice. In the first place, the criteria by which status is accorded are often incommensurate. It is all very well to say that the status of X is measured by the ranking which Y and Z assign to him and that if they are asked to rank him relative to A, B and C then the weighting of the various criteria finds expression in the final score which they give. But Y and Z may quite properly refuse to give a single score of this kind; and even if they are prepared to, the investigator may have doubts as to whether, let us say, their disparagement of X on grounds of racial purity ought not to be given more weight relative to their professed admiration for his attainments in other spheres than they themselves are disposed to give it. Furthermore, the criterion of ranking is likely to vary qualitatively not only over time but also within even a single culture at a single time. The prestige of the distinguished celebrity is not like the rich man's wealth: as one French author has put it, 'L'éminence se définit par la réputation, donc par un phénomène social qui varie selon le milieu et les échelles de valeur'.[1] How, therefore, can it ever be legitimate to construct a uniform, let alone a cross-culturally valid, prestige scale?

Secondly, it may in any case be impossible to translate behaviour symbolic of inequality of status into the sort of prestige scale required. The existence of distinguishable status-strata is generally held, following Weber and others, to involve differential life styles and upbringing, commensalism and endogamy, and social exclusiveness in general. But how is a distribution of status to be constructed from these, even where there is no question that the several groups are vertically, and not merely horizontally, differentiated? It may be possible, for example, to construct a 'ritual pollution scale' for the ranking of Hindu castes,[2] or to establish the existence of a 'hierarchy of preferences among shades of skin color' among Negroes by means of an appropriate psychological experiment and non-parametric statistical test.[3] But what are we to say if the castes are not after all amenable to Guttman scaling, or the results of the psychological experiments conflict? And in any case, it will only be within a caste-like system where status-equilibration is rigidly maintained that a single scale of exclusiveness will be capable of furnishing all the answers required. In the same way, sociometric choice may in some situations furnish an operational index of prestige. But it is only where 'popularity', in this sense, is a sufficient criterion of status that no further questions will arise. In general, it is only where exclusiveness can be assumed to correlate directly with esteem that anything like a dis-

---

[1] Claude Lévy-Leboyer, 'Les déterminants de la supériorité', in Alain Girard, *La Réussite sociale en France*, Institut national d'études démographiques, Cahier no. 38 (Paris, 1961), p. 32.

[2] Pauline M. Mahar, 'A ritual pollution scale for ranking Hindu castes', *Sociometry*, XXIII (1960), 292–306.

[3] Sidney Siegel, *Nonparametric Statistics for the Behavioral Sciences* (New York, 1966), pp. 49 50.

tribution of status analogous to the distribution of wealth can be plotted at all.

Thirdly, there may be a difference in kind not merely between the attributes selected as relevant to status or the forms of behaviour to which the recognition of these attributes gives rise but also in the nature of the recognition itself. There may be significant differences between societies where status is awarded in terms of, say, 'esteem' (defined by reference to performance in a specified role) as opposed to 'prestige' (defined by reference only to the role itself),[1] or 'praise' (defined as zero-sum) as opposed to 'respect' (defined as non-zero-sum),[2] or differentials of prestige deriving from 'sacred' values, in a Durkheimian sense, as opposed to 'secular' values (the distinction which, rather differently expressed, underlies G. M. Young's description of 'the philosophic man, like Mill and Fawcett, who will admit no inequality of status unless some utilitarian cause can be shown'[3]). These are not differences in the choice of attribute to which high or low status is assigned, although they may in practice correlate with one type of attribute rather than another. They are differences, broadly speaking, in the nature of the ideology·which underlies the choice of attributes. Sometimes these differences are very difficult to locate and define, even with a thorough knowledge of the history and culture of the society under study. But even if we assume that the investigator is sufficiently knowledgeable to detect not only the attributes held relevant to status and the forms of behaviour in which it finds expression but also the nature, in this sense, of those forms, how is he to express this in measurable terms? How, for example, could he compare the distribution of status in a modern industrial community with that in ancient Sparta, or among the Kalahari Bushmen, or in feudal Europe, even if we assume that he has available to him all the evidence that he could ask for? It is not that different attributes are taken to be relevant or that different modes of speech and behaviour are culturally prescribed so much as that the kind of status itself is different. We still wish to speak of inequality of status in each of its divergent forms; but there is no common yardstick which will make it possible to speak of the social distance between superiors and inferiors in one case as greater or smaller than in another. Even when all the evidence is in, there will be no way to describe the different distributions of status except in terms more or less valueless for the purpose of precise comparison.

Fourthly, there is the difference between those systems in which the

---

[1] K. Davis, 'A conceptual analysis of stratification', *American Sociological Review*, VII (1942), 309–21.

[2] W. G. Runciman, '"Social" equality', *Philosophical Quarterly*, XVII (1967), 221–30.

[3] G. M. Young, *Victorian England* (London, 1960), p. 155.

members of the inferior strata do, and those in which they do not, accept the ranking which they are assigned by the strata above them. This is not a difference which will be reflected in the investigator's map of prestige rankings or sociometric choices. Where the criteria of ranking are not in dispute the problem of intensity of feeling is solved by the translation of esteem or prestige into a score whose range will reflect the extent of variation among those whose rankings constitute the status-system in question. But what are we to say when the dominant ideology is passionately rejected by those whose inferior position it is held to justify? Indeed, it may be that in no society can those at the lowest level of status be said to be satisfied with their position, for even if they do not reject the ideology which assigns this rank to them they will envisage the possibility of securing at least a slightly higher rank within the accepted system. To pursue these differences of attitude further would lead into problems in the psychology of relative deprivation which are outside the scope of this paper. But they raise yet a further difficulty in the classification and comparison of hierarchies of status. It may be said that a man's resentment of the feelings of others towards him is irrelevant to the location to which those feelings consign him; although, in the words of Hobbes, 'every man looketh that his companion should value him at the same rate he sets upon himselfe', he cannot in any way require his companion to do so. But it is at the same time difficult to argue that where the members of an inferior stratum reject either the criterion by which they are ranked or the rank which they are assigned there is not an important difference of kind from a status hierarchy in which they are willing to accept their place.

This leads on to a fifth difficulty. When the ideology of the dominant stratum is rigidly exclusive and strongly held, the legitimacy of upward mobility may be denied altogether. It is this denial which is sometimes held to mark the difference in kind between 'class' systems and 'caste' systems: Myrdal, for example, in *An American Dilemma*, defines caste as consisting in 'such drastic restrictions of free competition in the various spheres of life that the individual in a lower caste cannot, by any means, change his status except by a secret and illegitimate "passing"'.[1] The phenomenon of passing is in a sense only a symptom of the previous difficulty: it arises only because the members of an inferior stratum refuse to accept the place assigned to them. But it raises a further problem for the investigator who is trying to locate every person, or at any rate every group, along a continuum of status. To treat those who pass as members of the stratum to which they are aspiring is to reflect correctly (for as long as they are not discovered) the prestige assigned to them by their fellows. But it is surely a distortion of the reality to

---

[1] Gunnar Myrdal, *An American Dilemma*, 2nd edition (New York, 1962), pp. 674–5.

categorize them as though they were, so to speak, 'genuine' members of the superior stratum. The problem is particularly acute when there are no overt signs by which those of inferior social origin can be recognized. The Burakumin of Japan, for example, are indistinguishable as members of a pariah caste except to the extent that their origin may be betrayed in such nuances of manner and attitude as are the product of their own awareness of their origin. Their difficulty in passing lies in concealing their place of birth or residence which others will be able to identify as a ghetto. Hence a distinction has to be made between 'lateral mobility', where the anonymity of a new milieu conceals but does not abolish the home ties of a Burakumin, and 'true vertical mobility' which will require a transfer of family registry as well as a permanent change of residence.[1] In other cultures, 'passing' may require a change of name. Indeed, if a person can conceal his family, then 'passing' can become relatively easy even within a caste system: thus, it has been said of outsiders in a Sinhalese village that 'if their kinship connections are unknown, and if they choose not to state their caste, then by changing their caste-linked names and occupations they can pretend to be anything they fancy. And they can get away with it.'[2] If, of course, the characteristic is unmistakable, like colour, individual mobility is only possible by overriding the fact of origin as opposed to denying it (whence the saying in Brazil that 'money whitens'). But the phenomenon of passing is one which is peculiar to the dimension of status, and makes it curiously difficult to say whether a person does or does not occupy a certain position. People cannot in this way pretend to have wealth or power; but if they can behave in such a way as to be treated by their fellows as other than they are, then they have to this extent to be accorded *de facto* equality of status.

Sixthly, there is the difference between those systems where there is, and those where there is not, an explicit legal sanction which underlies and sustains differences of status. However true it is that social recognition and esteem are not matters which are subject to legislative regulation, where mobility between strata which are distinguished from each other in social prestige is restricted not merely by custom but by law, there is an evident qualitative difference from those systems where custom alone furnishes the sanction. It is this difference which underlies the remark of Marc Bloch that 'If in France we speak today of the upper middle classes as a capitalist aristocracy, it is only in irony'.[3] Where

[1] George De Vos and Hiroshi Wagatsuma, *Japan's Invisible Race* (Berkeley and Los Angeles, 1966), p. 248.
[2] Nur Yalman, 'The flexibility of caste principles in a Kandyan community', in E. R. Leach (ed.), *Aspects of Caste in South India, Ceylon and North-West Pakistan*, Cambridge Papers in Social Anthropology, No. 2 (Cambridge, 1960), p. 99.
[3] Marc Bloch, *Feudal Society*, tr. Manyon, 2nd edition (London, 1962), p. 283.

every person is treated by law as inheriting the privileges of his father, and where those privileges serve to define a family's rank in terms of status as well as wealth or power, the very notions of exclusiveness, mobility, *déclassement* and so forth take on a different meaning. Of course, it is possible for the members of the society to deny the implications of the law in the sense that they may refuse to accord social esteem to the holders of inherited privilege. But it is a significant fact that they have, as it were, actively to refuse it. Thus when, for example, in imperial Rome it was ruled that a free woman cohabiting with a slave could be claimed, together with any child of the union, by the slave's owner, this will have served institutionally to reinforce the exclusiveness of which endogamy is a characteristic symptom and thereby to increase the social distance separating slaves and free. It will be difficult, and perhaps impossible, to tell just what importance changes of this kind may have in determining the distribution of status within the society at large, given that the attitudes and feelings of individual people never do correlate precisely with those tacitly enshrined in the law. But it can hardly be denied that the role of the law as it bears upon the hierarchy of status constitutes yet another difference of kind which undermines the validity of any ostensibly quantified comparison between one system and the next.

This list of the difficulties is not exhaustive, and will in any case have probably struck the reader as obvious. But it serves to show how the most intractable difficulties in the analysis of stratification arise within the three separate dimensions rather than in the relations between them. The analysis of inequalities of status is problematic not so much because they cannot be described in isolation from inequalities of power or economic class, but because they so seldom lend themselves to the kind of description which would make measurement and comparison possible.

VIII

If this is true of inequalities of status, it is hardly less true of inequalities in the dimension of power. The distribution of power is strictly speaking the province of political science, just as the distribution of wealth is the province of economics; but whether from the inherent difficulty of the subject-matter or because of the relative backwardness of political science, we are scarcely better placed than Aristotle or Hobbes to measure and compare inequalities of power between man and man or stratum and stratum. This has led some writers to voice the suspicion that the term 'power' is somehow inherently inaccurate or misleading, and would be better dropped altogether. But, as with status, it is difficult to deny that the many forms of special relationship habitually labelled in terms of it do all manifest an inequality of a common kind, however difficult to specify precisely. It would, of course, be absurd to suggest that the distribution of power in a society or even a relatively small organization could be plotted on a Lorenz curve as though it were an inequality of wealth. Even an ordinal scale analogous to a social distance scale can be plausibly constructed only under extraordinarily restricted conditions which have little application outside the psychological laboratory. But the various definitions of power which are current in the recent literature, however far they may be from being entirely adequate, all presuppose the meaningfulness of a distribution of power such that some people can be ranked above others by reference to it. The difficulty, as in the dimension of status, lies in the precise allocation of these rankings.

So difficult is it, in fact, to place the members of even a single community in an order of power that many of the writers on 'community power structure' have been justly criticized for falling into the error of simply assuming *a priori* that there is a correlation between the hierarchy of power and the hierarchy of economic class. But to rank the members of a community in order of power it will be necessary to show empirically and in detail both that some are better able than others to bring about actions and decisions on the part of others which conform to their wishes and also that those actions and decisions can be of a kind which those carrying them out are more strongly disposed to resist. The various definitions of power which are offered all agree, whatever their differences, that it has something to do with the capacity to bring about intended states of affairs; and most of them agree that what we mean in speaking of power in terms of more and less is that the more powerful man is both able to determine more actions of more people against stiffer resistance on their part and also to resist more successfully any such attempts made by others on himself. But it is not at all easy to say just what evidence is needed to answer these questions or how it might make possible even an ordinal ranking. Even worse, to the extent that we do know what evidence is called for we are likely to find that it is impossible to obtain.

The researcher cannot restrict himself to the actual performance of those whom he is studying, since the notion of 'having power' involves by definition a capacity to do, or bring about, something if one wishes (which one very well may not). It is not difficult in principle to discover a person's wealth, if he is prepared to co-operate in the enquiry, and even his status can in principle be ascertained by asking the right questions of the other members of his society or group. But it is impossible to discover a person's power without experimental evidence. Where there are satisfactory precedents, or where the scope and limits of the

power attaching to a specific role are clearly laid down within a fixed
institutional framework, then a person's power can to some degree, at
least, be measured. We can say that he can decide more actions of more
people than can others of his fellow-citizens; or that for a given number
of such actions and people he can call on such agencies as will overcome
stronger resistance should those affected be moved to put it up; or that
he is able where others are not to avoid arrest or detention, the forced
levy or extortion of goods, compulsory or directed labour, military
service, and things of this kind. But although it is differences in these
respects which justify the assertion that in a given social system one
group or stratum has more power than another, they leave us still a long
way from the precise description and assignment of weights which would
be necessary for the purpose of comparison; and to establish these it
would be necessary to have available an enormous number of examples
in which the whole range of analogous conditions were precisely and
systematically varied and which even then would only furnish a quasi-
experimental justification for a ranking in order of power.

There is thus at best a limited value in attempting a quantified
analysis of the distribution of power whether defined in the generally
accepted sense which I have tried to summarize or reformulated in such
more sophisticated terms as the probability of an outcome which would
not otherwise come about[1] or the latent capability to inflict sanctions[2] or
the ability to adopt those courses of action which will show the maximum pay-off.[3] The last of these approaches, which derives from the
mathematical theory of games, has the advantage of yielding very
precise differences in winning capacity between one player and another
in the situations to which it can be applied. But the problems of bluff,
coalition, log-rolling and so forth which have been shown to be amenable to formal treatment along these lines merely constitute a further
difficulty in an attempt at a broader appraisal of the power of one
person or group relative to another. It is not impossible that a market
model which draws on primarily economic notions of cost, benefit and
equilibrium may turn out to be applicable over a broader field than has
been shown hitherto. But in general it seems likely that successes will be
bought only at the price of reducing its bearing on those conventional
relationships of power which people tend to have more often in mind
when speaking of the power of one person or group 'over' another.
Indeed, this is one reason why there are so many other terms which are
employed to characterize particular kinds of relations of power—
influence, threat-advantage, control, authority and so on. All fall some-

[1] Robert A. Dahl, 'The concept of power', *Behavioural Science*, II (1957), pp. 201–15.
[2] Karl W. Deutsch, *The Nerves of Government* (New York, 1963), pp. 120 ff.
[3] William H. Riker, *The Theory of Political Coalitions* (New Haven, 1962), pp. 21–3.

where under the broad intuitive definition, but none furnishes an adequate criterion of measurement.

Two further general difficulties are related to these: first, the varying importance of numbers, and, second, the problem sometimes posed by intensity of feeling. Inequalities of either class or status can in general be much more adequately described by reference to roles than can inequalities of power. Power tends to be a function either of personality and circumstances or of numbers and organization, and to learn a person's role may tell the researcher surprisingly little about where he stands relative to others in the hierarchy of power. Not only does the power attaching to a role vary with number in the sense that in an open pluralist society the member or official of a large organized group has in general more power than the member or official of a small one; but even within the Indian caste system, the relative power of Peasants and Brahmins may be a function of their numerical proportions within their community. This might seem at first sight to make the problem of measurement and comparison easier. But even where the significance of number is not influenced by variations in the structural context, there is no way of weighting aggregation, in the sense of the ratio of actual members of a group to possible members, with either concentration, in the sense of the ratio of members to sub-groups or leaders who can be said effectively to speak for them, or numerical importance in the simple sense of the ratio of members of the group to the society at large. And once the structural context is taken into account, number itself in the sense of number of members may become less important than the number of non-members, or in other words the public at large, whose interests the members are in a position to affect: to borrow an example from Gerth and Mills, the elevator boys of Manhattan, whatever their relative wealth or status, are a more powerful group than its violinists.[1] Thus although numbers are indeed important and although they automatically make possible comparisons of a certain kind, they serve in effect only to complicate still further the problem of elaborating how far one person, or role, or group, or stratum can be said to be higher or lower in power than another.

The problem of intensity is in one sense accommodated by defining a person's power not only by reference to the number of people or actions he can modify but by reference to the strength of the resistance which he may encounter. But this may, if feelings run strong enough, give rise to a paradox, for as Tawney observed, to destroy power 'nothing more is required than to be indifferent to its threats'.[2] If X is in a position to require Y to do whatever he wishes on pain of death, and Y is unable to

---

[1] H. H. Gerth and C. Wright Mills, *Character and Social Structure* (London, 1954), p. 329.
[2] R. H. Tawney, *Equality*, 4th edition (New York, 1961), p. 176.

offer resistance to him, then it would be natural to say that X has absolute power over Y. But suppose that Y feels so strongly about being made to do what X wishes that he not merely tries unsuccessfully to escape from X, or evade his instructions, but submits to being killed by X rather than compromise his pride, or his religious principles, or whatever it may be. X may well decide to modify his instructions in this circumstance for he may recognize that if his aim is that Y should do as he wishes he is not achieving it any better by killing him. But do we then have to say that so far from X having more power than Y, Y has more power than X? This sort of paradox is, of course, familiar in formal theories of non-cooperative games. But as I suggested above, to interpret power strictly in these terms is to restrict its meaning too far. Power is not simply the chance of winning, but a relation between persons. If it is interpreted entirely in terms of probabilities of winning, it will merely create still further paradoxes of its own. For instance, it can be formally shown that under certain conditions a war of all against all will give the weakest player the best chance of survival. But it would be at least as absurd to say that he is therefore the most powerful person as to say in the hypothetical example just given that Y had, after all, more power than X.

Yet a further difficulty is that even where the power vested in a particular role can be readily assessed, the power of individuals in the society in question may be held to be measured relative not merely to that role but to their chance of occupying it. Whatever the prerogatives of office, the individual citizen will presumably be said to be less unequally placed if he has a chance, however slight, of occupying the position himself than if he has none whatever. The most egalitarian system, on this basis, will be one in which all offices are filled by lot. The least egalitarian will be one in which political decision rests with one man only, and only the one successor designated by him is eligible to take his place. In between is a whole complex of gradations of what is sometimes called 'politicization' according to which the adult citizen is more or less involved in the processes of decision-making and more or less likely to become so either by standing for office himself or by coming to be in a position where he may influence others who do. The likelihood of office can then be used as itself an index of the relative power of any chosen category of citizens. If an overwhelming majority of successful candidates for office are drawn only from certain restricted groups, whether in terms of wealth, race, occupation or anything else, then this will furnish an obvious criterion for saying that the members of that group should be collectively ranked above others in the hierarchy of power. In a way, this is an analogous measure to the probability of future wealth which requires to be built in to any measure of economic inequality. But where in the economic case the value of this future wealth can be directly related to the monetary yardstick in whose terms a person's position in the commodity and labour markets is expressed, in the political case the chance of office cannot be simply added to the other information acquired about the relative power of a person or group. Once again, although a quantitative measure is possible it does not significantly help to yield the cardinal ordering which an effective three-dimensional model of stratification would require.

Even if a political structure can be clearly described in terms of the power assigned to the various offices within it and the chances of the representative member of any designated group coming to hold one of these offices, it will still be possible to make only a limited and partial comparison between the distribution of power in one society and another. Even such a relatively simple, relatively homogeneous and relatively well documented set of cases as the traditional kingdoms of Africa cannot be compared with each other except in very broad and largely qualitative terms. When it comes to societies as large, complex and sophisticated as those of the advanced industrial nations, then the advantage of greater possibilities of quantification within limited areas is more than offset by the intricacy and incommensurability of the other areas which the researcher must take into account if he is to attempt to plot inequalities of power on even the most rudimentary kind of scale. This is not to say that progress will not be made in the comparative morphology of political systems. But it is hard to see how the generalizations to which subsequent research may lead will ever make possible the rigorous measurement, explanation and comparison of institutionalized inequalities of power.

As in the discussion of status, this review of the difficulties will probably have struck the reader as not only sketchy but obvious. But its moral is the same. The notion of power raises difficulties which make the construction of a satisfactory theory of social stratification exaggeratedly difficult not because we cannot isolate inequalities of power from inequalities of class or status but because having done so it is virtually impossible to make the kinds of comparison and measurement which would be necessary to justify it.

IX

Accordingly, we are now in a position to ask why it is that the three-dimensional framework, although both conceptually and empirically valid, is neither universally accepted nor widely used. The first answer follows directly from the discussion in the preceding sections: the difficulties which arise within the separate dimensions are by themselves enough to undermine any hope of adequately representing the structure of a society in terms of the box on its corner which I described at the beginning. But there are two others reasons also. The first is that the three-dimensional framework is often unnecessary. The second is that it is often uninteresting.

It is often unnecessary simply because of the closeness of fit between the three dimensions alike in industrial and pre-industrial societies. Wealth, power and prestige tend to go together, and this tendency itself is reinforced by a continuous feedback. One obvious example is the position of women. As anthropologists since Lowie have reminded us, their inferior position can be significantly discrepant even as between very similar cultures. But it is still true that women are less privileged than men in almost all known societies; they are less highly regarded, less able to participate in political decision-making, and less wealthy; only in a few cases do they even enjoy the unfettered right to direct inheritance from their fathers; and the separate inferiorities of class, status and power each serve to make the other more difficult to remedy. In some societies, indeed, the three dimensions are so closely interwoven at all levels and in all respects that the system is virtually one-dimensional, particularly where role differentiation is slight. To take only one example, it has been said of Peru in the Inca period that 'the degree of fit between the three sub-cultures (of 'wealth', 'authority' and 'prestige') was so close that they scarcely had any independent meaning'.[1] Often, moreover, the mechanisms for maintaining the fit are quite explicit. A recent study of Ruanda describes how the 'pretence to natural superiority' on the part of the Tutsi is upheld when one of them is unable to maintain himself in the style of life appropriate to his caste by making him the client of a richer Tutsi and thus in turn the patron of a few inferior Hutu.[2] Even where it might be less readily expected, the fit is still apt to be preserved. In ancient Athens, despite its notoriously democratic constitution, voters tended to elect as generals men of wealth and aristocratic birth rather than seasoned professional soldiers: democracy or not, 'the Athenian people', in the words of A. H. M. Jones, 'were rather snobbish in their choice of leaders'.[3] Indeed, the example of Athens serves to show how the fit may be preserved as much by the attitudes of the less privileged as by the policies and ambitions of the élite.

In industrial societies, the index of fit is furnished above all by the hierarchy of occupations. There are, of course, some familiar exceptions.

---

[1] Eugene A. Hammel, *Wealth, Authority and Prestige in the Ica Valley, Peru*, University of New Mexico Publications in Anthropology, no. 10 (Albuquerque, 1962), p. 96.

[2] Jacques J. Maquet, *The Premise of Inequality in Ruanda* (London, 1961), pp. 141–2.

[3] A. H. M. Jones, *Athenian Democracy* (Oxford, 1957), p. 49.

An aristocracy of birth may retain much of its status even when its wealth and power has declined; some bureaucratic or organizational roles may carry undue power relative to their status or pay; some highly regarded occupations may still be badly paid.[But on the whole, a man's occupation is a reliable index of his relative position in all three dimensions.] Perhaps, because of the peculiar difficulties raised by power, it would be safer to say that if and where occupations can be ranked in terms of power, their rank will generally correspond to their rank in the hierarchies of wealth and prestige. But occupations can on the whole be very adequately graded in terms of a 'composite of social and economic attributes that tend to cluster together':[1] in the United States there has been shown to be a correlation as high as $\cdot 91$ between the prestige of occupations and a combined measure of education and income.[2] It is not surprising, therefore, that many researchers have deliberately chosen to work with an index of 'socio-economic status' rather than with separate measures of status and class.

The analysis of social stratification in terms of occupation is equally justifiable whether it is the causes or the consequences of the nature and distribution of occupations which are to be assessed. To explain the distribution of occupations is largely to explain the social inequalities found in industrial societies, and to explain its consequences is to explain how it is that these are modified or preserved. Occupations are the mechanism by which the influences of natural endowment, upbringing and education are translated into differences of wealth, power and prestige, and the most significant moves which the individual can make in all three dimensions will be by means of a change from one occupation to another. Thus occupations are at once the most obvious symptom and the most effective predictor of differential location within the structure of social inequalities, whether considered in terms of income and economic *Lebenschancen*, or life-style, commensalism and endogamy, or autonomy and authority. Whether occupation or some more elaborate measure of 'socio-economic status' is used, there is little need to sift out the separate elements of class, status and power in any of the usual areas of social research in education, politics, demography, criminology and the rest. The fit is too close, and a composite indicator is too useful, for it to be called for.

[The reason why, besides this, the three-dimensional framework is often uninteresting is simply that so many of the most interesting problems in the study of stratification are irrelevant to it.] To see this, it is

[1] Joseph A. Kahl and James A. Davis, 'A comparison of indices of socio-economic status', *American Sociological Review*, xx (1955), p. 321.
[2] O. D. Duncan, 'A socioeconomic index for all occupations', in A. J. Reiss *et al.*, *Occupation and Social Status* (New York, 1961), p. 124.

only necessary to draw up a more or less haphazard list of topics in the field and then count how few of these involve more than very indirectly the distinction between the three dimensions. A number of topics of which this is true have already been touched on in the earlier sections, and the reader will no doubt be able to think of many of his own. But such questions as the following may serve as examples: why did the Greeks base citizenship on birth but the Romans on residence? why was the rate of manumission very much higher in Rome than in Athens? how far can the relations of dependence in feudal Europe be accounted for in military terms? why is the organization of pastoral societies more hierarchical than that of hunting and gathering societies? how important are patron–client relations in pre-industrial societies? how did Denmark, which had had a feudal system, become as egalitarian as Sweden, which had not? what is the importance of religion in sustaining the acceptance of inequality by the underprivileged? how far is this importance related to the stage of technological development? what in general is required to engender a perception of joint interest among those who share a common social location? does the permeability of adjacent strata during industrialization depend on whether urbanization is 'orthogenetic' or 'heterogenetic'?[1] does industrialization diminish or exacerbate racial discrimination? under what circumstances will the privileges of a bureaucratic élite within a centralized state be maximized? what are the principal psychological determinants of occupational mobility? In none of these questions is the distinction between class, status and power more than marginal. Furthermore, this will hold even if large-scale cross-cultural comparisons are to be attempted. The relevant column entries in Murdock's world ethnographic sample[2] are based not on class, status and power but on the presence of slavery, of a hereditary aristocracy, of 'important' distinctions of wealth, and of a complex subdivision into three or more 'classes' or 'castes'. As it happens, these headings are far from adequate for the sorts of comparisons from which valid and useful large-scale generalizations about stratification could ever be extracted. But such a search would nonetheless be at least as likely to be fruitful if conducted along these lines as if conducted along the lines of an elaborate and careful distinction between inequalities of class, status and power.

[1] Robert Redfield and Milton Singer, 'The cultural role of cities', *Economic Development and Social Change*, III (1954), 53–73.
[2] G. P. Murdock, 'World ethnographic sample', *American Anthropologist*, LIX (1957), pp. 664–87.

X

It almost seems, then, as though we are left with the paradox that a fundamental distinction which is conceptually and empirically valid is either inapplicable or simply irrelevant. But this conclusion would be too extreme. If it is easy to construct a list of topics to which the distinction is largely irrelevant, it is no less easy to construct a list of topics to which it is indispensable. What is more, many of these are topics which are difficult or contentious largely because the distinction has been given less attention than it deserves.

This applies not least to the ordering of occupations, which I have just cited as the most familiar example of closeness of fit between class, status and power. It is perfectly true that the familiar exceptions are, indeed, exceptions. But their significance is often out of proportion to their frequency, and they call in any case for explanation no less than do the more usual cases from which the rule has been constructed. It is not simply that as between different occupations the correlation of class-situation with status-situation may not always be exact, or that, as it is sometimes put, the separate 'statuses' bound up with a single occupation are not 'congruent'. Sometimes, an explicit condition of status is the diminution or loss of superiority in economic class; and conversely, sometimes an explicit condition of advantages of class or power is an inferiority of status. An example of the latter is the position of court eunuchs in imperial Rome and China; an example of the former is the position of the *sanyasi* within the Indian system of caste. These cases should not be confused with those where status or power are purchased at a relatively small cost to those who are already rich. Thus, decurions in the later Roman Empire (after 390) were more than willing to bear the very heavy expenses which senatorial rank then entailed because it also brought them both elaborate privileges of precedence and address and also effective immunity from the orders of the provincial governors. But this is closer to the sale of privilege as practised by, say, François I or Lloyd George, which serves more to illustrate how status and power can follow wealth than how a serious forfeiture of economic class can be a condition of it. The more interesting cases are those where there is not simply a lag which is in due course either personally or institutionally remedied, but a permanent discrepancy, such as the wealth accruing to members of despised but essential professions, the rejection of economic gain by the ruling élite in favour of martial glory, or the refusal of commensurate reward to highly esteemed occupations. These can all be documented for a wide range of societies both pre-industrial and industrial, and they call for explanation precisely because they involve an intrinsic and significant non-correlation between two or more of the three fundamental dimensions of stratification.

Where, in particular, there is a discrepancy between the status of a person or group and either their power or their economic class, it is essential to maintain the distinction. Perhaps the most important example is the study of race relations. No explanation will be adequate which attempts to account for this form of stratification simply by assuming *a priori* that inequalities of status are a function of economic exploitation or political dominance without reference to the psychology of purity and pollution. Indeed, this can likewise be said of the position of women. How far it may be possible to generalize on these matters is an open question. The psychology of pollution is by no means fully understood; nor are the social conditions by which the practice of segregation is more or less likely to be broken down. But without precise analysis of the interrelation between the separate dimensions of stratification it will be impossible to understand either the nature of the inequalities to which such relationships give expression or the prior inequalities from which they derive.

More generally, the importance of the three-dimensional distinction becomes clear whenever stratification requires to be discussed in terms of greater or less inequality as opposed to a specific analysis of a qualitatively distinct form of unequal social relationship such as that between master and slave or patron and client. This is true most of all in the discussion of 'classes'. Of course, a part of the difficulty here may be ideological. The views of even the most self-consciously academic observers are likely to be coloured by their approval or disapproval of the particular society in which they live, and there is a persistent tendency for the spokesmen of all kinds of régimes to overstate the degree of egalitarianism within them. Thus, as has often been pointed out, in the Soviet Union there has developed a doctrine of 'non-antagonistic classes' according to which the abolition of private property has eliminated the conflict of interest between hostile strata; and in the United States, correspondingly, there has developed a doctrine of 'classlessness' according to which the absence of hereditary privileges on the European model has allegedly made it meaningless to speak of 'class' membership at all. But there is in fact no need for such apologetics to confuse the issue once the distinction between the dimensions of stratification is strictly maintained. It is only necessary, first, to distinguish stratification from differentiation and, second, to establish as an empirical matter how far some people must be ranked above others in class-situation, status-situation and power. It is true that there will remain the practical difficulties which I have already described. But it is at least roughly clear what sort of evidence we need to answer the question how far state ownership of property in the Soviet Union has diminished inequalities of economic class, or how far the United States, although still permitting marked inequalities of economic class, has (among Whites) a more egalitarian status-system than other countries. The two further questions where, and on what grounds, a division should be made between one particular 'class' and another, and how far the members of these 'classes' perceive and act on a common interest, are, as always, a separate matter.

As before, the reader will be able to think of many instances for himself where the distinction between the three dimensions is appropriate and useful. But it may be worth citing a few current topics of controversy where a thoroughgoing recognition of the validity and application of the distinction could help to sift out much, if not all, of the purely verbal confusion which bedevils the argument. Consider, for example, the following questions: how far is the social structure of the Soviet Union going to become like that of the United States? have British manual workers and their families become middle-class? does the Negro population of the United States constitute a separate caste? can social stratification be shown in some way to be functional for social systems as a whole? are all societies controlled by an élite? These questions are, to be sure, very ill-defined. But they are very ill-defined in the literature where they are fully and extensively discussed. Once it has first of all been established to what extent they do relate to stratification and not simply to differentiation, then they will be effectively answered only by reference to the distinction between class, status and power. Theories of 'convergence' between advanced industrial nations must take account of how far similarities in the distribution of wealth within a highly differentiated occupational system may be compatible with marked dissimilarities in the distribution of power. Theories of *embourgeoisement* must show how far similarities in style of life made possible by equalization of class-situation may be compatible with continuing hierarchical distinctions of commensalism, endogamy and relations of friendship. Attempts to include the position of the American Negro within a more general theory of 'caste' must show how far the relation between the economic, political and status hierarchies found in the Indian system are paralleled in the United States. A 'functional' theory of stratification will have to show whether and to what extent it is an unequal distribution of economic rewards, social esteem, or institutionally vested authority which is claimed to be necessary for the adaptation of societies to changes in their environment. The argument between 'élitists' and 'pluralists' must establish empirically not only how power is distributed and governmental decisions influenced but to what extent this distribution is or is not causally related to the distribution of wealth and status.

These remarks may seem so obvious that they ought to be wholly un-necessary. But it is precisely because the distinction between the three dimensions of stratification has often been neglected that the discussion of these topics has often been unnecessarily confused. The fact that, for the reasons we have seen, the distinction cannot be rigorously applied is in no way a sufficient reason to ignore it.

Whether there will ever be a general theory of stratification is of course a further question. But if there will, it follows from the validity of the three-dimensional distinction that any general theory will have to be expressible in terms of it. Unless it is somehow shown that class, status and power are not conceptually and empirically distinct, or else that there is some further dimension in which organizations and societies are strati-fied, then the content of a general theory of stratification can be nothing other than such general propositions as will furnish an adequate and comprehensive explanation of any institutionalized inequalities observed anywhere and at any time—that is, of any and all 'conventional' rela-tions of class, status and power. This would include, moreover, all those relations which I have cited as qualitatively distinct, for even if the explanation of, say, patron/client relationships were to require the application of terms not found elsewhere within the theory, it would still be true that the superiority of the patron and the inferiority of the client can only consist in some combination or other of the three fundamental kinds of inequality. Even those questions which may not appear to require direct reference to the distinction could be conclusively an-swered only by reference, as more or less special cases, to the laws from which all variations in the nature and degree of institutionalized in-equalities would in principle be predictable. To this extent, therefore, the irrelevance of the distinction to many of the specific problems with which students of stratification are concerned is simply a mark of the present inadequacy of our knowledge of the necessary and sufficient conditions of the phenomena we are attempting to observe.

In any event, there is little purpose in speculating about what a general theory of stratification might look like. The necessary limitations on the extent of rigorous, comprehensive and publicly testable know-ledge which the historian or sociologist is ever likely to attain renders the hope utopian from the start; and the extent to which it will ever be ful-filled is an empirical matter which, as the relevant knowledge increases, will take care of itself. For the moment, we are not even in a position properly to answer the elementary question by which the social theorists of the nineteenth century were so strongly divided: does indus-trialization increase inequalities, as was believed by Marx and Engels, or decrease them, as was believed by Tocqueville and J. S. Mill? When there is so much still to be learnt, it may seem less important to argue about terminology than to set about collecting the facts. But in the field of stratification, as in others, many of the facts that we have would be much more useful to us if they had been collected with closer attention to avoidable confusions of terminology and logic. If the argument of this paper is correct, it will have shown that the researcher who ignores the distinction between the three separate dimensions of stratification must show good reason for doing so; and even if it is not, I hope that it may at any rate put the onus of argument on those who deny that this is so instead of those who assert it.

4

PRESTIGE, PARTICIPATION AND
STRATA FORMATION[1]

S. N. EISENSTADT

PART I

In this paper I shall attempt to present a preliminary analysis of the relation between two aspects of social life which have always been presented in sociological literature as basic components of social stratification—first social division of labour, functional social differentiation and the concomitant differential evaluation of roles and tasks,[2] and second, the division of society into several groups or strata which are arranged in some hierarchical relations or orders. Such groups or strata have been designated as 'classes' in Marxian terminology, as classes, estates and parties (or political groupings) in Weber's nomenclature, or classes and castes as used in some American community studies.[3]

Although these two approaches deal with similar or even identical

[1] The present article is part of a wider work on institutional analysis and stratification in which I have been engaged for some time. The initial stage of this work has been undertaken together with Dr E. O. Shild, and has been summarized in an unpublished paper 'Stratification and exchange' and in a series of working papers we have prepared together. Some parts of the present article (and especially pp. 66–67) are to some extent based on that paper. In the later stages of this work I have benefited from the collaboration of Mrs Y. Atzmon, Y. Carmeli, Miss M. Korelaro and G. Yatziv. Miss M. Korelaro has helped me in the preparation of the present paper. I am especially greatly indebted to Professor Edward Shils for very detailed comments and annotations of an earlier draft of this article.

[2] See for instance K. Davis and W. E. Moore, 'Some principles of stratification', *American Sociological Review*, vol. 10, 2 (1945), pp. 242–9; M. M. Tumin, 'Some principles of stratification: a critical analysis', *American Sociological Review*, vol. 18, 4 (1953), pp. 387–94; T. Parsons, 'A revised analytical approach to the theory of social stratification', in T. Parsons, *Essays in Sociological Theory* (Glencoe, Illinois, 1954). For the best single collection of the basic materials on stratification see R. Bendix and S. M. Lipset, *Class, Status and Power* (2nd edition) (New York, 1965).

[3] See for instance K. Marx and F. Engels, *Manifesto of the Communist Party* (N.Y., 1932), H. H. Gerth and C. W. Mills (eds.), *From Max Weber, Essays in Sociology* (New York, 1958), esp. ch. 7. For illustrations of American community studies see W. L. Warner and P. S. Lunt, *The Social Life of a Modern Community* (New Haven, 1941); W. L. Warner, M. Meeker and K. Eels, *Social Class in America* (Chicago, 1949); R. and H. Lynd, *Middle Town* (New York, 1925) and *Middle Town in Transition* (New York, 1937). For a critique of most of these community studies see S. M. Lipset and R. Bendix, 'Social status and social structure: A re-examination of data and interpretations', *British Journal of Sociology*, vol. 2 (1951), pp. 150–68, 230–54.

phenomena and to a large extent also use similar or identical nomenclature, so far there have been, on the whole, few systematic attempts to explain the one in terms of the other. True enough, strata have usually been defined as consisting of people occupying positions which are similar on some evaluative scale or in terms of the degree of their control of different resources, but there have been few attempts to explain how the process of differential evaluation of roles and tasks gives rise not only to a hierarchy of roles within any specific group but also to some such hierarchy of strata in the broader macro-societal setting, or conversely how the existence of such strata influence or shape the social division of labour and social differentiation. In the following pages some preliminary indications about the relations between these components of stratification will be presented.

The basic aspects of social structure most relevant for the study of social stratification have usually been designated first as the fact that any social system is composed of interconnected roles, the incumbents of each of which are expected to perform different tasks, and second what has been called in sociological literature the differential allocation of rewards to the incumbents of these roles. It is probably a universal fact of social life that in all groups and societies different positions receive differential rewards—be they differential esteem and deference, different amounts of services or commodities given to them by other people or different amounts of obedience they can command from their fellows, i.e. different amounts of power, which are allocated to them according to some socially relevant or accepted criteria or values. Third is the fact of the existence of differential access, among different individuals, categories or groups of people in a society, to the various positions or roles which are differentially evaluated or rewarded. Fourth is the possibility that the existence of such a differential allocation of rewards and access creates, within any group, some type of hierarchy of roles which may perhaps coalesce into some broader categories of people, into some groups or quasi-groups, with some common identity and continuity, usually called strata.

Already this relatively simple enumeration of the major characteristics of social stratification indicates some of the basic and most difficult problems in its analysis. First: which positions or which holders of which positions are differentially evaluated or rewarded? Second: what is the nature of these rewards; of what do they consist; how can they be used; how do they influence the evaluation of different positions and the access to them? Third: what are the criteria on which such differential rewarding of roles rest? Fourth: why are these particular criteria used, and how were they developed, i.e. how and by whom have they been established, and how have they become accepted? Last: under what conditions do such positions develop into some sort of hierarchy and what are the mechanisms through which the incumbents of such positions coalesce into some sorts of groups or into 'strata'—whatever their exact definition may be. Of these problems those which seem to be of special importance from the point of view of the conditions of strata formation will now be considered.

Perhaps the easiest problem—at least in a first, preliminary approach— is the designation of the types of social positions which tend, in all societies, to become the focuses of such differential evaluation. These are, in all groups or societies—albeit in different degrees—the various positions in the major institutional spheres, i.e. political, economic, cultural, religious, educational, etc.; those positions which are related to the central spheres and symbols of a society, and which represent the community; as well as positions which designate membership in certain primordial-social categories (like age) or collectivities (ethnic, racial, national, etc.). Somewhat more complicated is the problem of the nature of the rewards which are differentially 'allocated', of the ways in which these rewards can be used by the people who receive them and of the relevance of such uses for various aspects of social stratification.

What are these rewards? Although they may, of course, vary greatly in detail, on the whole they can be—and have been—classified by most sociologists in similar ways. As has been briefly listed above, people may get from other people particular services and/or particular commodities, and/or general means (media of exchange) of which money is, of course, the most general and important; some general facilities, like education, through which such services or commodities can be obtained; general obedience—i.e. be invested with authority to give commands to other people—at least in some spheres of life. They can also be given 'deference' or in common sociological parlance be invested with some 'esteem' or 'prestige'. These different types of rewards have been classified in the 'classical' triplet of power, wealth and prestige which have been designated in almost all studies of stratification as the major types of rewards allocated to different roles and presumably indicating their differential evaluation and standing. They have also often been designated as the bases or roots of such evaluation.

Despite the relative simplicity of the definitions of these major types of rewards, they really contain many problems and difficulties. One such problem, most important for the study of stratification in general and comparative perspective in particular, is, as we shall see in greater detail later (p. 68), the extent to which the rewards which are given in any face-to-face group, in any partial organization, in any parochial setting, are also meaningful beyond it, are evaluated outside it in the same way as inside, and can accordingly be used outside it. Do the power, services, commodities or the deference that a leader of a street corner gang has in his group provide him with any means through which he can gain some commodities, power or prestige in other groups or in the macro-society—or are they of little value in this respect? There may be, as we shall see in greater detail later, great differences, in various societies, between these three types of rewards, i.e. between power, wealth and prestige.

Before turning to this problem, it might be worth while turning to the problem of the different types of uses of such resources and the implication of these uses for the process of strata formation. Such rewards may be used in three ways. First, they can be directly consumed. Second, they can be used for 'symbolic consumption'; and last, for 'exchange'— for getting something else, some other service, commodities or privileges. The first way of using such resources—direct consumption—is seemingly the simplest and least problematic one. People may 'consume' the various commodities which they receive, i.e. use the services of others for their own enjoyment, command the activities and obedience of others in order to enjoy the subservience of others, or they may simply 'bask' in the deference given to them by others. Such consummatory use of rewards merges into the second type of their use—that of symbolic consumption—insofar as activities become conspicuous to outsiders and thereby tend to call forth evaluative judgments. The consumption acquires thereby a symbolic significance and it might even become motivated by considerations of that significance. In such cases a great stress may be laid on the exclusiveness of such consumption, i.e. to its being limited to certain groups of people, so that the very use of such patterns of consumption symbolizes their being different, possibly 'better', from others.

The terms 'conspicuous consumption' and 'style of life'—as well as the phenomenon of sumptuary laws—have often been used to illustrate this type or aspect of consumption. But beyond these two uses of the various rewards, which stress the fact that they may be seen as goals which people desire or the objects of acts which people admire—there is another way in which they can be used—a way which stresses their being also resources through which other services or commodities can be obtained, i.e. they may serve as resources or media of exchange in social, institutional, interaction. The variety of the ways in which these rewards-resources can be used in exchange is, of course, very great,[1] but at this point of our discussion we would like to emphasize only one way which is of special importance in the analysis of stratification—namely the possibility to use such rewards or resources in order to gain access (for themselves or for other people—especially, but not only, their

[1] See S. N. Eisenstadt, *Essays on Comparative Institutions* (New York, 1965), pp. 22–35.

children and relatives—who are seen as an extension of themselves, who share some primordial identity with them) to some of the more highly evaluated or rewarded positions—whether the same positions which they hold or other 'high' positions or roles, and to exclude others from getting access to such positions.

The use of various resources for regulating access to position may be done in principle in several different ways. One way is to satisfy (or to purchase means for satisfying) the requirements of access to a certain position for the actor himself or for other. Second, and no less important, is the use of these resources for the definition of the requirements of access themselves, for the setting up of norms which can limit in various ascriptive ways, institutional interaction in general and access to positions in particular.[1]

The differential allocation of rewards to various roles and positions, the 'symbolic' consumption of such rewards and their use for control of access to the higher positions—constitute the basic components of stratification on a macro-societal level, the starting points of the processes of strata formation. However, the relations between these various processes have not been fully explored in the literature. Even the first two approaches—which emphasize the differential allocation of rewards on the one hand and the differential access to positions on the other— have not been too closely connected in the analysis of stratification. They have gone separate ways—each usually engendering different lines of research and enquiry although in some analyses a rapprochement between the two can sometimes be discerned.[2]

Only recently has it been more perceived that these two constitute two basic and interconnected aspects of any system of stratification. For instance, Fallers has emphatically stressed this, designating differential evaluation of positions as the primary aspect of stratification and the regulation of access to positions as its secondary aspect.[3] But on the whole—and even in Faller's exposition—there have been but few attempts to study systematically the structural, long-range linkage between these two aspects of stratification—beyond the assertion of the

[1] On ascriptive restrictions see R. Linton, *The Study of Man* (New York, 1936), ch. 8; T. Parsons, 'A revised analytical approach to the theory of social stratification', in T. Parsons, *Essays in Sociological Theory*. For a criticism of the conception of ascription in relation to stratification, see M. G. Smith, 'Pre-industrial stratification systems', in N. J. Smelser and S. M. Lipset (eds.), *Social Structure and Mobility in Economic Development* (Chicago, 1966), pp. 141–76.

[2] For some of the classical illustrations of attempts at such rapprochement see J. A. Schumpeter, *Imperialism and Social Classes* (New York, 1951), part II; Gerth and Mills (eds.), *From Max Weber: Essays in Sociology*. For a more recent approach see D. H. Wrong, 'The functional theory of stratification: some neglected considerations', *American Sociological Review*, vol. 24, 6 (1959), pp. 772–82.

[3] L. Fallers, 'Equality, modernity and democracy in the New States', in C. Geertz (ed.), *Old Societies and New States* (Glencoe, Illinois, 1963), pp. 161–8.

general fact that people (or children of people) who occupy higher positions in a certain institutional sphere, usually have better chances of access to high positions in the same or another institutional sphere. Or, in other words, there have only been a few attempts to analyse systematically the nature of the mechanisms through which these two aspects of stratification are linked in different societies; to analyse the ways— and the extent—to which differential evaluation of different positions and the different types and degrees of rewards which such positions receive within a society influence both the short and long range intra- and inter-generational differential access of their incumbents (and/or their children) to other or (in the case of their children) similar institutional positions. Similarly, while it has been recognized in the literature that the symbolic consumption of rewards is a very important component of stratification, yet the relation between such symbolic consumption and other aspects of stratification—such as regulation of access to position, although often mentioned—have not been fully investigated. In order to be able to explore the linkage between these three major aspects or components of stratification, it is necessary first to analyse in greater detail the nature of one of the major types of resources or rewards mentioned above, namely that of prestige.

Prestige or 'honour' has always been designated as one of the three basic rewards which is differentially distributed in any group or society. Moreover it has always been designated as constituting a basic symbol of one's social standing or status. And yet of all the different rewards it has been at the same time the least analytically specified. Both the bases (or criteria) of prestige and especially the structural implications of its differential distribution have been abundantly described but not fully and systematically analysed. They were to some extent taken for granted, often subsumed under, or related to, the concept of 'style of life'—which often served, like the concept of prestige itself, as a sort of general residual category in studies of stratification. Of all the different rewards it seems on the one hand to be most 'symbolic', most elusive, least concrete. It does not seem to have the hard-core structural and organizational features that characterize money and commodities, power, coercion and obedience. Its most obvious expressions are symbolic—such as esteem or deference given to people, conferral of medals or of honorary titles, or keeping a certain distance from those who are bestowed with such prestige. It seems also to be the most directly consummatory of all the different rewards—i.e. it seems as if nothing can be done with it beyond the mere enjoyment of the deference, reverence or the special standing inherent in it.

And yet, on the other hand, in large parts of the sociological and historical literature on stratification, prestige manifest either in external symbols of status or in what is often called the 'style of life' of different people and groups, is presented as constituting a basic *structural* component or aspect of stratification. It is often presented as the focus around which some at least of the major organizations or structural aspects of strata tend to be formed. But the relation between these two aspects of prestige—the relatively purely consummatory symbolic one and its structural ramifications in terms of groups or categories of people—have not been fully explicated; although, needless to say, there exists in sociological literature an abundance of accounts or illustrations of both the personal and institutional bases of prestige. But in most of them prestige has often been seen as a derivative either of personal attributes, or of various institutional (i.e. economic, power, cultural, etc.) positions, or of the performance of functionally important tasks, without having a more autonomous, independent, societal and symbolic base. And yet a closer look at any group or society will show that within most, probably all, groups or societies at least three such specific, distinct societal bases of prestige can be discerned.

The first base of prestige is the very membership in any collectivity (or sub-collectivity), group or society. Almost all groups and societies differentiate between members and non-members and attempt to endow members with some special symbols which designate their special status or standing. A second source of prestige is the ability of controlling the collectivity, of representing it, of defining its goals and its central activities and symbols, or in other words to be in a sense in its 'centre'.[1] Although such 'centrality' is very often closely related to power, the two are not, as we shall see, analytically identical. The third specific societal root or base of prestige is the proximity to or participation in some broader socio-cultural—cosmic or religious, scientific, etc.—order, which is defined as relevant for the definition of a given collectivity or for its members. It is very often those who seem to be closest to or representing the essence of such order, tradition or 'mystery', who are knowledgeable about it and are the holders of the most prestigious roles. These three sources have one common denominator—namely, the quality of participation i.e. participation in a collectivity, in its centre or in some broader cultural order, even if the nature and quality of such participation may greatly differ with regard to each such 'source'.

Thus, according to this view, the sources of prestige, of the deference

---

[1] See E. Shils, 'Centre and periphery', in *The Logic of Personal Knowledge*, Essays presented to Michael Polanyi (London, 1961), pp. 117–31. Of relevance in this context, and especially in the study of traditional societies, are the concepts of Great and Little Traditions as developed by Redfield and Singer: R. Redfield, *Peasant Society and Culture* (Chicago, 1956); 'The social organisation of tradition', *The Far Eastern Quarterly*, xv (1955); R. Redfield and Milton Singer, 'The cultural role of cities', *Economic Development and Cultural Change*, III (1954), 53–73.

which people render to others, are rooted not only in their organizational (power, economic, etc.) positions or in some purely personal qualities, but also in their differential participation in one of these types of order which constitute the institutional focuses of what may be called the charismatic dimension of human and social existence, in their contribution to the development and maintenance of such orders or in their representation of the qualities of such orders.[1]

But such participation is not only a base of prestige: it constitutes one major aspect of prestige as a reward. The reward which is expressed by giving deference, by endowing somebody (whether an individual, a role or group) with prestige, is the recognition of his right to participate in any of these orders, or of his special contribution to them. In this view prestige becomes less symbolic and more structural, closer to the use of other types of resources and to the regulation of differential access to positions.

This can be seen first in the ways in which this conception of prestige throws some light on the structural implications of the desirability of prestige. As in all the major types of rewards, prestige also constitutes one of the many discrete desiderata and goals of individuals. It may, however, also become the focus of personal and collective identity,[2] and as such also have important broader, more generalized structural implications from the point of view of stratification. The most important of such implications are first the attempts to link the regulation of the desiderata or goals pursued by people with the degree to which they are allowed to participate in these collectivities, orders and centres. Needless to say, many discrete goals or desiderata—economic, political, 'social' or cultural—can be pursued, even in the most ascriptive societies, by people who do not belong to a certain category or group. And yet, there seems to be, in every society, some *combination* of desiderata which is perceived by the members of such groups (or by people belonging to certain social categories), as well as by others, as being peculiarly bound to those who share certain types of personal and collective identities, i.e. some combination of personal qualities or attributes on the one hand, with differential participation in these collectivities, orders and centres on the other. The most important structural manifestations of such

---

[1] See E. Shils, 'Charisma, order and status', *American Sociological Review*, vol. 30 (1965), pp. 199–213. See also S. N. Eisenstadt, 'Charisma and institution building: Max Weber and modern sociology' (Introduction to a selection from Weber's work to be published in The Heritage of Sociology Series by University of Chicago Press, 1968 (forthcoming)).

[2] *Ibid.* For some of the basic exploration of identity see Erik H. Erikson, 'Childhood and society', 2nd edition, and 'Identity and uprootedness in our time'—both in *Insight and Responsibility* (New York, 1964). For a systematic attempt to explore some of the social dimensions of identity, see D. R. Miller, 'The study of social relationship, situation identity and social interaction', in S. Koch (ed.), *Psychology: The Study of a Science*, vol. 5 (New York, 1963), pp. 639–737.

claims to pursue certain goals by virtue of such differential participation is the upholding of different styles of life—a concept which
we have encountered already above and which we shall explicate later
on.

But, secondly, the view presented here does explicate the structural
implications of prestige not only as a desideratum but also as a medium
of institutional interaction and exchange. Here prestige becomes in
some respects not entirely dissimilar from money or power. It can also
serve as a media of exchange, as a basis for getting other commodities—
such as money or power, or services. True enough, prestige is not usually
directly exchangeable for power or money; very often any attempt to
use prestige in such a way would entail its loss. But those having prestige
can often use it as starting points for specially favourable bargaining
positions, for the acquisition of other types of services, commodities or
media of exchange.

The man who has prestige may get some services, commodities or
obedience which would be inaccessible to others, or at a 'price' greatly
different from that which is demanded of others for such a commodity.
Moreover, prestige—the right of participation in different collectivities,
socio-cultural orders and centres—can also be used to assure one's access
to other institutional positions, such as economic or power ones, and to
attempt to limit the possibilities of other people having such access; the
illustrations of this are too numerous to need any documentation.

On the other hand those who have other resources—be they power or
money—may attempt to use them in such a way as would enhance their
chances of receiving prestige—even if it cannot usually be *directly*
acquired by such means. It is indeed the various attempts to link, in
some indirect way, the ownership of other resources with the attainment
of prestige that constitutes the major structural implication of prestige as
a medium of exchange in society.

It is these attempts to link prestige with other positions or resources
which constitutes the evaluative component of stratification. Such
evaluation is rooted in the assessment of any single position or sets of
positions in terms of one or several such bases of prestige. It is through
such evaluation that any specific position may become endowed with
some broader meaning and the rewards which it receives may become
legitimized in terms of some such meaning. But our preceding analysis of
the structural derivatives of prestige indicates that such evaluation is not
purely 'symbolic'. It is manifest in a very distinct structural mechanism
in the various mechanisms which attempt to link structurally prestige, in
the sense defined above, with other positions and resources.

The most important aspect, from the point of view of stratification
analysis, of these mechanisms is the institutionalization of the upholding

of the different styles of life discussed above and of various ascriptive limitations on institutional interaction, exchange and access to positions and on participation in exchange.[1] In most general terms such ascriptive restrictions on access mean that entry into a position is contingent not only upon satisfying requirements which can be satisfied in open interaction and exchange, but that in addition or in place of such requirements the candidate must belong to a certain social category or be an incumbent of certain other positions. Ascriptive restrictions on exchange means that an actor, even if he possesses the commodities relevant to a given exchange and is willing to enter into the exchange, is excluded because of his belongingness to some group or category of people.

It is the various structural derivatives of prestige analysed above that constitute some of the most important mechanisms through which the different aspects of stratification outlined above—the differential evaluation of positions; the uses of the rewards received for the regulation of access to positions; and for symbolic consumption which denotes the upholding of certain styles of life—become interconnected, albeit in different degrees, in different societies, and become the starting points of the process of strata formation. Or in other words that the process of strata formation can be viewed as that aspect of the general process of institution building which tends to establish such ascriptive limitations on exchange in terms of the setting up of basic individual and collective identities, of their arrangement in some hierarchical order, of specification of the desiderata which are 'tied' to such identities and which are manifest in different styles of life, and which tends to establish ascriptive limitations on access to positions. Although most of these elements of strata formation can be found in all relatively continuous social groupings, they become especially articulated in the macro-societal order where the crystallization of the basic personal and collective identities assumes several additional dimensions.

First, these identities become here closely related to participation in some primordial—family, kinship and territorial—groups which constitute the starting point from which possibilities of participation in other types of social or cultural units and orders tend to branch out. Second, on the macro-societal level, individuals' various desiderata include not only a great variety of discrete goals but also the propensity or sensitivity to some—usually differential—participation in all the major types of socio-cultural orders and centres. Third, in the macro-societal order the relations between the positions which a person occupies in all institutional spheres becomes very important both from the point of view of the individual's personal identity as well as from the point of view of broader integrative and regulative problems of the social order.

[1] See, in greater detail, Eisenstadt, *Essays on Comparative Institutions.*

It is these various elements specified above that constitute the major starting points of strata formation on the macro-societal level.

Strata (be they estates, castes, or classes, or political groups)[1] have usually been designated as categories or groups of people who are incumbents of institutional positions or roles which enjoy a similar broad evaluation, who receive similar differential rewards, and/or have a similar degree of control over some of the basic resources (i.e. economic, political or cultural) who tend to some extent to transmit such positions to their children or to other persons who are seen as extensions of their primordial identity and who, to some degree, are or seem to be organized in some hierarchical order. But any 'classificatory' approach to strata formation in terms of relative standing of a certain category or group of people with regard to any one resource does not enable us to understand how this is related to its standing with regard to the distribution of some of the other resources.

In any macro-societal order there necessarily arises, as we have seen, the problem of the relation and linkages among the different positions in the major institutional spheres. The effecting of such linkage constitutes one basic aspect or component of any strata formation. Its most crucial aspects are, as we have seen above, the attempts to monopolize or regulate, directly or indirectly, the conversion of resources among such different institutional positions, the historical or some wider meaning on various specific institutional positions, and the setting up of the rules of access to them, according to some ascriptive criteria which stress components of personal and collective identity which are defined as common to the incumbents of the given positions. These tend to be, as we have seen above, defined mostly by the combination of certain personal attributes and of differential participation in the major types of societal and cultural orders that exist in every macro-societal setting.

Out of these starting points the two major structural derivations of stratification, the upholding of styles of life and the regulation of access to positions, become crystallized in processes of strata formation. The emphasis on the upholding of a certain style of life denotes the symbolic consumption which manifests the differential participation of those who use them in such a way in various collectivities, socio-cultural orders and centres and their having attained some of the qualities which define these orders and centres. It does also bestow some broader meaning, in terms of such participation and qualities, on different specific institutional positions.

On the other side of this picture are also the attempts, by such groups, to deny—or at least make it difficult for—other groups to undertake

---

[1] For some of the major 'classical' definitions of strata see: Schumpeter, *op. cit.*; Weber, *op. cit.*; Warner and Lunt, *op. cit.*

these types of exchange, to attain such goals and as well to be able to acquire the requirements for those positions which may imply or necessitate the pursuance of such goals. Thus the development and upholding of such styles of life necessarily contain a very strong element of inclusiveness and exclusiveness—of inclusion of some people and of the concomitant exclusion of other social categories or groups. But such exclusiveness does not mean total isolation from other categories or groups, from other roles or people. The very emphasis on exclusiveness connotes a certain type of relationship with them—basically a certain type of 'unconditional' yet complementary relation with them.

A second crucial aspect of strata formation—most specifically articulated on the macro-societal level—are the attempts to transmit the right of conversion of resources and the access to the various positions occupied by certain categories or groups of people, to others who share some primordial identity. The most important (but not the only) type of such transmission is that through intra-familial, intergenerational units, as in most total societies (as distinct from more partial groups) the extension of one's identity is mostly—although not entirely—effected through the primordial family and kinship units. These units perform, from the point of view of stratification on the macro-societal level, several different functions which need not, however, always go together to the same degree. First, as they serve as the most general agency of socialization, it is from within them that basic orientations to different desiderata, as well as basic components or ingredients of personal and collective identity, are inculcated in individuals.

Second, they may also serve as agencies through which the access of positions is transmitted, either directly (i.e. through ascriptive, hereditary access), or, more indirectly, through the provision of resources which facilitate the acquisition of skills and attributes which tend to be necessary prerequisites for such positions. Third, is the limitation of intermarriage through the rules of exogamy, endogamy and hypergamy which are found in some way in most societies, and which very often constitute a very important aspect or focus of stratification. The importance of all these rules is rooted in the fact that the family and interfamilial relations may serve as the starting point for the development of strata solidarity which focuses around the common style of life, symbolized as it is in symbolic consumption on the one hand and in differential participation in different collectivities and socio-cultural orders and centres on the other.

Thus it is the combination of the ownership of resources with the control over the uses of such resources, over the conversion of such resources from one institutional sphere to another, from one group to another, from micro-social settings to the macro-societal order, with ascriptive regulation of access to their respective positions, and with the stress on a common identity with some strong primordial components that constitutes the crux of the process of strata formation in macro-societal terms. But the establishment of such identities and the con-comitant regulation of desiderata is not something 'given' in any society; it is in itself part of a continuous process of social institutional interaction. Here of crucial importance is the acquisition of the rights to establish the criteria according to which different positions are evaluated and different styles of life are legitimized. The institutional settings within which, in groups and especially in the macro-societal setting, such rights tend to become located, are the various social or cultural centres. Hence such centres necessarily are of crucial importance in the process of stratification in general and in that of strata formation in particular.

It is such centres which attempt to control both the differential participation of various categories of people in the major collectivities and cultural orders, as well as the conversion of various resources into other resources, and into chances of access to various institutional posi-tions. While, needless to say, such centres are not the only mechanism through which such conversion is being effected, and many other mechanisms—such as market or bargaining processes—are also very important from this point of view, yet the centres play a crucial role in this process. The special place of the centres for stratificational purposes is rooted in the fact that they combine or may attempt to combine the setting up of the basic symbols of personal, societal and cultural identity, the control of participation in the various collectivities and socio-cultural orders, together with the setting up of societal goals[1] and with more 'mundane' regulation of economic, legal, etc. relations within a society.

From the preceding discussion several general conclusions about processes of stratification and of strata formation—which I shall be able to explore here only in a very preliminary way—can be derived. The first is that it does not make great sense to talk about stratification —and especially about strata formation—in those societies in which the problem of such conversion of resources and of access to positions is very small. This is especially true of those societies (among 'total' societies, various types of primitive societies)—or in those spheres thereof—to which access is either distributed more or less equally among all mem-bers of a society, or in which the 'rates' of such conversion in general and the rules of access to positions in particular are ascriptively fixed to such a degree that there is very little scope for different ways or for

---

[1] See, in greater detail, Eisenstadt, *Essays on Comparative Institutions* and 'Charisma and Institu-tion-Building', *loc. cit.* See also the bibliography in the notes on p. 68.

changes of conversion of various resources and of regulation of access to positions. In such societies there may exist social differentiation but not social stratification and especially not processes of strata formation in the sense used here.[1]

The second conclusion is that the problem of strata formation arises when there does not exist such *automatic*, fixed conversion of resources and of access to positions, and there exists the possibility of different ways of converting the resources or the rewards derived from one set of positions to others.

Third is that the crystallization, through such processes of conversion of some broader, solidary groups or strata with common identity, is closely related to the existence of some common points of reference among them, i.e. of some types of centres, to which they share some common orientations, and that therefore the structure and contents of such centres play a very prominent role in such processes of strata formation.

Fourth is that although the process of strata formation combines all the various components outlined above, i.e. the setting up of identities, the regulation of access to positions and of their ascriptive transmission through some familial or semi-familial arrangements, the upholding of styles of life and the concomitant transmission of orientations to desiderata and goals through the major agencies of socialization, yet they need not always go together to the same extent in all societies; and one of the major differences between societies lies exactly in the extent to which they tend to coalesce together.

Fifth, the preceding analysis has some interesting implications for the problem of the extent to which there may exist a single hierarchy of status in a society. As is well known, sociological literature, following Weberian terminology, has distinguished three major dimensions of types of strata: 'classes', 'estates' and political groups. It has indeed been usually recognized in the literature that, in any society, each of these types of strata formation involves a different type of resources or of different types of institutional types of positions on which they are based. But there have been few attempts to indicate exactly how the three are connected: how, to what extent, in what ways do these different formations coalesce or diverge in different societies.

The picture that one may get from large parts of the literature dealing with this problem tends to waver between two extreme views—one which stresses that each of these formations constitutes a separate entity or hierarchy, and another in which they tend basically to coalesce and merge into one another. It is only recently, in the literature on congruence of status, that it has been recognized that these need not always

[1] See on this: M. G. Smith, 'Pre-industrial stratification systems', *op. cit.* pp. 53 f.

go together.[1] But even this literature, because of its stress on the 'dysfunctional' results of such incongruence, assumes that such congruence and a concomitant unified hierarchy constitutes in a way the natural order of things. However, our analysis which stresses the multiplicity of starting points of institutions, resources and positions on the one hand, and of different centres on the other, does imply that in any macrosocietal society there does not exist only one but several such hierarchies which tend to converge or to overlap to some, but only to some, degree and that the extent to which they converge or overlap again constitutes one of the major foci of comparative research.

PART II

We shall attempt to illustrate the utility of the approach presented above by comparing the process of strata formation in several societies which can be said to belong to one rather common broad type—that of Imperial or semi-Imperial societies—such as Imperial China, Russia, India or Western European Societies in the Age of Absolutism.[2] These societies had several common characteristics which distinguish them from other societies and which do therefore facilitate the comparison among them. One such common characteristic was a not dissimilar level of technology and hence also a similar basic range of occupational positions. Another such common characteristic was their traditionality as evident in the structure of their centres.

The basic categories of institutional-occupational positions sharing some common life chances and which can be found in these systems are the following:[3]

(a) The peasantry, comprising the majority of the population, living in free or servile village communities; sometimes subdivided—from the point of view of legal ownership and wealth—into various subgroups, such as gentry, middle or lower groups of peasants and a possible agricultural proletariat.

(b) Various upper or middle urban economic or professional groups such as merchants, craftsmen (again possibly divided into big and small ones), and some professional groups such as lawyers, doctors, etc. In

---

[1] See for example E. Benoit Smyllan, 'Status, status types, and status interrelations', *American Sociological Review*, vol. 9, 2 (1944), pp. 151–61; G. E. Lenski, 'Status crystallization: a non vertical dimension of social status', *American Sociological Review*, vol. 19, 4 (1954), pp. 405–13; I. W. Goldman, 'Status consistency and preference for change in power distribution', *American Sociological Review*, vol. 22, 3 (1957), pp. 775–81. For a somewhat new approach, akin to the one presented here, see W. G. Runciman, *Relative Deprivation and Social Justice: A Study of Attitudes to Social Inequality in Twentieth-century England* (London, 1966).
[2] For a general analysis of social and political systems see S. N. Eisenstadt, *The Political Systems of Empires* (New York, 1963).
[3] *Ibid.*

most of these societies these groups tend to be organized in some sort of corporate units.

(c) Lower urban groups composed of labourers, unskilled workers, etc.

(d) Cultural or religious groups and especially priests and officials of organized religions or of more local cults; members of religious orders, castes, organizations etc., and men of learning concentrated in academies, universities or in religious or secular centres. These last might be closely related to some of the professional groups.

(e) The various administrative and political echelons—especially on the central but also on the local levels.

(f) The 'upper' groups or strata composed in most of these societies (with the exception of China and the very partial exception of India) of aristocratic lineages possessing control over land and to some extent also over central political and cultural resources.

(g) The upper political élite centred around the King or Emperor, which may or may not have overlapped with some of the aristocratic and upper religious groups and which by definition had the highest degree of control over the centre or centres as they were established in these political systems.

These varied categories of positions or roles existed, even if in different degrees, in all the societies studied here. But the details of their organization, and especially the ways in which they crystallized into strata, differed greatly among these different societies. As has been pointed out above all these societies were also 'traditional' societies with some very specific types of structural connotations or derivatives of traditionality.

Perhaps the most important of these structural derivations was the symbolic and structural differentiation between the centre and periphery—and the concomitant limitation on the access of members of broader groups to the political and religious centre or centres and on participation within them. In these societies tradition served not only as a symbol of continuity, but as the delineator of the legitimate limits of creativity and innovation and as the major criterion of their legitimacy —even if in fact any such symbol of tradition might have been forged out as a great innovative creation which destroyed what till then was perceived as the major symbol of the legitimate past. These connotations of traditionality were not, however, confined only to purely cultural or symbolic spheres; they had definite structural implications. The most important was first that parts of the social structure and some groups were—or attempted to become—designed as the legitimate upholders, guardians and as a manifestation of those collective symbols, as their legitimate bearers and interpreters and hence also as the legitimizers of any innovation or change. In the more differentiated among the traditional societies these functions became crystallized into the symbolic and institutional distinctiveness of the central foci of the political and cultural orders as distinct from the periphery. It was this continuing symbolic and structural differentiation between the centre and periphery—and the concomitant limitation on the access of members of broader groups to the political and religious centre or centres and on participation within them—that constituted the most important structural derivation of the traditionality of these societies.

These characteristics of these societies had several important repercussions on some of the basic features of the structure of stratification within them in general and of strata formation in them in particular. The relatively sharp difference between centre and periphery stressed the crucial importance of the various centres for the regulation of the 'conversion' of different resources on the macro-societal level. The first result of this distinctiveness of the centre was the tendency to segregation between participation in central and peripheral spheres, i.e. in the attempts of the centre to control the process of the conversion of resources of the periphery, and to arrange relatively fixed conditions of entry into major central institutional spheres and of participation in them; and to assure, in so far as possible, that the mobility in the society in general and into the centre in particular would be mostly processes of sponsored mobility.[1]

Second, in close relation within the former characteristics, in all these societies there developed, albeit in different degrees, the tendency to combine an expressly metaphysical or theological evaluation of different groups and roles with some legal or semi-legal definition and fixation of various positions and status. This was especially true of those components of status which are important from the point of view of strata formation, i.e. of regulation, through ascriptive and/or legal injunctions, of access to at least some of the most important institutional positions; of the regulation of the symbolical use of resources by different groups as evident in the tendency to promulgate sumptuary laws; and even in restrictions on the use of some resources and exchange activities as most clearly seen in the regulation of the output of guilds.

But despite the fact that both the range of basic institutional (and especially economic and administrative) positions, as well as of the structure and 'traditionality' of their centres, seem to have been, to no small degree, common to all the societies studied here, yet there did also develop among them many differences in the basic characteristics of their respective strata with regard to almost all the components of the

---

[1] On this terminology see R. Turner, 'Sponsored and contest mobility and the school system', *American Sociological Review*, vol. 25, 6 (1960), pp. 855–67, especially p. 856.

processes of strata formation. They differed in the criteria according to which different positions and strata were evaluated in the extent of the autonomy of the strata; in the components of their identity and in the strength of their internal solidarity; in the extent to which they develop distinct styles of life and in the extent to which these styles of life were explicitly normatively prescribed and/or legally fixed; in the extent of country-wide strata consciousness; in their access to the different centres; in the place of family and kinship groups in the process of strata formation; in the patterns of inter-strata relations in general and of social mobility in particular.

We shall not be able, of course, to analyse here all such differences. We shall attempt only to see how far some at least of these differences can be explained in terms of the nature and structure of the centre or centres of these societies, and especially of (*a*) the predominant orientations and goals of the centre; (*b*) the multiplicity of the centres in the societies and the relations between them; and (*c*) the accessibility of different groups to the centre. The orientations of the centres will be classified according to the major type of resources or desiderata which we have delineated above; for example, as orientations to power, wealth and different types of prestige (i.e. of participation in collectivities, social and cultural orders and centres) or to various mixtures or combinations thereof. With regard to the number of such centres and of their interrelationships, already our preceding analysis has indicated that in any such society there usually existed several centres—the political, the religious or cultural and even the 'social' ones, i.e. centres of communal collective identity, as well as many local subcentres—the centres of the various Little Traditions, localities and regions. From the point of view of our analysis the most crucial aspect of the relations among the—both central and local—centres is their relative predominance, as well as the degree to which membership in one centre entailed the possibility of access to another.

In order to understand how these characteristics of the centre or centres influence the process of strata formation in these societies we shall work on the assumption that the incumbent élites in all such centres attempted to maintain their own monopoly of access to the centre, and to uphold those orientations and societal goals which they saw as representing the essence of their own collective identity, the source of their legitimation, and to the implementation of which they were committed. One of the most important ways and mechanisms through which any such incumbent élite of a centre attempted to attain these goals was by making that commodity or resource which was most closely related to their basic orientations (i.e. power in case of a power oriented centre, prestige in case of a centre oriented to the maintenance of participation

in some social or cultural order) the most hard to get, the most expensive, within the framework of the existing institutional exchange. This aim could be achieved in a great variety of ways. We shall only mention here those which are most important from the point of view of analysis of strata formation.

The most general and most important mechanisms of this kind was the attempt—already alluded to above—to control the process of conversion of the various resources which were at the disposal of the various groups in the society, from one institutional sphere to another, and from within various micro-societal and peripheral settings, to the level of macro-societal markets and of their respective commodities and media of exchange.

This general mechanism was subdivided in a variety of more concrete ones. The first was to limit, but only to some degree, the right of other groups to receive the central commodity, and to have access to the centre. Such limitation was always only partial, because no élite—except in cases of a pure conquest one—could afford to deny entirely to the broader groups the right of some access to the centre. If they did so they would have been able to exert other resources from the broader groups or only through coercive measures which, in their turn, could make excessive demands on the resources of the centre or would limit its ability to implement various collective goals in which it might be interested.

Therefore most élites attempted to attain some balance between the development, within the broader groups, of some quest for such central desiderata and for participation in the centre on the one hand and for keeping such quest within very strictly prescribed limits on the other hand. This could be achieved first by attempts to prescribe, through legislation, especially of sumptuary laws, proper 'style of living', of various groups and strata. Such legislation tended to emphasize on the one hand the ways in which different groups could 'properly' use the resources at their disposal in a way which would emphasize the degree to which they could have orientations or access to the centre, as well as their distance from the centre, and the concomitant relatively low evaluation of their own positions in contrast to the more central ones.

Second, and closely related to the first, this could be achieved through attempts to maintain in the hands of the centre the control of access to those central positions which were the bearers of the highest rewards, be they political, religious or cultural. Such restriction on access to central positions could be achieved in several ways. One was to make the resources or rewards at the disposal of any group almost totally irrelevant for the acquisition of such more central commodities and positions—leaving it at least in principle entirely to the centre to establish the criteria of such selection and to select the incumbents for these positions, as well as to prescribe their social life.

The other, closely related but not identical way, was to make the access to such positions contingent on the unconditional giving up by their 'new' incumbents of some at least of the resources at their disposal and especially the giving up of the right of converting these resources into the more central ones. The third way was to make the price for access to these positions very high, so as to minimize the ability of those who attained such positions to use these resources for taking some sort of an independent stand with regard to the élite. Although these last two ways may seem to be almost identical, they are, as we shall yet see in greater detail later, very often antithetical in their effects on strata formation.

Last was the attempt to direct or influence various groups to use the resources at their disposal for acquisition of non-central commodities and positions.

This does not mean, of course, that the centres were always successful in their endeavours in these respects, that their attempts were fully accepted by all groups or strata in their respective societies. As is very well known in all these societies there have existed many groups which were marginal in the central institutional core, which maintained their own traditions without very much reference to the centre. Similarly, within all these societies there existed and developed various groups and subcentres which developed orientations differing from those of the centres or even contrary and opposed to them. Moreover, the very institutionalization of any given centre or régime tended to give use to various 'counter-centres'.[1]

But in our present analysis our main concern will not be to analyse the conditions under which they were or were not successful in these endeavours, but rather firstly, insofar as they were successful and they became predominant and their orientations were accepted to some degree in the society, how did they concretely influence the process of strata formation in these societies; and secondly how the differences in some of the basic characteristics of the strata can be explained by the differences in the orientations and structures of their respective centres.

As has been pointed out already above we shall distinguish these societies first of all according to the basic orientations and structures of their centres. We shall accordingly distinguish here between states based on power, taking Russia (especially from the period of Ivan the Terrible and Peter the Great up to the beginning of the 19th century)[2] as the

---

[1] See on this S. N. Eisenstadt, 'Institutionalization and change', *American Sociological Review*, vol. 29, 2 (April 1964), pp. 49–59.

[2] On Russia in this period see especially M. Beloff, *The Age of Absolutism* (London: Hutchinson's University Library, 1954), ch. 6, and 'Russia', in A. Goodwin (ed.), *The European Nobility in the Eighteenth Century* (London, 1953); B. H. Summer, 'Peter the Great', *History*,

major illustration of this type; on a combination of power and a universalistic-traditional 'cultural' orientation (taking Imperial China as the major illustration of this type of centre);[1] a centre based on closed ritualistic religious orientation, taking India as an illustration,[2] and a society with multiple centre orientation, taking Europe (especially Western and Central) as the main illustration.[3]

PART III

Russia

We shall start with a brief analysis of Russia (from the time of Ivan the Terrible or Peter the Great, till the end of the eighteenth century) as an Imperial society, the evolution of which in this period tended—for reasons which we shall not deal with here—to make power the basic orientations of the centres. Its rulers attempted to define the basic orientations and goals of the polity in terms of the combinations of centre and power; to define the centre very largely in terms of such monopolization of power and in terms of pursuance of goals oriented to the

xxxii (1947), 39–50 and *A Short History of Russia* (New York, 1949). I. Young, 'Russia', in J. O. Lindsay (ed.), *The New Cambridge Modern History*, vii (1957), 318–38; M. Raeff, *Origins of the Russian Intelligentsia: The Eighteenth Century Nobility* (New York, 1966); J. Blum, *Lord and Peasant in Russia* (Princeton, 1961).

[1] E. Balazs, *Chinese Civilization and Bureaucracy: Variations on a Theme* (New Haven, 1964); D. Bodde, 'Feudalism in China', in R. Coulborn (ed.), *Feudalism in History* (Princeton, 1956), pp. 49–92; K. Eberhard, *A History of China* (London, 1960) and *Conquerors and Rulers: Social Forces in Medieval China* (Leiden, 1952); J. K. Fairbank (ed.), *Chinese Thought and Institutions* (Chicago, 1957); D. S. Nivison and A. F. Wright (eds.), *Confucianism in Action* (Stanford, 1959); K. A. Wittfogel, *Oriental Despotism: A Comparative Study of Total Power* (New Haven, 1957); A. F. Wright (ed.), *Studies in Chinese Thought* (Chicago, 1953).

[2] On Indian civilization with special reference to the caste system see Max Weber, *The Religion of India*, Hans H. Gerth and Don Martindale (Glencoe, Illinois, 1958); L. Dumont, *Homo Hierarchicus—Essai sur le système des castes* (Paris, 1966), and the nine issues of *Contributions to Indian Sociology* (ed. L. Dumont) (The Hague, 1957–66); also Milton Singer, 'The social organization of Indian civilization', *Diogenes*, vol. 45 (Winter 1964), pp. 84–119; M. Singer (ed.), *Traditional India—Structure and Change* (Philadelphia, 1959). Some of the earlier expositions of caste system can be found in J. H. Hutton, *Caste in India* (London, 1946); H. M. C. Stevenson, 'Status evaluation in the Hindu caste system', *Journal of the Royal Anthropological Institute*, vol. 84 (1954), pp. 45–65; E. A. H. Blunt, *The Caste System of Northern India* (London, 1931).

For some of the more recent discussions see F. K. Bailey, 'Closed social stratification', *European Journal of Sociology*, iv (1963), 107–24; A. Beteille, 'A note on the referents of castes', *European Journal of Sociology*, v (1964), 130–4; McKim Marriot, 'Interactional and attributional theories of caste ranking', *Man in India*, xxxix, no. 2 (1959), pp. 92–107.

For the most comprehensive analysis of the changes between the traditional and the modern Indian caste system see: S. M. Srinivas, *Caste in Modern India* (Bombay, 1964), and *Social Change in Modern India* (Berkeley, 1966).

[3] See M. Beloff, *The Age of Absolutism* (London: Hutchinson's University Library, 1954); J. O. Lindsay (ed.), *New Cambridge Modern History*, vii (1957); G. Clark, *The Seventeenth Century* (Oxford, 1929–59), and *Early Modern Europe (1450–1720)* (London, 1957); A. Goodwin (ed.), *The European Nobility in the Eighteenth Century* (London, 1953); B. Barber and E. G. Barber (eds.), *European Social Class: Stability and Change* (New York, 1965).

maintenance and accumulation of power.[1] Hence, the major problem of the ruling élite here was how to limit and control the access of other groups both to power as a generalized commodity and to the positions of central institutional power.

The Russian centre attempted to attain these results by creating a general situation in which the access to power in general and to power positions in particular could not, in a way, be 'bought', except through the very exercise of power; power could be used to get other resources but it was much more difficult to get power through such other resources. Those groups who had other resources at their disposal had to give up these resources, as demanded by holders of powers without themselves being able to 'buy' such power of their own volition.[2]

This was here attempted by several ways which seem to be specific to a power-system. First was the attempt to limit very seriously the extent to which the participation in the centre constituted a part of the identity of other groups and an active desideratum on their part. The rulers encouraged the development, especially but not only, among the lower levels of society, of only very passive orientation towards the centre. They attempted to attain this by allowing them but few independent possibilities of active independent orientation to the centre, by making the styles of life of different collectivities as relatively closed and segregated from one another as possible, and by making the participation in central activities both entirely dependent on the centre as well as different for each 'local' or 'status' collectivity.

In order to attain its aim the centre attempted to control not only the desiderata and identities of these groups but also the use, by them, of the resources at their disposal. Here the power centre tended to encourage the spending, 'wasting', of such resources, in various patterns of conspicuous consumption. But unlike the case of other types of traditional centres, it did not tend to encourage the development by these groups of very rigid styles of life sanctioned by the norms and symbols of the centre. On the contrary, it tended to minimize the legitimation of such styles of life and tended instead to encourage a rather 'indiscriminate' dispersal of the resources. It tended to be relatively permissive

---

[1] For details of Russian civilization in this period see the bibliography in the footnote on pp. 81–2; fuller references can be found in the bibliography of Eisenstadt, *The Political Systems of Empires*.

[2] Here the difference between 'traditional', Imperial power-oriented and modern totalitarian régimes stands out. The ruling élites of the latter have, often despite their natural 'power' tendency, to buy the various resources of the broader strata, because of, first, the nature of their legitimation which entails a potentially widespread quest for participation; second, they have to do so because of the scope of their goals which continuously create new organizational 'needs' and exigencies and which necessitates the mobilization of resources from these strata. Hence the totalitarian élite has to permit such wider groups to participate in some of the 'central' spheres so as to have some access to the power positions.

with regard to the use of such resources for various 'segregated' desiderata—so long as these were not too ostentatious; as they did not tend to create too great a demand for new 'skills' which could create too many new independent positions which in their turn could become foci of independent central markets, or of new collective identities; and so long as they did not impinge on access to the power central positions.[1] The third major mechanism used by this power élite to attain its aims was to set the price for entry into power positions and for maintenance of such positions in such a way that once somebody got into the power structure he had to give up unconditionally most convertible resources at his disposal and was then, in the power market, at a relatively low 'bargaining position' *vis-à-vis* the major holders of power—i.e. in principle the tsar.[2] These varied mechanisms through which the predominance of the power centre was being upheld had several repercussions on the process of strata-formation in Imperial Russia up till the end of the eighteenth century.

Perhaps the most general such influence was the lack of or weakness of what may be called society-wide class or strata consciousness and organization. This could of course be most clearly seen among the lowest groups—the peasants—where there was almost no way of extending participation from their own local collectivities into some wider country-wide frameworks, despite many various informal social ties and common traditions between peasants of various villages or regions. But this was also the case among various urban groups. Here the most important indicator of this weakness was the lack of common organization even among the 'middle' occupations of the same city and the great dependence of any specific occupational group (guild) within any locality (city or region) for the development of their own organization, on the official sanction of the centre.[3] The self-identity of most of these groups was mostly based on such narrow occupational and local bases, with only minimal wider, even local—and certainly, society-wide—orientations. Insofar as any such wider, more than minimal and latent, and based only on common customs, society-wide orientations may be found, they seem to have been grounded in the legislation of the centre.

Significantly enough, this applies also, even if in a somewhat lesser way, to the aristocracy.[4] The aristocracy had, of course, a much higher standing and a greater control of resources than any other social group. Moreover, by virtue of its very proximity to the centre on the one hand, and of some remnants of its own (pre-Mongol) semi-feudal traditions on

---

[1] Raeff, *The Origins of Russian Intelligentsia*; Blum, *Lord and Peasant in Russia*, esp. ch. 13.
[2] See Beloff, *The Age of Absolutism*, and Raeff, *op. cit.*
[3] For a general account see Young, *op. cit.*
[4] See Raeff, *op. cit.*; and Belof in Goodwin (ed.) *op. cit.*

the other, it did have some more country-wide links. Yet even it did not have very strong widespread country-wide autonomy or stratum-consciousness. Whatever autonomy it did maintain from the pre-absolutist period was shattered by the tsars who succeeded in making it an almost pure service aristocracy, and whatever elements of such autonomy developed later were also mostly entirely fostered by the tsars. It was only at the end of the eighteenth and the beginning of the nineteenth century that this situation began to change.[1]

This was very closely connected with the second major characteristic of strata formation in Russian society, namely the very high degree of segregation among the various status groups—the different local or occupational groups. Each of such groups tended to maintain its own identity, with but few common meeting points among them. Third, there did not develop within most of these groups a 'closed', normatively prescribed style of life encompassing all their varied positions and designating definite patterns of consumption. In fact there did of course develop, especially among the aristocracy and among some of the urban groups, certain such customary patterns. Similarly the peasantry, living in the various village communities, tended to follow old, traditionally accepted patterns of life. But these patterns were on the whole neither fully regulated by internal or external normative sanctions nor were they upheld as models and symbols by those who participated in them.[2]

Among the aristocracy some such normative prescriptions tended to develop in the capital when they were in state service, by virtue of participation of the life of the Court—but only to a smaller degree in their own domains. Thus, for instance, there were here but few—if any—normative restrictions on the engagement of aristocrats in business or in commercial activities of the kind known in France. Such restrictions did not apply to the peasantry—or even to the serfs—so long as they could buy their freedom from their lords or received their permission to engage in such activities.

This weakness of normatively prescribed status style of life was also quite closely related to patterns of inter-group intermarriage. From the available—true enough rather meagre—evidence, indications may indeed be derived which show that there was a relative paucity of injunctions against inter-stratum intermarriage. Cases of such intermarriage were known, although *de facto*—but not so much *de jure*—there was a very large extent of 'strata' endogamy. The situation naturally tended to be more rigid on the upper level—that of the aristocracy—but even here it was far from being clear-cut.

---

[1] See Raeff, *op. cit.* and Beloff in Goodwin (ed.), *op. cit.*
[2] Blum, *Lord and Peasant*, chs. 15, 23; and Raeff, *op. cit.*

The preceding analysis brings us to another crucial aspect of the Russian status system—namely the place of the family or kinship groups in the system of stratification. As in all traditional (and probably in other) societies the family or kinship group constituted, of course, the major primary agency of socialization within which the major desiderata and cultural and social orientations were inculcated in individuals. Moreover, family groups belonging to the same stratum probably usually formed the actual framework of social intercourse and of intermarriage within a given locality or region. But given the relative weakness of the *normative* prescription of life styles of strata and of country-wide consciousness of strata, families did not fulfil very important roles from the point of view of inculcating active, broader, strata collective identities. They were specially weak in interlinking any such identities with some broader, active orientation to participation in the centre or centres. Similarly, although *de facto* there was probably quite a lot of intergenerational occupational continuity within most families, yet most families could control access to such positions not through some hereditary rights of access but for the most part indirectly. They could do this either by force of custom or by making the proper use of the resources for the acquisition of such positions. Resources at the disposal of the family—including its status—could easily restrict the available opportunities but in themselves did not yet assure the access of the sons to the 'better' positions of the fathers.

Whatever the validity of the preceding analysis—and because of the paucity of systematic data it is necessarily rather conjectural—they seem to some extent to be borne out by some of the available indications —also rather scarce—on patterns of inter-strata mobility in Russia. Given the relative free use of resources, it was mostly hampered by the legal status of some groups (especially the serfs) and much less by their ability or willingness to use such resources in order to acquire higher positions or resources.[1] Insofar, however, as such mobility did take place, it usually gave rise to the creation of new 'segregated' patterns of local and occupational group life and much less to the establishment of either new common, country-wide, strata consciousness or of meeting points between different groups and strata and patterns of participation common to them.[2]

---

[1] The most important indicators here are the so-called serf entrepreneurs of the late eighteenth and nineteenth centuries. See on this H. Rosovsky, 'The serf entrepreneur in Russia', *Explorations in Entrepreneurial History*, vi (1953), 207–39.

[2] Of special importance in this whole context was, of course, the Church. It constituted the major channel of mobility from the lower strata—but it seems that the basic pattern of mobility was repeated also here. Entrance into the Church entailed on the one hand severance of most actual ties with the family of origin and the giving up of its style of life but it did not provide any foci for formation of common social links with other strata.

On the whole such mobility tended to emphasize both the segregation among different local or occupational status groups as well as the relative weakness of normative prescription of the styles of life of such groups. This seems to apply also to mobility into the aristocracy and state-service, although here some additional characteristics stand out. The most important characteristic of this mobility has been that it was a clear instance of 'sponsored' mobility. The concrete expression of this sponsored mobility among the upper classes of Russia was of course the almost total initial control of access into the bureaucracy—and in principle also into the aristocracy—by the tsars.[1]

Although in principle most scions of the aristocracy were expected to enter into some sort of state service, the choice was, in principle, not theirs but the tsar's; and the mere fact of belonging to an aristocratic family did not entitle—although it certainly facilitated—the access to such positions. However, once such access was obtained the style of life of the aristocrat in the capital, in state service, differed greatly from his life on his local estates—not only in the daily details but mainly in terms of the strength of its symbolic and normative prescription of the appropriate style of life. This courtly prescription of such style of life tended to emphasize disassociation from the family life of aristocrats in their localities. Thus many aristocratic families evinced in the life-time of their members a pattern of continuous disassociation and segregation between the style of life of family of origin (in the local aristocratic estates) and its point of destination (in the higher court positions) which characterized the general pattern of mobility in Russian society.

China

The second case in our comparative analysis will be the Chinese Imperial system as it developed from the period of Han (c. 206 BC) until the fall of the Ching dynasty in 1911.[2] Here again, without going into an historical analysis of the development of this centre, it will suffice for our analysis to indicate that from the Han onward this centre was defined in terms of the combination of political power and of the participation in a traditional cultural order—the Confucian-legalistic one. As in the case of any other traditional order its contents were conceived as given and fixed in the framework of its basic precepts and orientations. But in several

Although in principle it could provide close access to the centre and to political power, yet on the whole the Church was not permitted to become either an independent political or 'social' inter-strata identity. The basic limitations on access to power-position also seemed on the whole, with some minor exceptions, to apply to it.

[1] See Raeff, *op. cit.*

[2] For general bibliography see footnote 1 to p. 82. A fuller bibliography is given in Eisenstadt, *Political Systems of Empires.*

other aspects this cultural order was among the most open among all known traditional societies.

First of all, this order was conceived as a semi-secular one, oriented towards the upholding and the continuous cultivation of a tradition whose basic contents were indeed given in the activities and precepts of its Founding Father but within the framework of which there was indeed place for continuous cultivation and elaboration—mainly through learning and not, as for instance in India, through purely fixed or ritual activities. Second, this order was conceived as encompassing and enfolding—even if in different degrees—all strata and parts of the population and as open to all of them. Its relations to political power were twofold. On the one hand it tended to find within the confines of the Empire its natural focus and framework; on the other hand it was also the major legitimator of the political order.[1]

Hence, in China—unlike in Russia—the absolutist centre was defined in terms of both political power and of culture or tradition, each of which constituted independent bases of access to the centre. Whatever the vagaries of individual emperors and the lack of security of individual officials the centre was the arena of continuous interplay between the holders of purely political power and of representatives of the cultural order, the representatives of each attempting to control the access of the other to the centre—but not being able to deny the validity of the other and its relative independence.[2]

The possession of power, be it by virtue of hereditary standing, military power, individual ability, or of proximity to the Imperial household, did assure the possibility of access to the centre—but did not assure in itself the tenure of position within it. Power in itself had to buy access to the centre by participating to some degree at least in the cultural tradition. Similarly, those who were in possession of the prestige of participation in the cultural tradition and order had the right of entry into the central positions but within it they had to assure their place by giving up—even if only some of—their independent standing.

Thus there existed in China both a more multiple orientation of the centre than in the Russian case, as well as—and this is probably much more important—a somewhat greater heterogeneity of criteria and avenues of access of members of the sub-centres to the centre itself—although on the whole it was a very closed and monolithic centre, with very sharp distinctiveness from the periphery. But perhaps the most

[1] See on this in greater detail: Balazs, *Chinese Civilisation and Bureaucracy*; Fairbank (ed.), *Chinese Thought and Institutions*; Nivison and Wright (eds.), *Confucianism in Action*.
[2] W. T. de Bary, 'Chinese despotism and the Confucian ideal: a seventeenth-century view', in J. K. Fairbanks (ed.), *Chinese Thought and Institutions*, pp. 163–204; C. O. Hucker, 'Confucianism and the Chinese Censorial System', in Nivison and Wright (eds.), *op. cit.* pp. 182–208.

important aspect of the structure and orientations of the Chinese centre was not only the continuous interplay between the upholders of the pure political power and those of the cultural tradition, but the fact that cultural order which the centre represented was conceived as potentially encompassing all the groups and strata of the population.

Hence there existed here—to a much larger degree than in the Russian (or similar power-based) case—some basic affinity between the definition of the identity of various peripheral collectivities and that of the centre. Some—and not entirely passive—orientation to the centre and to participation in it constituted a basic component of the collective identity of many local, occupational groups. Here, unlike in a traditional power oriented centre, there did not exist a basic separation between the societal order represented by the centre and that embedded within the various types of peripheral collectivities.

Moreover the various peripheral collectivities were encouraged- at least in terms of the official ideology—to have some of their members participate more actively in the centre—mainly through the advancement in learning, by undertaking the official examinations and by graduating as literati.

Thus, because of this almost total universality of participation in the cultural tradition, the centre (part of which was anyhow composed of the central cultural groups) was not able—as in Russia—entirely to control the access to its own position. Rather it had to regulate the prices which could be exerted for the right of entrance—so that it could indeed assure that whatever other resources were accumulated and could become foci of new, independent desiderata, would mostly have to be invested in the quest of participating in the centre.

Unlike in the Russian case, the 'price' for such access was not the giving up of the right to 'convert' one's resources into the possibility of access to high position. Here this right was, in a sense, given and even encouraged—but at the same time the amount of resources necessary for its attainment was very high. It did also greatly differ for different groups and strata, according to their standing in the official ideological evaluation of positions that developed in China, and the highest prices were exerted from those groups—especially the merchants and military —which on the one hand were at the bottom of the 'ideological' scale of evaluation but who could accumulate many 'free' resources. The various institutional consequences of the orientations of the Chinese centre which were discussed above have greatly influenced some of the characteristics of strata formation in Chinese society.

The first such general characteristic of Chinese strata formation was the development of a relatively clear ideological evaluation of different occupational positions based on their assumed ideological, or metaphysical, proximity to the basic tenets of Confucian order. According to this evaluation the literati (and to some extent the gentry) enjoyed the highest prestige, the peasants next and the merchants (and to some degree the military) very low prestige. Very closely related to this official evaluation of different occupations and groups was the development, in China, of relatively strong normative definition of the styles of life and collective identities of different collectivities and strata. Each such normative prescription of the style of life contained a very strong orientation to the centre and possible participation in it; the normative linkage of such participation with specific occupational positions on the one hand, and with a symbolic consumption of resources on the other hand.

A third important characteristic of the Chinese strata system was the place of family units within it. Unlike in Russia, the various family groups served not only as the main agents of initial socialization but also as foci of the different styles of life and of various strata or local cultures. But, perhaps even to a somewhat greater degree than in Rusia, they could not serve as automatic channels of transmission of access to high positions—although in fact there did exist a strong correlation between family status and the chances of such access. But this relation was not— even *de facto*, and certainly not in ideology—fully legitimized.[1] At the same time, given the fact that kinship units constituted the major foci of various broader collective identities, and that these identities did contain important orientation to the centre, it was indeed family and kinship groups that also provided the resources and the incentives for attempting to achieve such access.

Fourth—and again partially in contrast with the Russian strata system—was the nature of a country-wide strata consciousness and organization. At least among the higher groups, i.e. the literati and the bureaucracy, there did indeed develop a relatively high degree of country-wide stratum consciousness or solidarity. This was rooted first in the common cultural tradition; second in sharing common avenues of access; and third in the fact that the access to these channels—the schools and the academies—was to some extent autonomous, not entirely dependent on the political centre, but at the same time very strongly oriented to it. This common consciousness was also connected with some, even if a rather minimal, degree of autonomous organization in the various schools and academies.

It was for parallel but obverse reasons, i.e. because of the distance from the centre and the lack of direct access to it, that such common consciousness could not develop among the merchants or the other

[1] E. A. Kracke Jr., 'Region, family, and individual in the Chinese examination system,' in Fairbanks (ed.), *Chinese Thought and Institutions*, pp. 251–68; Ping-ti Ho, *The Ladder of Success in Imperial China* (New York, 1962).

urban groups. Here, as in Russia, these groups never coalesced into one common stratum—cutting across different occupational or local positions —although there existed, of course, many trans-local ties. Moreover, any such tendency to the development of any such broader conscious-ness or organization of their own was also greatly impeded by the strong orientation to the centre even among these groups—an orientation which, given their great distance from the centre, tended to deflect their activities and resources from building up their own broader collective identities.[1] Such consciousness and especially common organization could not also develop among the peasants. This was due not only to the lack of adequate channels of communication, but also because the access to the centre, although permitted and even officially encouraged, was not given automatically to the peasant groups as corporate entities but was only encouraged for individuals.

The preceding characteristics of the process of strata formation had also several repercussions on some general structural characteristics of the system of strata in China.

Perhaps the most important of such characteristics was the absence of legal distinction between free and non-free strata—evident in the absence of aristocracy on the one hand, and of servile peasantry on the other. As is well known, China was on the whole characterized by the relative absence of hereditary aristocracy and by the peculiar nature of the highest groups —the literati-bureaucracy group.[2] It was the nature of the 'ruling group' or élite that underlined the basic relative weakness in China, of hereditary ascription, the strength of the achievement orientations within the limits of a given tradition and the major charac-teristics of mobility to which we shall soon address ourselves. This was very closely related to the status and structure of the peasant groups. They were, as we have seen, relatively highly evaluated and were accordingly in strongest opposition to the Russian case, conceived as legally free—although in fact they may have often incurred various dis-abilities and disadvantages. Moreover, in the internal differentiation of the peasantry there was a somewhat continuous transition between the different subgroups, with their apex in the 'gentry', each of which had, within its own collective identity, some orientations to the centre and whose local traditions were to some extent upheld and legitimized by the centre.

All these characteristics of strata formation have greatly influenced the pattern of social mobility in China, which constituted probably one of the major mechanisms of the stability of the Imperial-Confucian

---

[1] See, in greater detail, the discussion in Balazs, *op. cit.*, and Eisenstadt, *Political Systems of Empires,* esp. chs. VI-XI and ch. XII.

[2] Balazs, *ibid.*; Eisenstadt, *Political Systems of Empires,* ch. XII.

system. Fortunately here we have more data than in the Russian case. Ping-ti Ho's analysis has provided us with some of the most comprehensive surveys of this problem and has indeed shown the wide scope of both upward and downward mobility, the vagaries of individual family life-histories, as well as the way in which this mobility upheld the ideal of open achievement.[1]

But of no less importance, from the point of view of our discussion, than the extent of circulation of élites that was effected by this mobility, are some of its structural aspects or characteristics. It has been obviously a very 'sponsored' type of mobility—directed as it was at the attainment of positions within a very fixed institutional framework and cultural contents—but the effects of this sponsored mobility on inter-strata relations were different here from those that we found in Russia. Unlike in Russia there was, at least from the point of view of the peasants but also of other groups, a greater continuity and possible overlapping between the styles of life of the group of origin of the mobile persons and their groups of 'destination', and no sharp dissociation from the group of origin was demanded. This, in a sense, facilitated even the acceptance of downward mobility.

This was reinforced by the fact that these processes of mobility were here also very strongly bound to their familistic bases and to the possible extension of family obligations and resources. As it was the family which served as the major mechanism of transmission of strata identity, the processes of mobility have, at least in some cases, served also as inter-linking points between different strata.

India

We shall now proceed to an examination of one of the most baffling and yet crucial systems of stratification within our comparative framework—namely the caste system of India. We shall not enter here into a detailed discussion of the problem which has preoccupied scholars for a very long period of time—namely whether the phenomena of caste has been confined to India or can also be found in other societies. There can be no doubt that, on the one hand, some of the elements of caste—such as the emphasis on occupational exclusiveness, endogamy and ritual pollution, can be found also in many other societies. But on the other hand it is also clear that it is only in India that these have become a focus of a total macro-societal order and system of stratification.[2] It is on this that we shall concentrate our brief analysis.

[1] Ping-ti Ho, *The Ladder of Success in Imperial China.*
[2] See the bibliography in footnote 2 on p. 82. The problem of the uniqueness of the Indian caste system is discussed most fully in Dumont, *Homo Hierarchitus.*

The ideological focus of the caste system in India has been, as is well known, the Brahmanic system of values, with its focus on the conception of parallelism between cosmic and social purity and pollution, and in the ideology of the varnai. This is seen in the manifestation of this parallelism in the ritual and social spheres through the differential ritual standing of different occupations or tasks and in the transmission of such standing through the basic primordial family and kinship units. This social-cultural (ritual) order was, unlike the Chinese one, closed both in the terms of contents, i.e. the definition of the cosmic and social order, and in terms of access to it. It was ideologically totally ascriptive with almost no possibility whatsoever of transcending its hereditary limitations of access to actual social positions.

It was this Brahmanic ideology that can be said to have constituted the major centre of Indian civilization, with the various political centres serving mostly as secondary and political centres and, except later under the Moghul and the British rules, rather discontinuous ones. Closely related to the nature of this order was the lack of any other continuous— i.e. especially political—centre. Such a centre developed only later, under the Moghul and the British rules. Thus we find here, in comparison with other Imperial societies, an almost unique situation in that whatever political centres tended to develop here, they were usually partial and relatively 'weak' in terms of the major orientations or the cultural systems and the commitments they could command thereby.[1]

This type of orientation and structure of the centres had several implications on the process of strata formation in Indian society. First, we find here, owing to the sharp emphasis on the linkage between family units and ritual-cosmic standing, a very sharp normative definition of the styles of life of different status-groups (castes). These definitions tended in principle to combine the definition of collective strata identity in terms of cosmic purity or pollution together with differential evaluation of occupations; and the proper symbolic consumption of resources with very strict, ascriptive, prescription of the rules of access to the major institutional positions. Second, there was, because of the strongly ascriptive and hereditary ritual emphasis, a very strong linkage between family and kinship groups and status identity and organization. The family and kinship group was here the major socializing agency, the major focus of status participation and of collective identity, and the major channel of transmission of ascriptive access to the major positions. This was connected with a very strong emphasis on caste endogamy or, in the 'worst' case, hypergamy and, as consequence of this, with almost total ideological negation of the possibility of inter-caste mobility. Third was the specific type of linkage between occupational positions

---

[1] M. Singer, *The Social Organization of Indian Civilization*; M. Singer (ed.), *Traditional India.*

and ritual status. In principle every occupational position—be it that of an agricultural labourer, landowner, artisan or merchant—was clearly assigned to some of the major status (caste-varna) categories; but, at the same time, these categories comprised many concrete occupations. Fourth, comes the nature of the country-wide stratum consciousness and organization of the major status-group of the castes. It is here, perhaps more than in any other sphere, that the difference between theory and practice not only stands out but is of crucial importance for the understanding of the working of the Indian system of stratification. In theory (i.e. especially in the varna ideology) the different caste categories or units were defined as country wide and therefore in principle also engendered a country-wide caste consciousness and organization. This was closely connected with a strong tendency to put some of the 'lowest' groups beyond the pale of the system, which could also sometimes, but not always, become connected with legal disabilities and servitude.[1] In reality, however, there did not exist such a unified country-wide hierarchy and caste organization—just as there did not exist such close interrelation between institutional functions and positions, ritual standing and use of resources as was assumed in the official ideology. (Curiously enough it was probably only the British who, by incorporating caste classification into their census, gave the sharpest push to the establishment of some such unified hierarchy.)

The Brahmin ideology and system of worship was, in a sense, India-wide, and served, as we have already indicated above, as a focus of the overall basic cultural identity of the society. Moreover, among the same Brahmin groups—as well as among other, especially higher, castes—there existed also, to some limited degree, some country-wide, or at least region-wide, contacts and intermarriage. But on the whole the basis of caste organization and interrelation was local. In practice there were hundreds, if not thousands, of caste organizations organized locally—in villages, regions, and principalities. Thus there developed here a sharp discrepancy between the relatively uniform, homogeneous, country-wide demands of the cultural order and the more dispersed and diversified political and economic systems.

The ideal of the caste of the division of labour, while focused on country-wide ritual order, could not be applied either on the more regional or more local levels. With regard both to the use of political power and money, there developed, on these levels, a great variety of activities which could not be bound by the ritual caste prescriptions. First of all there was no full correspondence between the various occupational positions, the number of which was very great and becoming more diversified, and caste categories. This very diversification often

---

[1] Srinivas, *Caste in Modern India*, and *Social Change in Modern India*.

tended to create somewhat independent hierarchies of status which could often undermine the status of local groups of Brahmins and serve as a starting point for the attainment of new caste-status, often changing the existing caste-order in general and the interrelations and mutual obligations between different castes in particular.

The relations between the Brahmin and the political powers bring out even more the limits of the pure ideological pattern in which the political was subservient to the ritual. While this remained true on the ideological level, yet the concrete dependence of Brahmins or the rulers for the upholding of their relative status was very great.[1] In many, if not most cases, it was up to the rulers to define the relative ritual standing of various caste-groups, individuals or of single family groups—but mostly a pattern of 'contest' mobility of broader kinship groups. This mobility took on the form of formation of new types of political and economic units, organizations and hierarchies on the one hand, but on the other it also took the form of continuous formation of subcastes. Thus, on the one hand, this mobility did undermine the actual status of any given local caste hierarchy as well as the ideal patterns of conversion of resources. But on the other hand many of these mobile groups aimed at attainment, for themselves, of relatively higher ritual standing, at 'self-Sanskritization', thus upholding the basic ideological assumptions of the system.[2]

This pattern of mobility can probably be attributed firstly to the combination of common orientations to the 'ideal' pattern of one centre, with the multiplicity of actual centres; and secondly to strong linkage between family and stratum identity.

Western (and Central) Europe

We shall now proceed to a very brief and preliminary analysis of the last case of 'Imperial' or 'absolutist' systems of stratification—and one which necessarily is of special interest for our comparative analysis— namely that of Western (and to some extent Central) Europe as it developed in the post-feudal and post 'Stände-Staat' stage, i.e. in what is usually called the Age of Absolutism.[3] For reasons of space we shall also dwell only on those characteristics which seem to be similar to all the European societies and to distinguish them from other 'Imperial' systems and shall not deal with the differences among them.

The most outstanding characteristic of most West European centres

[1] See B. S. Cohen, 'Political systems in eighteenth century India: the Banares region', *Journal of the American Oriental Society*, vol. 82, no. 3 (July-September 1962); and Srinivas, *Social Change*, especially chs. I and III.

[2] On patterns of caste mobility see Srinivas, *op. cit.* ch. III.

[3] See the general bibliography in footnote 3 on p. 82.

was that they were pluralistic both in the sense of having relatively multiple orientations and of being based on multiple, semi-autonomous subcentres. As in every political centre, there was here also a strong emphasis on power and on the extension of its scope. But additional orientations such as those to different types of prestige, as well as to some degree of economic orientations, were also of great importance. Among the types of prestige which were stressed by these centres was first, the participation in the universalistic cultural religious tradition of Christianity; second was the participation in, or the representation by the centre of, the collective identities of the different local or status groups carrying on the transformed, older tribal communal traditions. As a result of this multiplicity of orientations there tended to develop within these centres a continuous struggle over their relative predominance. Here the outcome differed, of course, in various European countries; but on the whole it seems that a combination of power with some type of prestige—mostly 'social' and cultural universalistic prestige—were the most prevalent, although economic orientations, especially when combined with participation in different territorial or kinship communities, did also play an increasingly important role.[1]

But perhaps the most important aspect of the structure of most European centres was not the mere multiplicity of the orientations predominant within them but the interrelations between the different subcentres and broader strata and the centre. Here the most important fact is that any group which had control over some resources relevant for these orientations had some legitimate and autonomous, even if *differentiated*, access to the centre. Not only the Church but also many local or status groups were at least to some degree autonomous in their ability to convert their resources from one institutional sphere to another and from the periphery to the centres.[2]

Among the components of the identity and styles of life of these last types of groups and strata, primordial kinship and territorial ties played an important role. But these identities and the concomitant organizational frameworks were not closed in themselves, or entirely ascriptively fixed in their relations to other groups and to the centres. They were open towards the various centres—both towards the (national or 'state') political centres and to various supranational ones. The autonomy of no group was ever 'total', and the regulation of access to the centre was but rarely left by the centre itself to any single group, and none of them had full access to positions of control over any institutional markets. There

---

[1] See especially J. O. Lindsay, 'The social classes and the foundations of the states', in J. O. Lindsay (ed.), *New Cambridge Modern History*, VII (1957), 50, and M. Beloff, *The Age of Absolutism*.

[2] See E. G. Barber, *op. cit.* and B. Barber and E. G. Barber (eds.), *op. cit.*

developed therefore a great extent of mobility and change within these settings, a continuous conversion of resources from one sphere to another and the creation of new types of institutional positions. These general characteristics of West European centres have greatly influenced the processes of strata formation within them.

Given the strong orientation of various groups towards the centre, as well as the strong element of power and prestige within the orientation of the centre, it was but natural that there tended to develop here a strong tendency to the development of ideological-legal hierarchies of strata and concomitant legal distinctions between different strata. Given also the strong component of primordial kinship and territorial elements in the identity of the various strata—and hence also the differentiation between them in terms of the relative importance of their respective kinship-territorial communities—many of the contractual or political arrangements that developed in the beginning of the feudal age between different local and 'functional' groups tended to crystallize into differences between legally free and non-free strata and to reinforce the strong ascriptive, 'caste'-like tendencies of many of these groups. But at the same time there worked, especially among the free groups, some strong forces—which have been already alluded to above—which counteracted these tendencies. Given the multiplicity of the orientations of the centre, and of the strata alike, as well as the partial autonomy of the subcentres and of their access to the centre, there could not on the whole develop here a unified, ideological evaluation of different positions—despite the strong tendencies to the development of such positions of, and to, concomitant status legislation. Each of the major autonomous units—be it the Church, the Court, the different strata or collective groups—tended to develop different scales of evaluations, each of which claimed some degree of centrality and potentially general validity. As a result of this there tended to develop here a multiplicity of hierarchies of status and of different patterns of status incongruity, as well as strong tendencies to obliterate the legal distinction between free and servile groups.

The second important characteristic of European strata—and closely related to the preceding one—was the existence among them of a very strong tendency to relatively 'unified', country-wide strata consciousness and organization. This was especially evident among the higher strata but certainly not absent among the middle and even lower 'free' (peasant) strata. The fullest expression of this tendency can be found in the system of representation as it culminated in the systems of 'Estates'.[1]

---

[1] Indeed it seems that the whole conception of a society divided into society-wide homogeneous and self-conscious strata which constitutes a basic premise of most modern studies of stratification is largely derived from this particular European experience.

The roots of this tendency are to be found in the possibility of political participation or representation of most groups in the centre by virtue of their very collective identities, as corporate or semi-corporate bodies and not only, as in the Chinese case, by being able to provide for some of their members the means through which access to the centre becomes possible.[1] Hence, unlike in the Chinese case, this country-wide 'consciousness' or organization was confined not only to the higher groups but could also be found among the 'middle' or lowest free groups and strata.

Third, unlike in the Chinese, or even Russian, case, but not entirely unlike the Indian case, there tended to develop a close relationship between family and kinship identity on the one hand, and collective-strata identity on the other; and family and kinship groups constituted very important channels, not only of orientation to high position but also of ascriptive transmission of such positions. Unlike in the Indian case, however, the degree of access of different groups or strata to the centre was not ascriptively fixed but constituted a continuous bone of contention of what one could call 'strata-conflict', i.e. conflict among different strata as *strata* about their relative prestige standing in general, and about the scope of their participation in the centre in particular.

Fourth—and here again very unlike the Chinese or Russian cases and more like the Indian case—each such stratum and especially the 'middle' ones (but sometimes also the aristocracy) tended to encompass a great variety of occupational positions and organizations and to link them in some common way of life and in common avenues of access to the centre. These common styles of life of various strata comprised, as we have seen, different types of combinations of participation in primordial, kinship-territorial as well as in broad universalistic cultural orders, of orientations to the centre and participation in it; and they were closely connected to various economic occupational activities and to the performance of various institutional and occupational tasks.

Fifth, in close relation to the preceding characteristics there developed the possibility of the differential, yet *common*, participation of different groups and strata, in different cultural orders and centres, which in turn gave rise to possible overlapping in the styles of life of different strata. This was facilitated by the availability of several different channels of access to the centres which could be used by the various strata—providing also points of contact among them. Closely related to the preceding characteristics of strata formation was the scope and nature of the process of mobility that developed in European societies. On the whole we find—among all strata—starting with the nobility (with the partial exception of the eighteenth century) a very high degree of family

---

[1] Lindsay, *op. cit.*

mobility between strata. This already had its roots, as Marc Bloch has indicated, in the feudal age and seems to have continued throughout European history up to the end or middle of the Absolutist era.[1]

The very fact of the existence of European, trans-society-wide strata consciousness and organization facilitated such family mobility and continuous changes in the family and ethnic composition of various groups.[2] This mobility has been, on the whole, more of the type of 'contest' mobility of families than of the pure sponsored mobility—although the latter element was also certainly not missing. But even the sponsored mobility was very variegated—as it took place through many channels such as the Church, political and administrative avenues, etc.

In great contrast to China, but in some way similar to the process of subcaste formation in India, there developed here not only a process of mobility within a relatively given, fixed system of positions but also—concomitantly—a process which in itself created new positions and groups which could in turn become foci of new status crystallizations. The most obvious illustration of this has been the development of cities, merchants' associations, professional cultural groups, as well as the continuous change in the scope of activities of the aristocracy. In many cases these processes of mobility seem here to have created not only new positions but also new points of contact between different groups and strata and societies as foci of crystallization of new strata consciousness and of new political expressions of such consciousness.

PART IV

We may now attempt to summarize—in a very brief and tentative way —some of the analytical propositions or hypotheses, which may be derived from our preceding comparative analysis, about the influence of the major orientations and structures of centres on processes of strata formation in Imperial societies. We shall attempt to do this by indicating how several basic components of centre formation, and especially the extent to which they develop distinct styles of life and the extent to which these styles of life are normatively prescribed; the patterns of inter-strata relations in general and of social mobility in particular; the place of family and kinship groups in the process of strata formation; the extent to which there developed a unified evaluative hierarchy; and the extent of country-wide strata consciousness have been influenced by the orientations and structures of the centres.

All the following hypotheses are based, as has already been indicated above, on the assumption that the centre has been relatively successful in

[1] Bloch, *Feudal Society* (London, 1961).
[2] Bloch, *op. cit.* and Barber and Barber, *op. cit.*

maintaining its predominance, that the major groups and strata shared, even if only passively, in its orientations, and that no major counter-orientations have developed among them—an assumption which, as we have already indicated, has always been at most only partially true. But the partial validity of these assumptions should not prevent us from exploring these hypotheses which can be derived from them—it should only remind us that this is only part of the picture. Contrariwise, inso-far as the centre is mostly oriented to power (or, to some degree—as is to be found in modern societies—to economic development), such emphasis on normative definitions of styles of life of different groups or strata will tend to be much smaller. The extent to which different status groups will be segregated from one another is also greatly predicated first on the structure of centre and, second, on its orientations.

The preceding materials indicate that a tendency toward a strong normative definition of styles of life of different status groups is very closely related to some predominance within the centre of orientations to prestige, i.e. to participation in some types of collective, social or cultural orders. Such emphasis on normative definitions of styles of life will be most encompassing—as in the Indian case, and to some degree also European case—in so far as the centre is based on a combination of different types of prestige and especially on the combination of partici-pation in a cultural order with that in primordial units.

The more monolithic a centre is in terms of its composition and its distinctiveness from various subcentres and from the periphery, the more it will tend to encourage the segregation of the styles of life and patterns of participation of different local, occupational and territorial-kinship groups. Insofar as a relatively monolithic centre has multiple orientations, this would probably increase the number of channels of access to it, but it will not tend to break down the segregation between such groups. On the other hand, the more pluralistic the centre and the greater the number of other subcentres with direct access to it, the greater will be the potential overlapping and meeting points between their respective styles of life and patterns of social participation.

With regard to the orientations of the centre, here also the importance of prestige, as against power, orientations in the centre stands out. A power-oriented centre will attempt to maximize such segregation, as against the centre oriented to prestige which will tend to encourage some meeting or overlapping among different local-occupational groups —but the scope of such overlapping and the degree to which it will dis-courage such segregation of styles of life will vary according to the nature of the prestige which is upheld in the respective centre. A centre which tends to uphold participation in a relatively open universalistic tradition, such as the Chinese, will tend mostly to bring together the higher élites which converge in the centre, and to keep some points of contact with other groups insofar as they are seen as potentially participating in this centre. At the same time it will tend to encourage segregation of different groups at more peripheral levels of social life.

A centre which tends to emphasize a combination of 'close' cultural ritualistic contents together with strong ascriptive regulation of access to them, based on primordial qualities—as the Indian one—will tend to stress the meeting of various groups, in a highly differentiated way, around some common foci of cultural or political identity, but this very meeting will stress their segregation in most of the social and cultural orders.

A centre with more multiple prestige orientations, especially insofar as among these orientations there is also one towards more universalistic, open, cultural or religious traditions—as was the case in the European one—will also tend on the whole to minimize the segregation of different groups and to maximize the possibility of their overlapping in their participation in different social and cultural spheres. The orientations and structure of the centre will also greatly influence the extent to which there may develop within a given society a unified hierarchy of status. While in no complex society can there develop a single unified status hierarchy, yet the scope and directions of such a hierarchy will also differ greatly among them.

In general the more monolithic a centre the more it will attempt to establish a relatively unified hierarchy —but the exact scope will differ greatly according to the basic orientations of the centre. Thus, a power-oriented centre will attempt to establish a uniform hierarchy with regard to the centre itself but will 'cut it off' as it were below, without necessarily attempting to impose a unified scale of evaluation on the various peripheral institutional positions and occupations. It will also tend, on the whole, to increase the steepness of the hierarchy both within the centre, between it and the periphery and to some degree also among the peripheral groups.

A prestige-oriented monolithic centre will attempt to encompass, in its official evaluative hierarchy, not only the central position but also others more peripheral ones. It will at least tend to evaluate them on some general scale even if leaving them to develop their own, secondary scales of evaluation with regard to their various internal subdivisions and roles. The steepness of the hierarchy evolved by such a centre will largely depend on the accessibility of different groups to the centre. In-sofar as many groups have some autonomous and not fully fixed access to the centre, then there will be a greater spread of such hierarchies. If such multiple access is not fully legitimized, as in India, these hier-archies will be mostly of secondary importance and will never fully develop into fully competing ones—as was the case in Europe, where such multiple access was much more fully legitimized.

The major variables which tend to influence the degree to which there tends to develop, within any society, country-wide consciousness and organization of different strata are the orientations of the centre and the degree to which different strata both evince strong orientation to participation in the centre and have some degree of autonomous access to it, i.e. can to some degree control the conversion of their own resources into access to the centre. The greater the degree of such autonomy of access of various groups to the centre, the greater also will be their tendency to such country-wide strata consciousness and organization. The degree and scope of such country-wide strata consciousness and organization will be greater the more such access is rooted in ascriptive corporate right of primordial kinship or territorial groups. The degree of such country-wide strata consciousness will also be influenced by the orientation of the centre. Other conditions being equal it will be greatest insofar as orientations to prestige are more important. Contrariwise, it will be smaller in a society whose centre is based on power and which tends to minimize such autonomous access to the centre.

The combination of the orientation and structure of the centre with the degree of access to it will tend also to influence greatly the degree to which family and kinship units will serve not only as the agents of initial socialization and placement of individuals in the social structure but also as a basic focus of stratum-consciousness as well as an ascriptive regulator of access to positions. A power centre will tend to minimize any such tendencies on the part of family and kinship units—i.e. to minimize the 'status' or 'class' components of family or kinship group identity. A centre oriented to participation in universalistic tradition will tend to uphold the relation between family and status identity but will tend to minimize the functions of the family as an ascriptive regulator or channel of access to positions.

A centre which is oriented to a more 'closed' tradition, and within which primordial qualities are conceived as part of the basic definition of the socio-cultural order, will tend to encourage almost all such connections between family and status. However, the more multiple orientations there are within a centre and the greater the number of units with relatively autonomous access to the centre, the stronger will be the forces counteracting such ascriptive tendencies of various primordial kinship groups, without necessarily undermining the predisposition of families to serve as foci of strata consciousness. Lastly the patterns and scope of social mobility will also be to a very large degree influenced by the orientations of the centre, as well as by the degrees of access to it by various groups.

Any monolithic centre will tend to encourage, at least with regard to access to the central positions, patterns of 'sponsored' mobility. The exact criteria and channels of such mobility as well as its effects on centre-strata and inter-strata relations (i.e. on the degree of their segregation) are mostly influenced by the contents of the orientations of the centre as outlined above. Contest mobility tends, on the other hand, to develop when the centres themselves have relatively multiple orientations and/or especially insofar as the primordial and kinship units serve as important and independent bases of access to the centre. Insofar as the criteria of such access are, as in the Indian case, ideally fixed, then this will be a contest mobility among wider kinship, territorial and/or occupational groups. In so far as these criteria are not fixed—as was the case in Europe—then this contest mobility will have the character of mobility of individual families and will tend to create—to a greater degree than in the former case—new types of institutional positions and multiple hierarchies of status.

The preceding conclusions have been mainly drawn on for the comparative analysis of Imperial or semi-Imperial traditional societies. We have not attempted to present here a full explanation of the analytical reasons for the impact of different types of orientations and structures of centres on processes of strata formation. This would have necessitated a more systematic analysis of the institutional or exchange properties of these different orientations—something which would be beyond the scope of this paper.[1] Similarly the analysis here was confined to a certain type of traditional society—and it is yet to be seen to what extent it may also be applied to modern societies where the general levels of resources, the general basic orientations of centres and strata alike, the basic patterns of the access of the broader social groups to the centre, as well as the conception of the centre, has been greatly changed from those prevalent in the traditional societies discussed here.

---

[1] This constitutes, however, part of the broader work which has been mentioned in the first footnote of the paper.

5

DEFERENCE[1]

EDWARD SHILS

DEFERENCE

Into every action of one human being towards another there enters an element of appreciation or derogation of the 'partner' towards whom the action is directed. It enters in varying degrees; some actions contain very little of it, some consist almost entirely of appreciation or derogation, in most actions the appreciative or derogatory elements are mingled with others, such as commanding, coercing, cooperating, purchasing, loving, etc.

Appreciation and derogation are responses to properties of the 'partner', of the role which he is performing, of the categories into which he is classified or the relationships in which he stands to third persons or categories of persons—against the background of the actor's own image of himself with respect to these properties. This element of appreciation or derogation is different from those responses to the past or anticipated actions of the 'partner' which are commands, acts of obedience, the provision of goods or services, the imposition of injuries such as the withholding or withdrawal of goods and services, and acts of love or hatred.

These acts of appreciation or derogation I shall designate as *deference*. The term *deference* shall refer both to positive or high deference and to negative or low deference or derogation. Ordinarily, when I say that one person defers to another, I shall mean that he is acknowledging that person's worth or dignity but when I speak of a person's 'deference-position', that might refer either to a high or low deference-position. What I call deference here is sometimes called 'status' by other writers. There is nothing wrong with that designation, except that it has become associated with a conception of the phenomenon which I wish to modify. The term 'deference', with its clear intimation of a person who defers,

---

[1] This paper is a further exploration of the theme of my earlier papers 'Charisma, order and status', *American Sociological Review*, vol. 30 (April 1965), pp. 199–213; 'Centre and periphery', in *The Logic of Personal Knowledge: Essays in Honour of Michael Polanyi* (London: Routledge, Kegan Paul, 1961), pp. 117–30; 'The concentration and dispersion of charisma', *World Politics*, vol. XI, 1, pp. 1–19; and 'Metropolis and province in the intellectual community' in N. V. Sovani and V. M. Dandekar (eds.), *Changing India: Essays in Honour of Professor D. R. Cadgil* (Bombay: Asia Publishing House, 1961), pp. 275–94.

brings out the aspect which has in my view not been made sufficiently explicit in work on this subject in recent years.

Deference is closely related to such phenomena as prestige, honour and respect (and obscurity and shame, dishonour and disrespect), fame (and infamy), glory (and ignominy), dignity (and indignity).

Acts of deference are performed in face-to-face relationships and in the relationship of actors who have no direct interactive relationship with each other but who are members of the same society. (It can exist too in the relationships of individual actors or collectivities in different societies, although to the extent that this occurs the societies in question cease to be totally separate societies.)

The granting of deference entails an attribution of superiority (or inferiority) but it is not the same as an attribution of goodness or wickedness. It does however often have such overtones; occasionally there is a suggestion that the superiority requires goodness for its completeness. It is an attribution of merit (or of defect); it is an assessment which attributes worthiness (or unworthiness) which is quite distinct from an attribution of moral qualities. What this worthiness consists in is an obscure matter.

To be the recipient of deference from another actor, whether in some tangible or clearly perceivable and discrete form of action from other persons, or to possess it in an autonomous symbolic form which is regarded as an 'objectification of deference' quite apart from the deferential actions of concrete actors, or to possess it by believing oneself to be entitled to it through the possession of the qualities which are conventionally accepted as the grounds on which deference is elicited or granted, is a widespread desire of human beings. It might even be said that the desire to be 'worthy' is a 'need' of human beings in the way in which affection, erotic gratification and the satisfaction of organic needs such as nutriment and bodily warmth are 'needs'.

To grant or accord deference is also a 'need' of human beings aroused or generated by the process of interaction and by the fact of living in a society which goes beyond the limited radius of face-to-face interaction. Just as they wish to be worthy and to have that worth acknowledged by the deference of other persons, so they also often have a need to live in a social world implanted with worthiness, to acknowledge the embodiments of that worth and to derogate those who are unworthy.

Deference of the sort which I discuss in this paper is a way of expressing an assessment of the self and of others with respect to 'macro-social' properties. By macro-social properties, I refer to those characteristics which describe the role or position of persons in the larger (usually national) society in which they live. The act of symbolization of deference is an attribution of deference-position or status in the total society. In acts of deference performed within face-to-face relationships or within limited corporate groups, the deference is often but not always accorded primarily with respect to status in the larger society. The deference accorded to a father as head of a family is not deference in my sense of the word when it does not make reference to the father's position in the society outside the family. The deference awarded to a superior or colleague within a corporate body is a mixture of deference with respect to intra-corporate status and to 'macro-social' status. The deference accorded to a woman or to women as a category or to a man or to men as a category is at the margin of macro-social deference. The deference accorded to age or youth is similarly marginal. Both age and sex are significant factors in the determination of the 'life chances' of a person and therewith of the likelihood that that person will receive deference. They are moreover themselves the objects of deferential judgments. Yet the deference granted to age or to sex seems to be of a different order from that deference which is an appreciation of worthiness or a derogation of unworthiness.

THE BASES OF DEFERENCE

The disposition to defer and the performance of acts of deference are evoked by the perception, in the person or classes of persons perceived, of certain characteristics or properties of their roles or actions. These characteristics or properties I shall call deference-entitling properties or entitlements. While they do not by themselves and automatically arouse judgments of deference, they must be seen or believed to exist for deference to be granted. Deference-entitlements include: occupational role and accomplishment, wealth (including type of wealth), income and the mode of its acquisition, style of life, level of educational attainment, political or corporate power, proximity to persons or roles exercising political or corporate power, kinship connections, ethnicity, performance on behalf of the community or society in relation to external communities or societies, and the possession of 'objective acknowledgments' of deference such as titles or ranks.

It is on the basis of the perception of these entitlements that individuals and classes or more or less anonymous individuals who are believed to possess some constellation of these entitlements are granted deference; it is on the basis of the possession of these properties that they grant deference to themselves and claim it from others. It is on the basis of simultaneous assessments of their own and of others' deference-entitlements that they regulate their conduct towards others and anticipate the deferential (or derogatory) responses of others.

Why should these properties be singled out as pertinent to deference?

What is it about them which renders them deference-relevant? Why are they and not kindness, amiability, humour, manliness, femininity, and other temperamental qualities which are so much appreciated in life, regarded as deference-relevant?

The cognitive maps which human beings form of their world include a map of their society. This map locates the primary or corporate groups of which they are active members and the larger society which includes these groups, but with which they have little active contact. The map which delineates this society entails a sense of membership in that society and a sense of the vital character of that membership. Even though the individual revolts against that society, he cannot completely free himself from his sense of membership in it. The society is not just an ecological fact or an environment; it is thought to possess a vitality which is inherent in it and membership in it confers a certain vitality on those who belong to it. It is a significant cosmos from which members derive some of their significance to themselves and to others. This significance is a charismatic significance; i.e. it signifies the presence and operation of what is thought to be of ultimate and determinative significance.

If we examine each of the deference-relevant properties with reference to this charismatic content, i.e. with reference to the extent to which it tends to have charisma attributed to it, we will see that each of these properties obtains its significance as an entitlement to deference primarily on these grounds.

Occupational role is ordinarily thought of as one of the most significant entitlements to deference. The most esteemed occupations in societies, for which there are survey or impressionistic data, are those which are in their internal structure and in their functions closest to the *centres*. The centres of society are those positions which exercise earthly power and which mediate man's relationship to the order of existence—spiritual forces, cosmic powers, values and norms—which legitimates or withholds legitimacy from the earthly powers or which dominates earthly existence. The highest 'authorities' in society—governors, judges, prime ministers and presidents and fundamental scientists—are those whose roles enable them to control society or to penetrate into the ultimate laws and forces which are thought to control the world and human life. Occupational roles are ranked in a sequence which appears approximately to correspond with the extent to which each role possesses these properties. The charismatic content of a given occupational role will vary with the centrality of the corporate body or sector in which it is carried on. The most authoritative role in a peripheral corporate body will carry less charisma than the same type of role in a more centrally located corporate body. The roles which exercise no authority and which are thought to have a minimum of contact with transcendent powers call forth least deference.

Of course, occupational roles and their incumbents are also deferred to on account of certain highly correlated deference-entitling properties such as the income which the practice of the occupation provides, the educational level of its practitioners, the ethnic qualities of its incumbents, etc. Conversely, occupational roles which are ill-remunerated and the incumbents of which have little education and are of derogatory ethnic stocks receive little deference on the grounds of these traits as well as on the grounds of the nature and functions of the occupational role itself. Nonetheless, occupational role is an independent entitlement to deference.

Beyond occupational role, accomplishment within the role is a deference-entitlement both micro- and macro-socially. To be not only a judge but an outstanding judge, to be not only a scientist but an outstanding scientist constitutes a further deference-entitlement. It does this not only because outstanding accomplishment renders its performer more 'visible' and therewith more likely to be the recipient of deference but much more because accomplishment is the realization of the potentiality of creative action. Creativity is a feature of centrality; creative action makes the creator part of the centre.

Wealth is deferred to—great wealth is greatly deferred to, and poverty is derogated—because it is powerful. But without association with charismatic occupation or with political power, wealth is not as much deferred to as when it enjoys those associations. Wealth which is manifested only by purchasing power is not as esteemed as wealth which embodies its power in the ownership and management of landed estates or in the directorship of great industrial corporations, employing many thousands of persons. Wealth is, in one important aspect, purchasing power and as such it is like income; it is also the power to employ and the power to dismiss from employment. These powers over physiological existence and access to dignity are tremendous but they are not peculiar to wealth and are quite compatible with the propertylessness of those who exercise these powers. Wealth also calls forth deference when it is associated with a certain style of life, for which it is indeed a condition.[1] Wealth is therefore both a derivative and a conditional entitlement to deference. It is derivative from occupation, from the exercise of power, over persons and over the soil; it is conditional to a 'style of life'. It is

[1] Wealth alone calls forth a qualified deference. Until the wealthy acquire an appropriate style of life and associations, they do not gain 'acceptance' by those whom they equal or exceed in wealth and who already have a high deference position. The contempt shown towards the *nouveau riche* is well known and it often takes a generation for wealth to acquire the appropriate education, religion, occupation and style of life which are necessary for assimilation into a higher deference-stratum.

also conditional to income;[1] it itself and alone is significant primarily as a potentiality of power. To gain the deference which sociologists often assert is the reward of wealth it must find completion in a wider complex of properties such as the actual exercise of power through an authoritative occupational role, through a 'validating' style of life, etc.

Income too is regarded as an entitlement to deference as a manifestation of power, but it is a limited and segmental power which is exercised in the specific buyer-seller relationship in the purchase of goods and services. Purchasing power, confined as it is to very specific exchange relationships, is not a very weighty entitlement to deference. Income alone possesses only potential deference-entitlement.[2] Nonetheless, a high income, like a large fortune, is regarded as a valid entitlement to deference when it is used to acquire what it can most legitimately be used for, namely the style of life to which it corresponds, or to acquire those other purchasable entitlements like educational opportunity, and associational membership. Income is therefore a *conditional* deference-entitlement which acquires deference primarily when manifested in another category. In itself it possesses as little charisma as an immediate specific potential power confers.

A style of life is a deference-entitlement because it is a pattern of conduct which is a voluntary participation in an order of values. A style of life is value-permeated; it demonstrates connection with a stratum of being in which true value resides. The conventional and long-standing deference given to the 'leisure classes' was not given because idleness was a virtue or because work or occupation was a burden but because leisure permitted the cultivation and practice of a value-infused pattern of life. Like an authoritative occupation, it was a value-generating and value-infused existence. More than authoritative occupations, it belongs, despite its material embodiment, to the realm of

[1] Cf. the anomaly experienced in the contemplation of very wealthy persons who do not *use* their wealth in the practice of an appropriate style of life, who exercise no power through its use (employing no one, exercising no control over the agricultural or industrial properties in which it is invested), and who practise no occupation. All they have is the potentiality which we know from the observation of other cases wealth possesses. They enjoy such deference as they receive—apart from what they might receive by virtue of their family name—because of the potentiality rather than the actuality of their exercise of power. Potentiality is less instigative of deference than actuality. As a result, they are the objects of an ambivalent judgment, deference granted for the potentiality of power which wealth confers, deference withheld for their failing to complete the potentiality of wealth by manifesting it in the fuller pattern which is incumbent on anyone who is high in any single distribution.

[2] Although all resources in particular distributive categories contains the potentiality of conversion into a position in another distributive category, they vary in their degree of specificity. Income can be used to purchase objects at relatively fixed rates, e.g. household furnishings, books, education, etc.; education is not equally specific in the response which it is thought to be entitled to call forth. Neither is political authority. In general we can say that the more diffuse a potentiality, the greater is its entitlement to deference.

culture. It included eating ('commensality') 'in style', living in the midst of an appropriate *décor*, in an appropriate quarter ('a good address'), surrounded by servants who provide not just labour power but a ritual environment.[1] In its highest form, 'style of life' was found in courts and palaces, in great country houses and grand bourgeois establishments. Style of life requires income as a condition but it is an entitlement to deference not as a direct function of wealth and income or simply as an indicator of wealth and income. It is facilitated by wealth and income but it enhances them and transfigures them. It does so because it partakes of a charismatic quality which they contain only in the potentiality but not in their sheer and specific actuality.

The level of educational attainment possesses deference-entitling properties partly because it is often conditional to entry into authoritative, creative and remunerative occupational roles but even more because it is an assimilation into an ideal realm. It is an assimilation into a pattern of values and beliefs which are part of the centre of existence. The 'possessor' of a large amount of education is often an incumbent of an authoritative occupation and as an actual or potential incumbent of such an occupation he receives deference; he also has the likelihood of a higher than average income and an appropriate style of life and as such he receives deference also.[2] The educated person is one who has received the culture of beliefs and appreciations which are central in the society. These beliefs may be scientific beliefs about the way in which the world works, they may be beliefs about the 'essential' nature of the society, its history, its religion, its cultural traditions and objectivations. Education is also the acquisition of skills which prepare for participation in the centre of the society through the exercise of authority, technological performance, the discovery and transmission of vital truths about the universe, man and society, in short for *creating* and *ordering*. Education is an autonomous, non-derivative entitlement to deference because it is integral to and testifies to its possessor's participation in the charismatic realm.

The exercise of power whether in an occupation or through the employment of purchasing power is determinative of the life chances of the persons over whom it is exercised; therewith it shares in the charisma which is inherent in the control of life. It is difficult to separate power from occupational role because much or even most power is exercised in

[1] Of course, 'style of life' can be shrivelled to hedonistic self-indulgence, 'conspicuous consumption' or sheer idleness, all of which are capable of gaining ascendancy within the pattern.
[2] The deference-entitlement of education is also affected by the institutions and countries in which it is acquired. Some schools and universities and university systems are thought to be more central than others. Those educated in them acquire more of a charismatically infused culture.

occupational roles, in corporate bodies, particularly if we include inherited, entrepreneurially initiated, appointed and elected incumbency
in roles in the state, church, armies, economic organizations, universities, etc. Authority exercised through occupational roles becomes more
diffuse the higher its position within any corporate hierarchy, whether
the hierarchy be religious, political, military or whatever. Its diffuseness,
which is another facet of its creating and ordering responsibility and
capacity, is crucial to its deference-entitlement.

There is undoubtedly some power which is not occupational in the
locus of its exercise. It might be worth while, therefore, to employ a
separate category for power as a deference-entitlement for those persons
whose charismatic ascendancy is not a function of an occupational role.[1]

Where everyone in a society or at least all adults stand in at least one
important respect in equal relationship to the exercise of authority in
government by virtue of citizenship, deference is dispersed. The sharing
of power and the attendant equalization of deference through citizenship does not abolish the inequality of power and thus the inequality of
deference associated with the unequal distribution of authoritative
occupational roles. It does, however, offset it and in some situations to a
very considerable extent.

Relative proximity to persons in powerful roles is another deference-
entitlement. The proximity may be a fiduciary relationship between the
incumbent of a very authoritative role and his 'personal staff'; it may
be a close personal relationship of friendship or affection; it may be little
more than the acquaintanceship of frequent encounter; it may be the
primordial tie of kinship. Whatever the content of the relationship, the
important thing is that the magnitude of its entitlement to deference for
a given person is assessed (a) by the deference-position of the person to
whom he stands in proximity and (b) the degree of proximity. To be the
son or cousin or the intimate friend of a person of no significant status
adds no status to those in that degree of proximity; indeed it makes for
the insignificant status of those who stand in such proximity. Being a
close friend or a frequently met colleague of a person of a high deference-
position confers more deference than would a slighter degree of friendship or a less intense collegial intercourse. The deference-position of the
person at the end of the chain is determined by the properties already

---

[1] Just as within occupations, there are inter-individual differences in creativity or productivity, so it is perfectly conceivable that this creativity can manifest itself avocationally and
outside the corporate bodies within which such activities are ordinarily carried on. There
are religious prophets who arise out of the laity, revolutionary politicians who are not
incorporated into the established political order, intimates of rulers who have no formal
political occupation and whose own occupations are not constitutively endowed with
power. All of these are exercisers of power in a way which is independent of their occupational roles. (Of course, the definition of occupation in this way has the danger of turning
occupational role into a residual category.)

referred to; the relationship is the channel through which a fundamentally charismatic quality is transmitted. Just as the member of a corporate body participates in the charisma of his organization, whether it be a university, a church or a government, so membership in a personal relationship or in a primordial collectivity (e.g. family) is constituted by or results from a diffusion of the charisma of the central person or role of the collectivity. Those who stem from 'famous' families, those who keep the company of important persons, who move in 'important' circles, share in the charismatic quality of those whose charisma gives fame to families and importance to circles. The three modes of linkage—primordial, personal and collegial—are all different from each other and yet each has been regarded as a legitimate channel through which charisma and, consequently, the entitlement to deference can be shared.

Ethnicity is very much like the kinship tie—they are both primordial, being constituted by the significance attributed to a presumed genetic connection and the primordial unity arising therefrom. Unlike kinship connection as an entitlement to deference, ethnicity does not refer to a genetic link with a particular important person or persons. It is a link with a collectivity in which a vital, charismatic quality is diffused. It is thought to represent the possession of some quality inherent in the ethnic aggregate and shared by all its members. Indeed the possession of that 'essential' quality as manifested in certain external features such as colour, hair form, physiognomy and physique constitutes membership in the aggregate. In societies which are ethnically homogeneous, the ethnic entitlement is neutral; in societies which are ethnically plural, the ethnic entitlement can only be neutralized by an overriding civility or sense of citizenship or by the disaggregation of the society to the point where it almost ceases to be a society.

Areal provenience whether it be rural or urban, regional or local, provincial or metropolitan can also be a deference-entitlement in a variety of ways. In some respects, it can be derivative from occupational roles and the exercise of authority insofar as particular occupational roles and the exercise of authority tend to be more concentrated—although not necessarily in the same locations—to a greater extent in some areas than in others. It might also be derivative from the greater proximity to authority and eminence which is more likely in some areas than in others. But the soil and the city might be independent entitlements, one gaining ascendancy over the other in accordance with prevailing beliefs concerning the sanctity of the soil or the charisma of urban existence.

Religious adherence or affiliation is similar to ethnicity in that it is a deference-entitlement referring to membership in a collectivity, but in this case the collectivity is constituted by the sharing of beliefs about sacred things and therewith by the sharing of the charisma of the church or sect. Whereas practically all societies are differentiated in occupational roles and in income and power or authority and are bound to be so by their nature as societies, ethnic and religious heterogeneity is not inevitable.

Indulgence conferred on the community or on society by protecting it from injury or by enhancing its position—power, wealth, deference—among communities or societies is regarded as an entitlement to deference for those who confer such indulgence. Successful military men, politicians and statesmen, diplomats, athletes in international competitions, literary men and artists are deferred to within their own societies in proportion to their external deference or their enhancement of the power of their own society *vis-à-vis* other societies. The enhancement of the deference-position and power of the society enhances the deference-position of its members by virtue of their membership in it. It is the same here as in the case of proximity to importance or membership in primordial collectivities. There is a sense of some shared essential quality with those who 'represent' the society.[1]

A title or emblem conferred by the major deference-bearing institutions of the society is an entitlement to deference—such are the criteria by which deference is allocated in societies. They are not all of equal importance in the formation of deference judgments nor do their relative weights remain constant through time or among societies. Ethnicity, area, religion might vary considerably in their significance in accordance with the strength of the sense of civility and the extent and intensity of religious belief. Education might become more important when a larger proportion of the population seeks education and possesses different amounts and kinds of education. The more equal the distribution of any given deference-entitlement, the less weight it has in differentiating the deference-positions of the members of a society. This does not mean that it loses its significance in the determination of the allocation of deference, only that it ceases to differentiate the worth of individuals. In fact, while ceasing to differentiate, it might at the same time raise the deference-position of most individuals throughout the society. But there is also a possibility that a particular criterion might become irrelevant, or at least diminish in relevance, to deference, losing its influence on the level of deference as it ceases to discriminate among individuals, groups and strata.[2]

---

[1] There is a deference-stratification among societies. It includes the deference-stratification of whole societies and an international deference-stratification system of individuals which is however extremely fragmentary.

[2] If we can imagine a society, the technology of which has become so automated that a large part of the gainfully employed population ceases to be differentiated by occupation, we are confronted by a situation in which occupations, at least for a large part of the population,

DEFERENCE BEHAVIOUR

The phenomena of the stratification system are generally thought of as so massive in their impact on the rest of society that it is only natural that they too should be conceived of as having a substantial existence. Indeed they are spoken of as if they possessed a continuous, almost physical, tangibility which enables them to be apprehended by relatively gross methods of observation. In fact, many of these properties are very discontinuous or intermittent in their performance. When they are not actual, they fall into a condition of 'latency'. The different entitlements vary in the continuity and substantiality of their performance or manifestation. And what is true of entitlements to deference applies even more to deference behaviour itself.

First of all, however, before considering deference behaviour as such, I should like to consider the substantiality and continuity of the entitlements.

Occupational roles are, for example, performed for from one- to two-thirds of the waking life of the human being so employed for most of the days of each week for most of the weeks of the year over a period of forty to fifty or more years, through youth, adulthood and old age. A wealthy person usually has his wealth in the form of real property, chattels or convertible paper, available to him whenever he wishes to call upon it and as long as he owns it. The receipt and expenditure of income is a less continuous property, not only because the amount of income received fluctuates or varies over the course of a decade or a lifetime but also because once expended it ceases to be available, and because when not being used it is not visible. Only the results of expended income are visible in the material or tangible components of a style of life. Income is *recurrent* and it can be regularly recurrent as a disposable sum but not *continuously* and it is not always *substantially* manifested.

The style of life of a person or a family is a pattern heterogeneous in its composition and pervasive in apparel, speech, domestic arrangements, physical, social and cultural. Its material apparatus is grossly observable. Like occupational role, among the deference entitlements, it is performed, enacted or lived in a larger proportion of waking time (and even sleeping time) than the other deference entitlements. Style of life is, with occupational role, the most substantial and continuous of the various deference-entitlements. It is, with occupation, the most visible.

have lost their capacity to confer different deference-positions in their practitioners. This does not mean that the entire gainfully employed population has become occupationally homogeneous, but for that section which has become homogeneous occupation will count for no more than race in an ethnically almost homogeneous society.

Level and type of educational attainment is a different kind of thing. It is like kinship in the sense that it is membership in a category which entails no present action. (Indeed kinship entails no action on the part of the actor in question. It is a *past* biological connection, a *present* genetic composition and classification by self and other.) Level of educational attainment insofar as it is a past qualification for present incumbency in a role has ceased to exist except as a marker of a past accomplishment, like a medal awarded for heroism in a long past battle. Where it is interpreted as an approximate indication of present level of culture, it refers to very discontinuously performed actions. Insofar as it refers to the number of years in which studies were carried on, to the subjects studied and certifications which attest to amounts, etc., it refers to past events which provide a basis for present classification by self and other. Thus, while to an external analyst the level of educational attainment is a stable property of a person, it is not continuously operative in that person's action or interaction with others. It is a fluctuating and intermittent quality, sometimes of high salience, sometimes latent. It need not be so in all societies, in all strata or in all individuals. In societies or strata which are highly 'education-conscious', it will be more continuously salient as a categorial property than in those which are less 'education-conscious'. Persons of a given level of educational attainment will manifest it more substantially in their speech, thought and conduct.

Power, which is so closely and often associated with the performance of occupational role, resembles it in this respect too, since it is often exercised or performed for significantly continuous periods, with sufficiently regular recurrence. (It is also like occupational role in the sense that it places its practitioner in a category which calls forth responses from self and other in situations outside the occupational or power-exercising role.)

The foregoing observations were intended to render a little more explicit than is usually done the temporal discontinuity of entitlements, their intermittence and periodicity of performance and visibility. I have done this because these characteristics of entitlement affect their probability of being perceived and therewith of calling forth deference. I have also done it because I wish to call attention to what appear to me to be important, even if not readily evident, features of deference behaviour.

The term *status*, when it is used to refer to deference-position, ordinarily carries with it, as I suggested earlier, overtones of the stability, continuity and pervasiveness which are possessed by sex and age. A person who has a given status tends to be thought of as having that status at every moment of his existence as long as that particular status is not replaced by another status. One of the reasons why I have chosen to use the term 'deference-position' in place of 'status' is that it makes a little more prominent the fact that status is not a substantial property of the person arising automatically from the possession of certain entitlements but is in fact an element in a relationship between the person deferred to and the deferent person. Deference towards another person is an attitude which is manifested in behaviour.

Acts of deference judgments are evaluative classifications of self and other. As classifications they transcend in their reference the things classified. A person who is evaluatively classified by an act of deference on the basis of his occupation is in that classification even when he is not performing his occupational role. The classificatory deference judgment, because it is a generalization, attains some measure of independence from the intermittence of entitlements. It has an intermittence of its own which is not necessarily synchronized with that of the entitlements.

Overt concentrated acts of deference such as greetings and presentations are usually shortlived, i.e. they are performed for relatively short periods and then 'disappear' until the next appropriate occasion. The appropriate occasions for the performance of concentrated acts of deference might be regular in their recurrence, e.g. annually or weekly or even daily, but except for a few 'deference-occupations' they are not performed with the high frequency and density over extended periods in the way in which occupational roles are performed. But does deference consist exclusively of the performance of concentrated deferential actions? Is there a 'deference vacuum' when concentrated deferential actions are not being performed? Where does deference go when it is not being expressed in a grossly tangible action?

To answer this question, it is desirable to examine somewhat more closely the character of attenuated deference actions. There are concentrated, exclusively deferential actions which are nothing but deferential actions just as there are exclusively power or style or life or occupational actions but in a way different from these others. Occupational actions are substantial; all effort within a given space and time is devoted to their performance. They can be seen clearly by actor and observer as occupational actions; the exercise of authority has many of these features, especially when it is exercised in an authoritative occupational role. Expenditures of money are of shorter duration but they too are clearly definable. The acts of consumption and conviviality which are comprised in a style of life are of longer duration but they too are also clearly defined. On the other hand, level of educational attainment and kinship connection and ethnicity are not actual actions at all, they are classifications in which 'objectively' the classified person is continuously present although once present in the class he does nothing to manifest or affirm.

But deference actions—deferring to self and other, receiving deference from self and other—are actions. They result in and are performed with reference to classifications but they are actions nonetheless. They are not however always massive actions of much duration. They occur more-over mainly at the margin of other types of action. Deference actions performed alone are usually very shortlived; they open a sequence of interaction and they close it. Between beginning and end, deference actions are performed in fusion with non-deferential actions. Through-out the process of interaction they are attenuated in the substance of the relationship in which the performance of tasks appropriate to roles in corporate bodies, to civil roles, to personal relationships, etc., occurs. Deference actions have always been largely components of other actions; they are parts of the pattern of speaking to a colleague, a superior or an inferior about the business at hand in an authoritatively hierarchical corporate body, of speaking about or to a fellow citizen, of acting towards him over a distance (as in an election). In other words, deference actions seldom appear solely as deference actions and those which do are not regarded, especially in the United States, as a particu-larly important part of interaction in most situations. Nonetheless, deference is demanded and it is accepted in an attenuated form.

This then is the answer to the question as to where deference goes when it ceases to be concentrated: it survives in attenuation, in a pervasive, intangible form which enters into all sorts of relationships through tone of speech, demeanour, precedence in speaking, frequency and mode of contradiction, etc.

Deference can, however, become extinct. A person who fails to retain his entitlements in the course of time also loses the deference which his entitlements brought him. He might not lose it entirely; ex-prime ministers, professors emeriti, retired generals, long after they departed from their occupational roles continue to receive some deference, although it is probably, other things being equal, less than they received while active incumbents. Kings in exile, great families fallen on hard times also lose much of their deference and some, sinking away into peripheral obscurity, cease to be known and their deference becomes entirely local.

The salience of deference behaviour is closely related to deference-sensitivity. Indifference to deference is a marginal phenomenon but individuals, classes and societies differ in the degree to which they demand deference—whether concentrated or attenuated—or are relatively unperceptive regarding its appropriateness, its presence or its absence. Snobs are persons whose demand for deference is great and for whom the deference-position of those they associate with is their most relevant characteristic.

It is one of the features of modern Western societies that they are moving in the direction of deference-indifference and attenuation. The movement is very uneven among modern societies with the United States, Canada and Australia in the lead, with other countries some distance behind but they too seem to be moving further along than they were a half century ago. The movement is also very uneven within societies, with marked differences between classes and generations.

The equalitarian tendencies of contemporary Western societies have not only witnessed the attenuation and retraction of deference, they have also seen it assimilated into the pattern of intercourse among equals. But can it be said that deference still exists in relations among equals? Is not equality a point where deference disappears? Concentrated and salient deference behaviour was a feature of the relations between the great of the earth and their subordinates. There is to be sure no elaborate ritual of deference between equals in contemporary Western societies and particularly in American society, except that which still obtains between heads of states, between heads of churches, heads of universities, on especially ceremonial occasions, etc.

Concentrated deference actions have by no means disappeared but they have become less elaborate and with their diminished elaboration they have been abbreviated. They have become less substantial and less separate from other actions. Ceremonial deference and formalized etiquette have diminished in magnitude and frequency.

The decline in the power of aristocracies and the diminution of the number of monarchies have been accompanied by a reduction in the amount or proportion of ceremonial deference in societies. Modes of spoken and written address have come to bespeak a more homogeneous distribution of deference throughout societies and in doing so they have moved towards simpler, briefer forms. The movement is not however all one way; the strata which previously were treated with the minimum of deference or indeed with negative deference have now begun to receive an enhanced deference although in the simplified and shorter forms of a less ritualized society.

The inherited rituals of deference tended largely to be concerned with the relations of superiors and inferiors. As an equalitarian outlook became more prominent, the rituals of deference fell into the same discredit as relationships which they expressed. It is however an open question whether equality or approximate equality is antithetical to rituals of deference. What seems fairly certain is that the relationships of equals can and do at present contain considerable elements of attenuated deference and can indeed not dispense with them.

Nonetheless, it would be wrong to fail to acknowledge that contemporary societies are less oriented towards their centres with respect to deference than their ancestors of a century ago. It is not merely on account of the decline of aristocracy and monarchy. These are only instances of a more general phenomenon, namely the diminution of the ruling classes in the various countries. When élites were smaller, educational opportunity more restricted and the kinship tie more respected than they are nowadays, the various sectors of the centre—the political, administrative, ecclesiastical, cultural and military élites—and to some extent the economic élite—were closer to each other through common origins, common institutional experiences, a shared conviviality and the linkage of kinship than they are now when the obligations of kinship are less observed in recruitment to the élite, when specialization has gone further and numbers greatly increased. One of the consequences of this pluralization of the élites is that their model is less imposing. Each sector is taken for what it is and, except for the very pinnacle of the head of state and the head of the government, the sense of difference in worth is felt to be less great than it once was.

THE DISTRIBUTION OF DEFERENCE

It has long been characteristic of the study of deference and of the de-ference-positions (status) which it helps to produce to ascribe to them a distribution similar in important respects to the distribution of entitle-ments such as occupational roles and power, income, wealth, styles of life, levels of educational attainment, etc. The entitlements are all relatively 'substantial' things which are not matters of opinion but rather 'objective', more or less quantifiable, conditions or attributes and as such capable of being ranged in a univalent and continuous distribu-tion. Every individual has one occupation or another at any given period in time or for a specifiable duration; every individual has—if it could be measured—such and such an average amount of power over a specifi-able time period. Every individual has some style of life, certain com-ponents of which at least are enduring and observable—and he either possesses them or does not possess them. There are of course cases of persons having two widely different kinds of occupational roles within the same limited time period ('moonlighting'), of persons having widely divergent incomes within a given period, but these and other anomalies can quite easily be resolved by specifiable procedures for the collection of data and for their statistical treatment and presentation.

Present-day sociological notions of deference (status, esteem, prestige, honour, etc.) grew up in association with the 'objective'[1] conception of social stratification. For reasons of convenience in research and also

---

[1] The 'objective' conception concerned itself with the relatively substantial entitlements, the 'subjective' with the 'opinion'-like elements.

because common usage practised a system of classification into 'middle', 'upper', 'lower',[2] etc., classes, research workers and theorists attempted to construct a composite index which would amalgamate the positions of each individual in a number of distributions (in particular, the distributions of occupational role and education) into some variant of the three-class distribution. The resultant was called 'social-economic status' (sometimes, 'socio-economic status').

The 'subjective' conception of social stratification appreciated the 'opinion'-like character of deference but for reasons of convenience in research procedure and because of the traditional mode of discourse concerning social stratification, the 'subjective factor' itself tended to be 'substantialized' and it too was regarded as capable of being ranged in an univalent distribution.[2] Sometimes as in the Edwards classification in the United States or in the Registrar-General's classification in the United Kingdom, this 'subjective factor' impressionistically assessed by the research worker was amalgamated with the 'objective factors' in arriving at a single indicator of 'status'. Status was taken to mean a total status, which included both deference-position and entitlements, constructed by an external observer (not a participant in the system). But this conception has not found sufferance because it is patently unsatisfactory. Deference-position—or esteem, prestige or status—does belong to a different order of events in comparison with events like occupational distribution, income and wealth distribution, etc. It belongs to the realm of values; it is the outcome of evaluative judgments regarding positions in the distributions of 'objective' characteristics.

The improvement of techniques of field work in community studies and sample surveys has rendered it possible to collect data, relatively systematically, about these evaluations and to assign to each person in a small community or to each occupation on a list a single position in a distribution. Research technique has served to obscure a fundamental conceptual error. As a result, since each person possessed a status (or deference-position), they could be ranged in a single distribution. Such a distribution could occur, however, only under certain conditions. The

---

[1] The prevalence of the trichotomous classification and variations on it is probably of Aristotelian origin. There is no obvious reason why reflection on experience and observation alone should have resulted in three classes. This might well be a case where nature has copied art.

[2] It is quite possible that this pattern of thought which emerged in the nineteenth century was deeply influenced by the conception of social class of the nineteenth-century critics of the *ancien régime* and of the bourgeois social order which succeeded it. In the *ancien régime* the most powerful ranks were designated by legally guaranteed titles which entered into the consciousness of their bearers and those who associated with or considered them. These designations were not 'material' or 'objective'. They did not belong to the 'substructure' of society. They were therefore 'subjective' but they were also unambiguous. They could be treated in the same way as 'objective' characteristics. By extension, the same procedure could be applied to the other strata.

conditions include (*a*) an evaluative consensus throughout the society regarding the criteria in accordance with which deference is allocated; (*b*) cognitive consensus throughout the society regarding the characteristics of each position in each distribution and regarding the shape of the distributions of entitlements; (*c*) consensus throughout the society regarding the weights to be assigned to the various categories of deference-entitling properties;[1] (*d*) equal attention to and equal differentiation by each member of the society of strata which are adjacent to his own and those which are remote from it;[2] (*e*) equal salience of deference judgments throughout the society; (*f*) univalence of all deference judgments.

Were these conditions to obtain, then the distribution of deference-positions in such a society might well have the form which the distributions of 'objective' entitlements possess. There are, however, numerous reasons why the distribution of deference-positions or status does not have this form. Some of these reasons are as follows: (*a*) Some consensus concerning the criteria for the assessment of entitlements might well exist but like any consensus it is bound to be incomplete. Furthermore criteria are so ambiguously apprehended that any existent consensus actually covers a wide variety of beliefs about the content of the criteria. (*b*) Cognitive consensus throughout the society regarding the properties of entitlements and the shape of their distributions is rather unlikely because of the widespread and unequal ignorance about such matters as the occupational roles, incomes, educational attainments of individuals and strata. (*c*) The weighting of the various criteria is not only ambiguous, it is likely to vary from stratum to stratum depending on the deference position of the various strata and their positions on the various distributions; it is likely that each stratum will give a heavier weight to that distribution on which it stands more highly or on which it has a greater chance of improving its position or protecting it from 'invaders'. (*d*) The perceptions of one's own stratum or of adjacent strata are usually much more differentiated and refined and involve more subsidiary criteria than is the case in their perceptions of remote strata. Thus even if they are compatible with each other there is no identity of the differentiations made by the various strata. (*e*) Some persons are more sensitive to deference than are others and this difference in the salience of deference occurs among strata as well. Some persons think frequently in terms of deference position, other think less frequently in those terms. Accordingly assessments of other human

---

[1] Where these three conditions exist, there would also exist a consensus between the judgment which a person makes of his own deference-position and the judgments which others render about his position.

[2] It also presupposes equal knowledge by all members of the society about all other members.

beings and the self may differ markedly within a given society, among individuals, strata, regions and generations with respect to their tendency to respond deferentially rather than affectionately or matter-of-factly or instrumentally. The arrangement of the members of a society into a stratified distribution as if each of them had a determinate quantity of a homogeneous thing called deference (or status or prestige) does violence to the nature of deference and deference-positions; it further obscures in any case sufficiently opaque reality. The possibility of dissensus in each of the component judgments—cognitive and evaluative—which go to make up a deference-judgment can, of course, be covered by the construction of measures which hide the dispersion of opinions. If all inter-individual disagreements are confined to differences in ranking within a given stratum, the procedure would perhaps be acceptable. But, if 80 per cent of a population place certain persons in stratum I and if 20 per cent place them in stratum I I, is it meaningful to say that the persons so judged are in stratum I?

The dissensus which results in inter-individually discordant rankings seriously challenges the validity of procedures which construct univalent deference distributions and then disjoin them into strata. This difficulty would exist even if there were agreement about the location of the boundary lines which allegedly separate one deference stratum from the other. But there is no certainty that there will be consensus on this matter, and the purpose of realistic understanding is not served by assuming that there is such consensus or by constructing measures which impose the appearance of such a consensus on the data.

The conventional procedure of constructing deference distributions has tended to assume a considerable degree of clarity and differentiated-ness in the perception of the distribution of deference-entitling properties through the society. But as a matter of fact perceptions are vague and undifferentiated. Terminologies and classifications, particularly in relatively 'class-unconscious' societies, are not standardized and terms like 'poor', 'working people', 'lower classes', 'ordinary people', etc., are used in senses which the user has not reflected upon and which do not have a definite referent. There is no reason—at least until further research has been done—to think that they are interchangeable with each other although sociologists do treat them as if they are.

If differentiation and specificity are slight in speaking about strata adjacent to one's own, they are even less developed in reference to remoter strata of which the judging person has no direct experience. This does not mean that deference-judgments are not made about these remoter strata; it does mean that such judgments are made with scant knowledge of the extent to which these deference-entitlements actually exist in the persons or strata so judged. The cognitive stratification map becomes vaguer with regard to those areas of the society far from the range of experience of the judging person. This too renders cognitive consensus impossible even if evaluative criteria were identical. What one judge looking at his own immediate stratification environment sees as highly differentiated, another who views it from a distance sees as homogeneous. Thus every sector of the stratification system is highly differentiated but only to those who are living in the midst of that sector.[1]

Up to this point I have cast doubt on the conventional treatments of the distribution of deference positions by referring to the diverse sorts of dissensus among individuals, strata, regional cultures, etc. But I wrote as if each of these agents of judgment spoke with a single voice. There is some justification for this since there *is* a tendency in many societies to regard the deference system as something objective, as *sui generis*, as existing outside the judging persons and independently of their own evaluations and appreciations of persons and strata. This tendency to 'objectivize' the distribution of deference is in part a product of the perception of the deference judgments of other persons in one's own society. But it also represents a tendency to believe in the 'objectivity', the 'givenness' of deference stratification which is a product of a tendency to believe that in addition to our own tastes and dispositions there is a realm of normative being which exists independently of those tastes and values.

But alongside of this tendency to believe in an 'objective' order of worthiness, there is a widespread alienation from that order and the acceptance and alienation exist very often in the same persons. This ambivalence is very difficult to apprehend by present-day techniques of research and it is even more difficult to deal with it systematically—at least for the present. It exists nonetheless and it is apt to become stronger as society becomes more differentiated and as the 'ruling class' in the sense of a set of persons intimately interrelated through kinship, common institutional experiences and long personal friendships, filling most of the positions at the top of the various distributions, gives way before a less unitary and therefore less imposing élite.

There is nothing pathological about this ambivalence. Submission to the ascendancy of the centre and to the standards which affirm it is painful because the indignity of inferiority is painful. The society which focuses on the centre imposes such indignity on the periphery. The more highly integrated a society ecologically, the greater will be the strain on the periphery, and the less imposing the élite at the centre, the more likely the emergence of the negative side of the ambivalence. The impli-

---

[1] The question arises therefore whether a distribution of deference positions incorporates the perceptions and categorizations which are applied to one's own and adjacent strata or those which are applied to remote ones. Whichever alternative is followed, the factitious character of the distribution so constructed is evident.

cations of this ambivalent attitude are far-reaching and they cannot be gone into here. Let it suffice to say the presently prevailing methods of describing deference distributions cannot accommodate these simple facts. Yet without these simple facts of ambivalence and alienation in the stratification system, how can class conflict and movements for reform by the re-allocation of deference and its entitlements be dealt with? And what is one to make of the anti-authoritarianism and antinomianism which has been a fluctuatingly frequent phenomenon of modern societies? How does this fit into a picture which portrays deference positions as univalently and consensually distributed?

Finally, I should like to conclude these reflections on the problems of deference distribution with some observations on equality. In general, the prevailing techniques for representing deference distributions proceed with a fixed number of strata or by means of scales which rank occupations or persons on a continuum running from 0 to 100. Both procedures assume a constant distance between the extremes and between the intervals or strata. This does not however seem to accord with the realities of the movement of modern societies towards a higher degree of equality of deference than was to be found earlier.

The range of deference-distribution probably varies among societies. Some are more equalitarian than others. In what does this equalitarianism consist apart from increased opportunities or life-chances for peripheral strata? Does it not consist in an appreciation of the greater worthiness of the peripheral strata—a judgment shared to some extent throughout their society. It is indeed a matter of opinion but it is an opinion of profound significance for the stratification system. I cannot go into the causes of this development;[1] I wish here only to call attention to its relevance to any realistic description of deference systems.

DEFERENCE INSTITUTIONS AND DEFERENCE SYSTEMS

Whereas most of the things valued by men become the explicit foci of elaborate institutional systems concerned with their production, acquisition, protection, maintenance, control and allocation, the same cannot be asserted of deference. Unlike economic or military or political or ecclesiastical institutions, deference institutions are marginal to the valued objects which they seek to affect. There is a College of Heralds, there are chiefs of protocol in departments of foreign affairs, there are *Who's Who's* and *Social Registers*, authors and publishers of books on deportment and on modes of address, there are advisers to prime

---

[1] I have attempted to explain the causes of this movement towards the narrowing of the range of dispersion of deference-positions in 'The Theory of Mass Society', *Diogenes*, 39 (1962), pp. 45–66.

ministers and presidents on the award of honours, there is an *Almanach de Gotha*, a great many states have a system of honours and many have had systems of titles and orders. Armies award medals and universities award earned and honorary degrees. Armies have titles of rank as do universities. Civil services too have ranks and designations which denote differences and ranks of authority but which are also titles of deference. Many of those institutions have handbooks which specify orders of precedence. All of these institutional arrangements confer or confirm deference; they seek to express deference, to create and legitimate claims to deference, to specify who should receive it and to entitle particular persons in a way which objectifies their claims to deference. Only a few of these institutions have sought explicitly to determine a 'generalized' deference position, namely those who sought to control and guarantee membership in nobilities or aristocracies. Others awarded deference for rather specific qualifications and although in many of these cases the deference was generalized, in others it remained an indicator of a quite specific achievement and thereby attained scarcely any measure of generalization. But at best, they have touched only a small part of the societies in which they have functioned and although they intensify and strengthen the deference system they cannot be said to create it or to manage it.

The deference system of a society extends throughout the length and breadth of that society. Everybody falls within it, yet very few of those have their deference positions determined by the deference-conferring and deference-confirming institutions. The actual really functioning deference system of a society envelops the deference institutions and takes them into account but it is not predominantly determined by them.

Most of the deference-behaviour—the behaviour which expresses deference—occurs in the face-to-face interaction of individuals and very few of those who receive some allocation of deference have any titles or medals. The deference which they receive is received from other persons who respond not to titles or honours of which they have heard or emblems of which they see on the garments of the persons deferred to, but to the entitling properties which they believe are possessed by the person to whom deference is given. Titles and medals might be taken into account and even when the title is used in full and correctly, the use of the title in addressing the person deferred to is at most only a part of the deference expressed. The title is thought to stand for something more than itself, for kinship connections, acknowledgment by the sovereign or occupational role and these too are not ultimate; they are evocative of other characteristics, of positions on various distributions.

The deference granted is as I have said earlier expressed in overtones of speech and action. Much of it is expressed in relations of authority and it appears together with commands and acts of obedience, with the giving of counsel and the taking of counsel, in the interplay of authorities and subjects, colleagues and neighbours performing the actions called for by authority, collegiality and neighbourliness. It is far more subtle and richer than the prescriptions for the ritual manifestations of deference and it is also often more impoverished. Being a duke or a professor or a colonel constitutes only one element—a quite considerable element —in the generalized deference which the incumbents of those ranks and the bearers of those titles receive. Those who associate with them and who defer to them respond to other things about them as well as to their ranks and titles. The excellence of their performance past and current, the power which they actually exercise or have exercised, the level of culture and their style of life, insofar as these can be perceived or imagined or are already known from previous experiences and from other sources, enter into the determination of the deference granted and expected.

Deference institutions are more important in some types of societies and in some strata than in others. In societies in which there is a sharp disjunction between centre and periphery, they will have more influence than in societies in which the periphery has expanded inwardly and overwhelmed the centre.

Deference institutions are especially important at or near the centre of society although ordinarily it is not the intention of those who manage them to confine their influence to that zone. But because deference is more intense in face-to-face relationships and direct interaction than it is in remote relationships, there is a tendency for deference systems to become dispersed in a particular way. Deference systems tend to become territorially dispersed into local systems which are more differentiated to those who participate in them than is the national system. I do not mean to say that the several systems ranging from local to national are in conflict with each other. Indeed they can be quite consensual and the local usually could not be constituted without reference to persons, roles and symbols of the centre. In the various zones and sectors of the periphery where the centre is more remote, the imagery of the centre still enters markedly into the deference system and local differentiations are often simply refined applications of perceptions and evaluations which have the centre as their point of reference. Thus, for example, local deference judgments will make more subtle internal distinctions about occupational role and authority, income and style of life than would judgments made from a distant point either peripheral or central. Still the distinctions will refer to distances from some standard which enjoys its highest fulfilment at the centre. It seems unlikely that centre-blindness can ever be complete in any society.

Nevertheless, the various systems do to some extent have lives of their own. The local deference system is probably more continuously or more frequently in operation than the national system—although as national societies become more integrated and increasingly incorporate with local and regional societies, the national deference system becomes more frequently and more intensely active.

In all societies, the deference system is at its most intense and most continuous at the centre. The high concentrations of power and wealth, the elaborateness of the style of life, all testify to this and call it forth. It is at the centre that deference institutions function and this gives an added focus and stimulus to deference behaviour. The centre adds the vividness of a local deference system to the massive deference-evoking powers of centrality. Within each local or regional deference system, there are some persons who are more sensitive than others to the centre and they infuse into the local system some awareness of and sensitivity to the centre.

At some times and at others, individuals whose preoccupations are mainly with the local deference systems—insofar as they are at all concerned with deference—place themselves on the macro-social deference map. This self-location and the perception that others are also locating themselves is the precondition of a sense of affinity among those who place themselves macro-socially on approximately the same position in the distribution of deference. The placement of others is made of course on the basis of fragmentary evidence about occupational role, style of life, or elements of these and the sense of affinity is loose, the self-location very vague, very inarticulated and very approximate. In this way deference (or status) strata are constituted. They have no clear boundaries and membership cannot be certified or specified. It is largely a matter of sensing one's membership and being regarded by others as a member. Those one 'knows' are usually members, and beyond them the domain spreads out indefinitely and anonymously in accordance with vague cognitive stratification maps and an inchoate image of the 'average man'; within each stratum, an 'average man' possesses the proper combination of positions on the distribution of significant deference-entitlements.

Thus the formation of deference-strata is a process of the mutual assimilation of local deference systems into a national deference system. It is through class consciousness that deference-strata are formed.

In the course of its self-constitution a deference stratum also defines in a much vaguer way the other deference strata of its society. It draws boundary lines but, except for those it draws about itself, the boundaries are matters of minor significance. Boundary lines are of importance only or mainly to those who are affected by the location of the boundary, i.e. those who live close to it on one side or the other. The location of a line of division in the distribution of deference is regarded as important primarily by those who fear that they themselves are in danger of expulsion or who are refused admission to the company of members of a stratum to whom they regard themselves as equal or to whom they wish to be equal and whose company they regard as more desirable than the one to which they would otherwise be confined. The members of any deference stratum are likely to be ignorant about the location of deference stratum boundaries which are remote from them and if they are not ignorant, they are indifferent.

The various deference strata of local deference systems are in contact with each other through occasional face-to-face contacts. They are present in each others' imaginations and this deferential presence enters into all sorts of non-deferential actions of exchange, conflict and authority.

In national deference systems too the different strata are in contact with each other, not very much through face-to-face contact but through their presence in each other's imagination. This presence carries with it the awareness of one's distance from the centre and it entails some acceptance of the centrality of the centre and some acceptance of the greater dignity of the centre. It is an implicit belief that the centre embodies and enacts standards which are important in the assessment of oneself and one's own stratum.

In some sense, the centre 'is' the standard which is derived from the perception, correct or incorrect, of its conduct and bearing. These remote persons and strata which form the centre might be deferred to, or condemned in speech, and the pattern of their conduct, bearing, outlook, etc., might be emulated or avoided. An 'objective existence' is attributed to the rank ordering from centrality to peripherality of the other strata and within this rank ordering one's own stratum is located. The ontological, non-empirical reality which is attributed to position in the distribution of deference makes it different from 'mere' evaluation and sometimes even antithetical to it.

On a much more earthly level, contacts between deference strata occur and in many forms—particularly through the division of labour and its coordination through the market and within corporate bodies and in the struggle for political power. This does not mean that the strata encounter each other in corporately organized forms[1] or that,

---

[1] Corporate organizations, membership in which is determined by a sense of affinity of deference positions and of positions in other distributions, seldom enlist the active membership of all the members of the stratum or even of all the adult male members of the stratum. Those who are not members of the corporate body are not, however, to be regarded as completely devoid of the sense of affinity with other members of their stratum. 'Class consciousness' in this sense is very widespread but it is a long step from this type of 'class consciousness' to the aggressively alienated class consciousness which Marxist doctrine predicted would spread throughout the class of manual workers in industry and Marxist agitation has sought to cultivate.

when there is interstratum contact in the encounter of corporate bodies, these bodies include all or most members of their respective strata. Much of this inter-stratum contact takes place through intermediaries who act as agents and who receive a deference which is a response both to their own deference-entitling properties and those of their principals. Those who act on behalf of these corporate bodies do so in a state of belief that they are 'representing' the deference-stratum to which they belong or feel akin.

A society can then have a deference system of relatively self-distinguishing and self-constituting deference strata, with the strata being in various kinds of relationship with each other. Such a situation is entirely compatible with the absence of the type of objective deference distribution which we rejected in the foregoing section. Each of the deference strata possesses in a vague form an image of a society-wide deference distribution but these images cannot be correct in the sense of corresponding to an objective deference distribution, which might or might not actually exist.

DIGRESSION ON PLURAL SOCIETIES

I have emphasized the importance of the self-constitutive character of the classes which make up a system of deference stratification. I have also emphasized the unreality of the construction of status distributions on which sociologists have expended so much effort and at the same time I have also stressed the elements of integration of the deference strata into a single system focused on the centre of society. Some writers contend that the deference system and the associated stratification systems of what are called plural societies are incompatible with this mode of analysis. By a plural society, they mean one in which various ethnic groups are so segregated from each other that they form societies separate and distinct from each other. Yet they do not go so far as to say that the various constituent societies are totally independent of each other; they acknowledge that they are integrated into a single economy and that they live under a single political authority. In that sense the constituent societies of a plural society are parts of a single society.

The problem which this poses for the study of deference systems is well worth consideration. What we find is that the ethnic entitlement is regarded in these societies, particularly by the more powerful, life chances controlling section of the dominant ethnic group, as so absolutely crucial, that it is made into such a salient criterion of deference that those whose deference-positions are affected by it are included into broad deference strata in comparison with which all other deference-entitlements are of secondary importance. These other deference-entitlements exist and they do determine differences in the allocation of deference but they are only capable of generating differences within each of the major ethnically determined deference strata. Each ethnically determined deference stratum is internally differentiated in accordance with the distribution of deference-entitlements within it. Each approximates a completely self-contained deference system but it does not become completely self-contained. It fails to do so because despite its highly segregated pluralism the society does have a centre and this centre constitutes a focus of each of the partially separate deference systems. The latter bear some resemblance to the deference systems of whole societies because of the differentiation of occupational roles within each of the ethnic sectors but the occupational structure of each sector is not the complete occupational structure of the total society. That total occupational structure is distributed between the ethnic sectors and there is indeed some overlap between them. It is because of these points of overlap—between the bottom of the super-ordinate deference stratum and the peak of the subordinate deference stratum—that conflicts arise. These conflicts could only arise because the sectors or strata are parts of a peculiarly integrated single deference system.

DEFERENCE SYSTEMS AND STRATIFICATION SYSTEMS

When it is not treated as an unreal, conceptually constructed amalgam of a number of positions on a variety of distributions, deference has often been treated as an epiphenomenon. It is often considered as having relatively little weight in the determination of conduct—apart from the choice of companions in conviviality or in the motivation of emulatory conduct. Yet it is deference which is responsible for the formation of strata or classes.

Deference is, as a result of its properties of a generalization, the crucial link in the stratification system. Without the intervention of considerations of deference position, the various very differentiated inequalities in the distribution of any particular facility or reward would not be grouped into a relatively small number of vaguely bounded strata. The very idea of an equivalence among positions in different distributions could not be realized if there were no generalization to cut across them.

By a stratification system, I mean a plurality of strata within a single society with some sense of their internal identity, of the internal similarity and of their external differences *vis-à-vis* other strata. The stratification system is constituted by strata which are formed by persons who have approximately similar positions on a variety of separate distributions. This approximate similarity of positions is a precondition of the sense of affinity—because it strengthens the sense of identity of the self from which the sense of affinity of many selves is formed. If each person were randomly heterogeneous in his cluster of positions the likelihood of identity and therewith of affinity would be much less than it is in fact.

The sense of identity is a vague perception of self and other and it refers to some pervasive qualities of those so identified. These qualities by which strata identify themselves and others are frequently referred to by a shorthand terminology such as 'wealth' or 'poverty' or 'rulers' or 'people' or 'workers' or 'bosses'. These terms refer to positions on particular distributions such as wealth and income, power and occupational role. Yet these terms have for those who use them a significance beyond the limited descriptive sense in which they are used. Each term stands for a position on each of a number of distributions and implies that positions in the various distributions are correlated and connected with each other. Those who are 'workers' are also 'poor' or in any case relatively low in wealth and income distribution. Those who are 'bosses' are also 'rich' or at least higher in the wealth and income distributions and they usually have more political power. Those who are 'well off' have more education and more authority through their occupational roles and through political participation.

The connections between the positions of an individual on the different distributions are of two sorts. One is the connection through 'life chances'. 'Life chances' are opportunities to enter into a higher position on any distribution from a lower position on that distribution or on several distributions. 'Life chances' are determined by the power of income, by personal, civil and kinship relationships and by occupational role and level of education. Any one of these can have a determinative influence on the allocation of 'life chances', i.e. on the opportunity to ascend on that distribution or in others.

A 'life chance' which arises from position on a particular distribution also affects chances for maintaining or acquiring 'life chances' for positions on other distributions. Income permits education to be purchased; the acquisition of education increases the probability of higher deference and higher income; higher education increases the probability of greater political influence; increased political influences increase the likelihood of a greater access to financial resources.

There is a widely experienced aspiration to bring positions on a series of distributions into an appropriate correspondence with each other. Each position provides resources for affecting positions on other distributions. Why should this be so? Why should there be thought to be an 'appropriate' relationship among positions, an equilibrium which should be striven for? Why, when a person has much political power does he not use his political resources exclusively to enhance or maintain his political power instead of expending them on bringing his style of life or the education of his children 'into line' with his political position?

(Of course, one reply to this question is to say that it is generally believed that improving positions on the non-political distributions is a necessary condition for maintenance or improvement of the position on the political distribution. But is not this very belief itself evidence of the belief in an appropriate pattern of positions which is thus a precondition for the more 'costly' political support necessary for further improvement in political position? Another reply to the question is that most human beings, given the opportunity, will strive to enhance their position in any particular distribution and that being in a better position on one distribution provides resources for betterment on others. But although there is some truth in this assertion it does not confront the fact that there is a sense of an appropriate pattern of positions on different distributions.)

The belief that it is appropriate that the several positions on the various distributions should be consonant or harmonious with each other is attributable to the belief that they each express a common, essential quality. An 'inappropriate' pattern of positions bears witness to the absence of the essential quality. There is something 'unseemly' or 'eccentric' or 'perverse' or 'unfortunate' about the individual or family whose positions are scattered at a variety of unequal points on the several distributions.

This common or essential quality is the charismatic quality which requires diffuse and pervasive expression in the various distributions. The cognitive element in an act of deference is the perception of the presence of this quality and its generalization beyond any specific manifestation in action is an acknowledgment of the apparent possession of charismatic quality by the person deferred to. The demand for deference is the demand for a diffuse acknowledgment of the diffuse charisma which is possessed in some measure by the self and which is above all in its earthly form resident in the centres of society. Self respect—deference to the self—is an acknowledgment of one's own charisma and of one's satisfactory proximity to the centre in an essential respect.

The cognitive and evaluative map of a stratification system is a differential allocation of deference to a series of aggregates of persons—for the most part anonymous—in accordance with their proximity to the centre and thus in accordance with the magnitude of their presumed charisma. The stratification system of a society is the product of imagination working on the hard facts of the unequal allocation of scarce resources and rewards. The charisma is imaginary but it has the effect of being 'real' since it is so widely believed in as 'real'. Deference which is basically a response to charisma is only a matter of opinion but it is an opinion with profound motivation and a response to profound needs in the grantor and the recipient of deference.

6

SOME MEASUREMENTS OF SOCIAL
STRATIFICATION IN BRITAIN

MARK ABRAMS

With one or two outstanding exceptions British sociologists have made little contribution to the theory of social stratification. At the same time, stratification is such a solid reality in our society that there is an abundance of empirical studies of the British people which have taken as their starting point the assumption that they can be divided into a handful of more or less self-contained strata that form an hierarchical order. These studies are to be found particularly in the two research fields of consumer behaviour and voting intentions.

Fundamentally the market researcher is concerned, usually through sample surveys, to identify among the population at large the determinants of differences in spending behaviour. Not surprisingly, working in a society long accustomed to considerable inequalities of income, he has taken for granted that the major differences in spending behaviour are to be explained by differences in income and that these differences in their turn are directly related to occupation. This approach has a long history and certainly antedates the emergence of market research. Even before the Registrar General in the Census of 1911 divided the population into social classes Charles Booth had set out an eightfold division of London's population ranging from the 1% of 'loafers, drunkards and semi-criminals' at the bottom of the income scale to the 18% 'lower and upper middle class' at the top. But the real forerunner of present-day stratification practices can reasonably be identified as F. G. D'Aeth, whose essay 'Present tendencies of class differentiation' appeared in the *Sociological Review* of October 1910.

In D'Aeth's view the traditional lines of demarcation between the different classes (derived from birth, family, estate etc.) had disappeared, and a new class structure, based upon different standards of living, had taken their place. To embrace the whole population he described seven such income/occupation standards and, to mark the break with the past, each structure was designated by a letter (A, B, C, etc.) and not by a word or phrase (e.g. 'the lower orders' or 'the gentry') that smacked of pre-twentieth-century English society. The general character of the members of each stratum was indicated in terms of occupation, income, housing, social customs, and what might be called intellectual ability. For example, two of his largest strata, C and D, were described as follows:

C. Artizan. *Standard*–45*s*. weekly; *Housing*–five-roomed house, with parlour; homely but comfortable furniture; *Occupations*–very varied: skilled labourers, foremen, petty officers, clerks, smaller officials, etc; *Social customs*–table set for meals: married children visit parents on Sundays; *Ability*–technical skill; a very fair general intelligence; shrewd at times; a simple mind, not following a connected argument; laborious procedure at business meeting.
D. Smaller Shopkeeper and clerk. *Standard*–£3 a week; Housing–above shop or £25 to £30 a year; *Occupation*–very varied: clerks, shopkeepers and tradesmen, commercial travellers, printers, engineers, etc. elementary school teachers, a few ministers; *Social customs*–furnish their houses; entertain visitors; some have a young servant; *Ability*–varied; either a high degree of technical skill; or a little capital and managing a business; shrewd in small matters; read magazines; express superficial opinions freely upon all subjects: *Education*–elementary school; in some cases a technical career.

In all, D'Aeth defined seven standards of living: A, 18s. a week; B, 25s. a week; C, 45s. a week; D, £3 a week; E, £300 a year; F, £600 a year; G, £2,000 and upwards.

The distinctive and highly original characteristics of D'Aeth's analysis were that he stratified the population essentially by income levels, that each stratum contained a variety of occupations, and that similarity of income was alleged to produce similarity of social and consumption habits. (His use of letter designations for the several strata had been anticipated by Booth.)

The first generation of university-trained market researchers began to appear in the early 1930's. All of them were educated at the London School of Economics and most of them were students of Bowley rather than of Ginsberg; in other words, they were social statisticians rather than sociologists, and therefore, almost as a matter of course, when in their new jobs, they were called upon to stratify the nation's consumers, they thought in terms of income differences rather than differences of speech, education, social and personal values etc. Indeed, in this respect they went further than D'Aeth and confined their definitions almost entirely to income levels that were associated with (or thought to be associated with) particular occupations. Thus, in the 'Home Market' (G. Harrison and F. C. Mitchell, Allen and Unwin, 1936) the authors divided all British households into three groups:

A, where the chief income earner received £10 a week or more— 5·3%; B, where the chief income earner received £4–£10 a week— 21·3%; C, where the chief income earner received under £4 a week— 73·4%.

The precision of the authors' figures and the readiness with which they were adopted by other market researchers in setting 'quotas' in sample surveys masked, however, one essential weakness in their reliability—they were largely derived, not from directly obtained statistics of people's incomes, but by imputing incomes to particular occupations. In fact, it was essentially a stratification by occupation of male heads of households.

When, after the war, market researchers resumed their enquiries their categories of description followed much the same lines but were more numerous (and, of course, they reflected the fall in the value of money). For example, in the series of Hulton Readership Surveys in the late 1940's the two pre-war A and B grades were re-aligned into three grades (A, B and C) to reflect 'usual income levels of head of household' of over £1,000 a year, £650 to £1,000 a year, and £400 to £649. At the same time the massive pre-war C grade was thinned down to segregate the 8% of households with incomes below £225 a year and largely dependent for their incomes on social benefits.

Methodologically the first substantial advance in market research stratification procedures took place in the middle 1950's when the National Readership Survey came under the direction of the Institute of Practitioners in Advertising (I.P.A.). In the first place, the survey was based on a probability sample of 16,000 persons drawn from the Electoral Registers for Great Britain. This did away with the need, inherent in quota samples, to provide interviewers with socio-economic descriptions of their respondents. Instead, armed with names and addresses, interviewers recorded the occupation of each respondent and the occupation of the head of the household of which the respondent was a member. This crystallized the fact that the stratification of respondents into six grades—A, B, C1, C2, D and E—was based exclusively on occupation (although the technical appendix to the report hazarded an estimate of what the income range was likely to be for the workers embraced by each letter-designated stratum).

Secondly, the 1956 survey carried out an experiement that aimed to assess the validity of attaching class descriptions to particular occupations. Twenty-two occupations were selected (e.g. doctor, journalist, elementary school teacher, coal miner, bricklayer, railway porter). Informants were first asked to describe which of the twenty-two (the order of presentation was randomized) they thought were middle class and which working class; secondly, they were asked to say which of the jobs they had described as middle class came nearest to being working class; then, about the jobs they had originally described as working class, they were asked which they thought came nearest to middle class. The results showed that most people (on average 92%) were still ready to attach traditional class labels to each of these occupations; that for fourteen of the twenty-two listed occupations the labelling was reasonably clear-cut (i.e. at least two-thirds of the respondents gave the same answer); but that some occupational descriptions (office clerk, small shopkeeper) were almost classless—in the sense that roughly equal proportions of the sample chose each of the four possible gradings— middle class, lower middle class, upper working class, lower working class; and, finally, that all subdivisions of the sample (men, women, old, young, etc.) gave almost identical answers. These findings suggested that while probably no harm was done by attaching class descriptions to most occupations, yet for many occupations clear-cut class identifications were non-existent—at least in the minds of the general public.

In much subsequent consumer research the I.P.A.'s sixfold division by occupation was adopted, but with a small though persistent under-current of doubt about its efficiency in circumscribing and predicting patterns of spending patterns. Everyday observation and an increasing supply of official statistics reminded the market research analysts that dockers earned more than school teachers, that the earnings of secretaries (at least in London) were just as large as those of young university-trained scientists and engineers. Up to a point the I.P.A. met this difficulty by making the estimated likely income ranges for some of its groups open-ended and overlapping—in particular those of its C 1 grade (lower-grade white collar) and C 2 (skilled manual worker). But this did not cope with the core of the problem—the feeling that the division of the population into head of household occupation-income groups does not necessarily coincide with a division based on spending patterns and that frequently the latter is more illuminating for marketing purposes. People thrown together in the same occupation-income group may differ widely in their life styles depending upon the size and composition of their families, their educational backgrounds, their cultural and recreational standards and behaviour, their age. Or, alternatively, people placed in widely differing occupation-income groups may have in some areas of consumption roughly similar tastes and behaviour.

Examples of both these anomalies can be found easily enough in studies of newspaper reading. Thus, among AB grade adults there are two very different groups; those with a terminal education age of 19 or more and these concentrate nearly 60% of their reading of morn-ing daily newspapers on the *Daily Telegraph*, the *Guardian*, and *The Times*; but people in the same AB grade but with a terminal education age of 15 or less (and they constitute one-third of all AB's) concentrate 70% of their newspaper reading on the *Express*, the *Mail* and the *Mirror*—a pattern of preferences matched almost exactly by people in the C 2 grade (skilled manual workers) with the same terminal educa-tion age of 15 or less.

Similarly the National Food Survey in its most recently published report (for the year 1964)[1] showed that within its A grade households weekly food expenditure per head ranged from nearly 50 shillings (for households made up of 1 man, and 1 woman) to 26 shillings (households consisting of 1 man, 1 woman and 3 or more children); and at the same time the average household expenditure for the A grade as a whole was exceeded by three out of the seven B grade types of household.

In the light of these anomalies, in 1960 the Market Research Society set up a working party 'to study and analyse all existing methods for determining Social or Socio-Economic Classes and to report on the validity' of each method and its usefulness in helping consumer research. Its first report was issued in October 1963. It identified the essential functions for a satisfactory stratification definition (for its members' needs) as: (i) classification into groups according to the amount of money available; (ii) classification into groups according to the way in which a given amount of money is likely to be expended; (iii) classification into groups to which may be attributed characteristics established in other surveys. With these criteria in mind the working party examined various stratification systems currently in use.

1. *Self-rating definitions*

It was clear from various British surveys that at least 95% of the adult population is prepared, irrespective of the form of questioning used, to ascribe to themselves a position in one of the middle or working classes and that about one-quarter of people in non-manual occupations describe themselves as working class, and about 35% of those in manual occupations rate themselves as middle class. In spite of the stability of these replies the group had to conclude that the self-rating approach failed to satisfy any of the three criteria largely because of the absence of relevant data.

2. *Occupation and/or subjective definitions*

Here what the group had in mind were the procedures used by many market research organizations and consists of a mixture of occupation and 'mode of living' where the assessment is usually made by the interviewer. Its conclusion was that on the first two criteria the method 'bears up quite favourably' but within each of the strata commonly used there is a wide dispersion of money available.

---

[1] The National Food Survey's classification is based on information obtained from the housewife about the head of household's gross weekly income; but if this is not obtainable it is imputed from occupation. In 1964 A grade = weekly income of £24 or more and accounted for 14 per cent of all households. B grade = £15 and under £24 and accounted for 35 per cent of all households.

3. Census of population definitions

The working party examined the two separate systems of classification used in the analysis of the 1961 Census of Population—'Social Class' and 'Socio-Economic Group'. Both are based essentially on occupation, but also in describing them the Registrar-General explicitly brings in a non-monetary criterion ('general standing within the community') and rejects the idea of any direct relationship between occupation and income. In his own words:

> The unit groups included in each of these categories (of social class) have been selected so as to secure that, so far as possible, each category is homogeneous in relation to the basic criterion of the general standing within the community of the occupations concerned. This criterion is naturally correlated with (and the application of the criterion conditioned by) other factors such as education and economic environment, but it has no direct relationship to the average level of remuneration of particular occupations.

As far as one knows the Registrar-General's office has not conducted any research to validate its categorization of occupations in terms of 'general standing within the community'—whatever that may mean in non-monetary terms. But a sample survey carried out by Research Services shortly before the 1961 Census suggests, on one formulation of 'general standing', that the adult population as a whole does not see eye-to-eye with the Registrar-General, and that different sections of the population differ substantially in their ratings of some occupations.

A national sample of 2,000 persons aged 21 and over were shown a list of nine occupations and asked: 'From the point of view of importance to the nation, how many marks out of ten would you give each of these occupations?' The accompanying table shows the proportions of the sample allotting 9 or 10 marks to each occupation; the figures indicate the answers of the whole sample and of four divisions of the sample classified by the I.P.A. occupation categories.

With an eye on their own criteria the working party examined the Census social class definitions (and the socio-economic gradings) by drawing upon some of the findings of a national probability sample survey carried out in 1960 by the British Market Research Bureau. From slightly less than 8,000 respondents aged 16 and over this survey obtained information about the occupation and the gross income of the head of the household, whether or not the respondent's household owned its dwelling, had a car, a washing machine, drank wine regularly (i.e. at least once a week) and read one of the three 'class' daily morning papers (*The Times*, *Telegraph*, *Guardian*). Table 2 presents the findings—

Table 1. *'Importance to the Nation'*

	All (%)	AB (%)	C1 (%)	C2 (%)	DE (%)	Registrar-General's 'Social Class'
Doctors	85	80	87	84	88	I
School teachers	63	63	62	63	65	III
Engine drivers	56	39	47	53	71	III
Bus drivers	48	32	39	47	55	IV
Dockers	38	28	28	38	48	IV
Draughtsmen	31	25	28	32	35	III
Civil servants	20	18	20	18	23	II
Accountants	19	15	20	17	21	II
Journalists	16	11	13	16	20	II

Table 2. *Registrar-General's 'Social Class' and B.M.R.B. survey (1960)*

Registrar General's Social Class	Average gross income of H.O.H. (£)	Proportion of adults owning			Proportion of adults who are	
		Home (%)	Car (%)	Washing machine (%)	Wine drinkers (%)	Readers of *The Times, Telegraph, Guardian* (%)
I Professional	1,250	68	63	64	20	46
II Intermediate: non-manual	1,030	60	57	59	14	27
III Skilled:manual	600	35	28	49	5	5
IV Partly skilled: manual	531	26	18	41	3	3
V Unskilled	430	15	13	28	3	3

but with some important omissions; we have left out at this point the findings for the minority subgroups in social Class II, III and IV.

The groups shown in the table represent 77% of all households and as they stand indicate that, despite his own account of the basis of stratification ('general standing' etc.), the Registrar-General has done a reasonably good job of stratifying the British people in terms of income groups and spending patterns. It is the other 23% that disturbs the picture. For example, the non-manual heads of households in Social Class IV have incomes only slightly larger than the average income for Social Class V but the proportions of them who drink wine and read 'class' daily newspapers are substantially higher than those prevailing among manual workers in Social Class III. Or, again, the agricultural heads of households in Social Class II (and they seem to be 14%

of that Class) have average incomes which are only 60% of the average Professional income but their proportions owning cars, homes, washing machines are almost identical with those in Social Class I; and, at the same time, their poor performance in wine drinking and reading a class newspaper brings them nearer the skilled manual class than it does to their alleged class equals—the non-manual workers in Social Class II.

The working party also compared the Census 16 socio-economic groups with the survey findings and concluded that both systems of Census stratification 'correlate moderately well with both "the money available" and "spending patterns" but not very highly with either'.

4. *Multi-dimensional definitions*

Finally, the working party considered a system of stratification which has rarely, if ever, been used in Great Britain. In the United States, however, several empirical sociologists (e.g. Havighurst, Lloyd Warner, Hollingshead) have developed definitions of social class based on a combination of characteristics—occupation, source of income, type of house, type of dwelling area, education, age, etc. Usually three or four of these are selected and each is given a weight; these are summed to give each respondent a score which determines his place in a scale of class groups. (Except for the quantification of the ingredients and scores, and the control of the characteristics taken into consideration, this method is much the same as the occupation-and/or subjective definition used by interviewers in some market research projects.) The working party concluded that while 'theoretically' the multi-dimensional method of stratification could produce a better correlation with money available and spending patterns than any other definition, yet, in the absence of any British data, it could reach no recommendation.

Since issuing its first report the working party (through J. A. Lunn, *Commentary*, July 1965) has issued the findings of some exploratory survey work conducted under its own auspices. Information from interviews, with a nationally representative sample of 1,000 housewives, was collected on: Interviewer's rating of class of district in which respondent lived and her overall rating of the respondent's social class; from respondent herself was obtained income of head of household, occupational status of head of household, number of earners in the home, presence of children under thirteen years of age in the family, size of dwelling, weekly expenditure on food, age at which formal education ended, respondent's self-rating in respect of social class, readership of various daily and Sunday newspapers, evidence of ownership and purchase of cars, television sets, telephone, refrigerator, other major household appliances, gramophone records, and household stocks of coffee, beer, wines and spirits.

Table 3. *Results of factor analysis*

Item	Factor loadings	
	Income included	Income partialled out
Interviewer's assessment	·61	·60
Occupation	·60	·50
Income	·53	—
Spirits in house	·51	·47
Class of district	·50	·60
Car	·46	·23
Telephone	·46	·34
Refrigerator	·46	·34
Beer in house	·41	·44
Wine in house	·41	·42
Self-rated class	·39	·48
Age on school completion	·38	·31
Sunday Times	·29	·40
Observer	·26	·34
Daily Telegraph	·24	·40
Sunday Telegraph	·18	·33

This information was analysed in two ways: (*a*) cross-tabulations against income, occupation, class self-rating and food expenditure were run for all variables. (*b*) An intercorrelation matrix was calculated between all the variables and factor analysed.

From the cross-tabulations, occupation showed more overall discrimination among the remaining variables than did the three other classifications (income, self-rating and food expenditure). The outcome of the factor analysis is shown in Table 3.

The appearance of interviewer's assessment as the variable with the highest loading suggests that interviewers (at least after they have obtained from the respondent information on all the other items in the table) have a high degree of proficiency in rapidly summarizing all the other variables and then stratifying the population. The factor analysis table indicates that, apart from interviewer's assessment, for most general purposes stratification of the population using the two dimensions of occupation and income (ascertained, not imputed) would divide British society into significantly different strata. A comparison of the right-hand column with the left-hand column suggests that in an exercise that wished to put prime emphasis on the income aspect of social class it would be well, in addition to income and occupation, to pay attention to those items where the loadings decline when income is partialled out—ownership of a car, telephone, refrigerator and terminal education age. On the other hand, the use, in addition to occupation and income of such items as class district, self-rated social class, and news-paper reading would produce a stratification with more emphasis on taste and background.

A good deal more work will have to be done along the lines of this first study—with larger samples and a wider range of consumer goods, but there is already a strong likelihood that the present market research methods of stratification can be filled out comparatively easily to provide an efficient stratification of British society.

Outside the field of consumption the market researcher's stratification system based on occupation, imputed income and interviewer's assess-ment has been widely used in the study of voting behaviour; this is not surprising since, at least in quantity, most of the British work here has been done by market research organizations. Consistently the findings of sample surveys have emphasized the fact that party voting in Britain at General Elections is very much class voting: in the ABC 1 grades (middle class) Conservatives usually outnumber Labour supporters by about 3 to 1; and in the C 2 DE grades (working class) Labour suppor-ters outnumber Conservatives by almost 2 to 1. This is so commonplace that much of the interest in analysing British elections is now focused on the deviant minorities—the ABC 1s who vote Labour and the C 2 DEs who support the Conservatives. As far as the working class 'defectors' are concerned this has been explained in part as arising from their feel-ing that they have materially prospered more than others and that while remaining members of the working class they are free to vote on a non-class basis. Part of the explanation is that some of the 'defectors' consider themselves, despite their occupations, to be middle class (even if they are not socially assimilated by the 'real' middle class) and accordingly they too vote for the middle class party.

A re-analysis of some of the survey material collected by Research Services for Almond and Verba in 1959 ('The Civic Culture') suggests that if a question on voting intentions were attached to consumer surveys another dimension might be added to the stratification at least of the working-class grades—one that indicated high or low conformity with the traditionalist outlook on life that distinguishes the Conservative-voting middle class.

For example, one open-ended question was: 'Speaking generally, what are the things about this country that you are most proud of?' The most frequent category of replies (given by nearly half all re-spondents) referred to the nation's political-legal system—its political stability, democratic character, justice, freedom, etc.; among ABC 1 Conservatives and DE Conservatives the proportions replying in these terms were 57% and 53% respectively, but only 32% of DE respond-ents gave answers of this kind.

Again, respondents were handed a list of possible replies and asked: 'Here are some important problems facing the people in this country: would you please tell me which one you feel is most important to you *personally*?' Of the total sample nearly two-thirds selected three of the eight proffered answers; on all three ABC 1 Conservatives and DE Conservatives saw eye to eye and gave a pattern of replies that differed sharply from that elicited from DE grade Labour supporters. The moral improvement of society seemed almost as important to Conservatives as the improvement of their personal circumstances. DE Labour voters, by contrast, showed little concern for the moral welfare of society but a great concern for their personal conditions.

Table. 4 *Problems facing this country*

	Conservatives ABC 1 (%)	Conservatives DE (%)	Labour DE (%)
'Improving conditions for your family'	25	26	50
'Moral and spiritual betterment'	23	17	8
'National defence, foreign affairs'	16	15	5

When they were asked to describe the sort of people who vote for each party DE Conservatives tended to be even more conventional in their replies than were ABC 1 Conservatives. The former saw Conservatives essentially as intelligent, altruistic patriots.

	Sort of people voting Conservative? Conservatives ABC 1 (%)	Sort of people voting Conservative? Conservatives DE (%)	Sort of people voting Conservative? Labour DE (%)	Sort of people voting Labour? Conservatives ABC 1 (%)	Sort of people voting Labour? Conservatives DE (%)	Sort of people voting Labour? Labour DE (%)
People interested in national strength	55	31	17	12	7	25
Intelligent people	36	39	11	7	5	18
People interested in welfare of humanity	24	32	7	21	13	43
Selfish people	—	3	30	24	26	2
Ignorant people	—	—	7	24	22	—

Findings of this kind suggest that although the working-class Conservative may be 'spurious' in the sense that he has not really been assimilated or integrated within the middle class (or the Conservative

Party), yet he has learned and accepted the 'correct' conventional middle class responses when called upon to assess the character and purposes of the British nation and its people.

If as the result of wider and more substantial research this suggested character of the working-class Conservative can be firmly established, then, apart from its contribution to political sociology, it looks as if the addition to consumer surveys of a question on voting intentions would strengthen the efficiency of a multi-dimensional system of stratification by adding socio-psychological flexibility to money available and spending behaviour.

7

STRUCTURAL CHANGES IN THE
WORKING CLASS

A situational study of workers in the Western
German chemical industry

FRIEDRICH FÜRSTENBERG

Recent studies in social stratification have been mainly focused both upon methodological devices for ranking and the interpretation of respective empirical data. Therefore the scaling of differential social and economic positions and opportunities has somewhat repressed the perception, already maintained by T. H. Marshall (1934), 'that the objectivity of class consists not in the criteria that distinguish it, but in the social relations that it produces.'[1] These social relations and their impact upon the relative social position of the individual can only be recognized through situational analyses. As each individual is involved in different social situations changing their scope and meaning during the course of life, empirical research necessarily must be limited through theoretical criteria to such areas of interaction which decisively influence relative life chances. Differences in relative social positions in society certainly are particularly manifest in leisure-time activities, realizing a given material standard of life and cultural goals internalized through the channels of socialization. However, the sector of work and occupational behaviour still maintains fundamental importance for determining individual and group life chances. Social roles and relations during active work life still are a major indicator of the relative position individuals or groups maintain within the social structure of a given society. We therefore need 'a typology of work relationships, without which no clear appreciation of class identification can be obtained'.[2]

Based upon comparative empirical research in seven chemical plants in the Federal Republic of Germany the present paper aims at situational and attitudinal analyses of those factors present in work structure and employee relations that determine the relative social positions of chemical workers. I do not intend to give a quantitative account of what

---

[1] T. H. Marshall, *Citizenship and Social Class and Other Essays* (Cambridge, 1950), p. 94.
[1] D. Lockwood, 'The new working class', *Arch. Europ. Sociol.* 1 (1960), 257.

workers think about class, social status and social prestige and how they rank themselves in a given frame of reference; but rather attempt to describe scientifically the social reality of a significant social stratum and the factors that influence the relative stableness of this reality.

The empirical data underlying this study were collected between March and September, 1966. Criteria for selecting the plants were: dispersion of size, age of equipment, level of technological advancement, mobility of personnel, position in the regional labour market and geographical location. Within each plant, all employees were the object of the study, in all 725 workers and 68 white collar employees. Within the period mentioned the workers were interviewed individually twice during work hours, leaving an interval of about three months between the two interviews. In the first interviewing phase (charts 3–10, 16) 601 workers (83% of all employed workers), in the second phase (charts 11–15) only 484 workers (67%) could be investigated. The remainder were missing due to sickness leave, holidays or, in less than 3% of all cases, were unwilling to co-operate with the research team.

Plant A consists of three completely automated and continuously producing crack-platforms and is part of a recently established enterprise with 1,900 employees. It is located in the highly industrialized Northern Rhine region. Plant B is the partly automated production unit of a newly founded plastics producing enterprise with 190 employees in South-Western Germany. Plants C and D are operating in linked production. Work processes are highly mechanized and partly automated. From plant C the intermediate product is transported to plant D, where it is polymerized. Both plants are part of a big corporation with 48,000 employees in the Rhine valley. Plant E is a highly mechanized part of an independent production unit (5,900 employees) of an international corporation producing synthetic fibres. It is located in a still mainly agrarian area with few employment opportunities. Plant F is the production unit of an old-established enterprise in the Northern Rhine region with 570 employees producing dangerous chemicals. While plants A–F only occupy male workers plant G is mainly operated by female workers. It is part of a pharmaceutical enterprise with 500 employees, situated in a Northern German city. There are many filling and packing operations, partly on conveyors.

In each of these plants the research team collected statistical data on the personnel and social policy of the enterprise and on the social structure of the employees, provided a job description for each work-place and work-flow analyses, twice carried out interviews with all workers present in the plant and conducted group discussions with a 10% random sample of all workers.

Analysis and evaluation of the data collected were based upon a theoretical frame of reference, defining the social position of a worker by his involvement in a given *work system* and his place in a given *social structure* of the plant. The work system is constituted by all work performances shaping the plant work flow. It determines the relative margin for each worker in·shaping his performances and likewise deter-

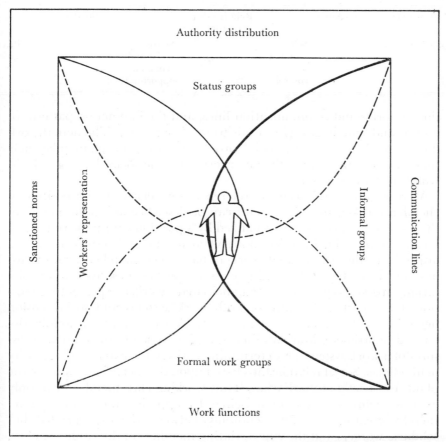

Fig. 1. The social tension field of the plant

mines the level of skill requirements, of responsibility and of physical as well as psychical burdens. The work system is decisively influenced by the expediency of technical equipment and the rationality of the work organization. It may be 'open', leaving substantial control functions to the worker, or 'closed', strictly predetermining work procedures and work effort.

The social structure of a plant is thought of as a tension field consisting of an institutionalized social framework of functions, authority, sanc-

Table 1.   *Work-situation and types of working-class patterns*

Work-situation	Work system		Institutionalized social framework		Interaction pattern	
Worker type	Closed	Open	Authoritarian	Co-operative	Dichotomized	Plural
'Proletarian' worker	Alienation	—	Relative de-privation	—	Solidarity	—
'Emancipated' worker	—	Self-initiative, self-control	—	Share in social and economic opportunity	—	Privati-zation

tioned norms and communication lines, and the interaction patterns of groups and individuals within this frame (see fig. 1).[1] The actual work flow as well as any other social processes within the plant take their shape according to the influence exerted by the social tension field in which they are located.

With regard to this frame of reference, the relative social position of chemical workers in a given plant can be described as a position within the respective work system actualized by a position within the respective social tension field. In order to arrive at meaningful results the actual attitudes of the investigated workers have been matched against two opposite ideal types of working-class properties, described as 'proletarian' worker type and as 'emancipated' worker type, both conditioned by specific structure of both work systems and social-tension fields (see table 1). The 'proletarian' worker type as, for example, described in orthodox Marxian literature, is exposed to the extreme pressures of a work system, predetermining entirely the extent and intensity of his efforts. Social relationships based upon the social framework of the plant are strictly authoritarian. Thus working-class members can only express themselves as human beings by opposing the whole system, thereby creating a social dichotomy between the expropriated but solidaric workers and the expropriating members of the capitalist class. Alienation from work, relative deprivation of its results and militant solidarity are the main attributes of this type. Over against this we may describe the 'emancipated' worker as being conditioned by an open work system leaving the worker some margin for performing his functions. He no longer serves the machines but rather supervises complete work procedures. Additionally the social framework of the plant has been reorganized into co-operative units with a fixed right of workers for

---

[1] For a more detailed exposition of components shaping the social structure of a plant see F. Fürstenberg, *Grundfragen der Betriebssoziologie* [*Fundamental Problems of Industrial Sociology*] (Köln und Opladen, 1964), pp. 22–44.

information, consultation and even participation in some decision-making processes. Thus, the labour force is differentiated into multiple functional groups with segmentalized social roles. The worker also no longer identifies himself totally with a given position within the plant but rather disposes of additional means of self-identification. As a result this worker type no longer feels the burden of alienation but is rather conscious of his share in social and economic opportunities offered through both management policy and the urge of his own re-presentatives. In his social attitudes he is less class-conscious and more self-conscious. He shows more or less 'privatized' attitudes.[1]

These two ideal types of workers offer an opportunity to interpret the findings of our research on German chemical workers by ordering them on an attitudinal continuum ranging from the 'proletarian' type to the 'emancipated' type. The analysis starts with a short characterization of the respective labour force, and is followed by a survey of worker re-actions towards the respective work system and social framework and of their own perception of interaction patterns. It will be continued by an evaluation of differences occurring between the different plants investi-gated, thus showing by comparison the main influencing variables which determine the perceived situations. Finally, some general hypotheses concerning the coherence between work system, social framework, inter-action patterns and type of worker will be formulated.

CHARACTERISTICS OF THE WORK FORCE INVESTIGATED

The distribution of the investigated workers according to age, sex and length of service within the firm shows significant differences between the plants (see table 2). The average age of workers in plants A–D is relatively low compared with the average in plants E–G. As already mentioned, plant G occupies mainly female workers. Length of service naturally is rather short in the recently founded plants A and B. Their share in workers hired before 1960 is entirely due to personnel taken over from the founding enterprises. Plant F has a remarkable percentage of workers with longer service periods.

As can be seen from table 4 the formation and occupational status of workers differs widely between the plants. While in plant A only 29% of the investigated workers had no vocational training, this share rose to 77% in plant G. Likewise the share of workers actually occupied in positions of skill grade 3 differs between 60% in plant F and 2% in plant G. Especially remarkable is the high percentage of gang leaders in plants B and C which reflects the greater number

---

[1] Valuable hints at the trend towards 'privatization' I owe to David Lockwood, who lectured on this subject at the University of Göttingen in 1965.

Table 2.   *Age, sex and length of service (percentage figures)*

	All plants	A	B	C	D	E	F	
I. Age								
1. Birth date 1901 and earlier	1	0	0	2	0	1	1	
2. 1902–10	9	0	5	4	9	14	15	1
3. 1911–20	18	11	11	30	14	17	22	2
4. 1921–35	50	56	49	50	45	58	42	4
5. 1936–45	20	30	34	14	28	9	17	
6. 1946 and later	2	3	1	0	4	1	3	
Total:	100	100	100	100	100	100	100	10
II. Sex								
1. male	88	100	100	100	100	100	100	
2. female	12	0	0	0	0	0	0	9
Total:	100	100	100	100	100	100	100	10
III. Date of entrance into plant								
1. 1940 and earlier	6	0	0	0	7	7	20	
2. 1941–44	1	0	0	0	0	3	1	
3. 1945–55	29	0	3	46	16	60	50	
4. 1956–60	25	47	11	27	30	12	25	
5. 1961–63	10	14	9	7	13	8	3	
6. 1964	14	9	49	9	13	9	0	
7. 1965 and 1966	15	30	28	11	21	1	1	
Total:	100	100	100	100	100	100	100	1
Total number:	601	100	101	56	56	105	101	
Percentage of all workers in the respective plants:	83	71	83	84	76	87	88	

of partly independent units within a highly mechanized and partly automated work flow.

The rather even distribution of workers in plant A between skill grades 2 and 3 is due to the fact that most workers had been hired within the past 5 years. Promotion to skill grade 3 is only possible either after completion of respective apprenticeship or after several years of experience on the job. If we consider the plant wage structure (table 4) we find plants A and B on top of the scale, while plant G entirely drops out of the average frame due to the fact that most female workers are working normal time and get hourly wages, while the wage rates for male workers in plants A–E are paid for shift work and are also much higher according to higher skill levels. In the investigated plants hourly and premium wages with additional shift payments prevail, only in plant E we find 19% of the investigated workers working on piece rates. This difference again can be attributed to the respective work system. In plants A–D the degree of integration of different functions into a complex work flow determined by large aggregates is so high that there is no direct relation between individual work performance

Table 3. *Formation and occupational status (percentage figures)*

Formation	All plants	A	B	C	D	E	F	G	Total chemical industry
1. No vocational training	53	29	41	56	57	58	56	77	
2. Commercial apprenticeship	4	4	3	5	4	2	1	12	
3. Industrial or trade apprenticeship	43	67	56	39	39	40	43	11	
Total:	100	100	100	100	100	100	100	100	
Occupational status									
1. Worker unskilled: wage group 1	1	0	0	0	2	0	0	5	12
2. Chemical worker semi-skilled: wage group 2	52	53	43	21	41	71	37	0?	31
3. Chemical worker skilled: wage group 3	36	46	27	39	48	28	60	2	26
4. Gang leader: wage group 4	9	1	23	36	9	1	3	1	31
5. Foreman	2	0	7	4	0	0	0	0	0
Total:	100	100	100	100	100	100	100	100	100

Table 4. *Wage structure (percentage figures)*

Gross monthly wage	All plants	A	B	C	D	E	F	G
1. under 600 DM	13	0	0	0	4	0	0	96
2. 600–799 DM	1	0	0	0	7	0	0	4
3. 800–999 DM	7	3	1	20	13	2	20	0
4. 1000–1199 DM	57	37	72	51	49	87	80	0
5. 1200–1399 DM	18	50	18	27	25	8	0	0
6. over 1400 DM	4	10	9	2	0	3	0	0
7. not known	0	0	0	0	2	0	0	0
Total:	100	100	100	100	100	100	100	100
Wage system								
1. Hourly wage/ shift	48	97	97	0	0	79	2	2
2. hourly wage/ normal work time	16	3	3	2	0	2	10	98
3. piece wage/ shift	3	0	0	0	0	19	0	0
4. premium wage/ shift	31	0	0	96	84	0	88	0
5. premium wage/ normal work time	2	0	0	2	16	0	0	0
Total:	100	100	100	100	100	100	100	100

and output quantity. In plant E, however, there are some work places where output can be influenced directly by the worker.

The diversity of data provided by tables 2–4 hints towards significant differences in the technical and social structures of the investigated plants. One group of plants with a high percentage of trained workers (A and B), a group with medium percentages (C–F) and one plant with low level of training (G) can be distinguished. Concerning actual work positions, plants B and C offer a greater number of higher ranked work places. The group with medium conditions is represented by plants A and D–F. Plant G again shows the lowest level. Average earnings are highest in plant A, higher than average in plants B–D, about average in plants E and F, while plant G shows remarkably low average earnings.

THE WORK SYSTEM: ALIENATION VERSUS SELF CONTROL

Based upon work descriptions and work-flow analyses, we can distinguish four types of work systems in the plants which have been the object of our study. Type I represents fully automated and continuously producing aggregates, integrating work functions not visually and directly (working 'hand in hand') but indirectly through technical devices. The whole plant is not divided into work places but rather into work areas which are covered by persons with mainly supervisory and registrary functions (reading off control instruments and taking notes of control data; adjusting pressure, temperature and quantity of material flow in case of emergency). Characteristically, this type of function is called 'driving' the aggregate, or 'driving' the control room. Indeed, work performance has some similarities with driving a vehicle to a designated goal by controlling instruments, observing the situation and adjusting the driving manner according to the rule of the road, the behaviour of the vehicle from moment to moment and external circumstances. Workers within this system are usually highly interchangeable. After two years they usually know the whole plant working in turn 3–6 months in different areas. Usually the work load is rather psychically than physically perceived, but this can change suddenly and entirely in case of emergency when all available personnel must act to maintain, or to regain control over, aggregates representing immense economic value and immense potential energy which can be extremely destructive. While the plant is operating normally, personnel supervision is not very close, it is more or less indirect through control of electronic registrations. We can find work systems of type I in plants A, B and C.

Type II is characterized by highly mechanized and partly automated serial work performances. There are short interruptions after each series. The different work procedures are closely linked by technical devices but there is no continuous work flow. Instead we find mechanical transportation according to the serial rhythm of production. In this work system we find designated work places. But work performances are not uniform during the shift. They alter with the different stages of a production series. They recur, however, in each new series. A worker operating a set of polymerization boilers, for example, spends two hours cleaning the boilers, checks the instrument-board for thirty minutes, supervises the adding of polymerization components for one and a half hours and then supervises the automatic heating of the boiler for three hours. The following ten hours are spent controlling the automatic polymerization process. This is followed by one hour degassing and one hour discharging the boilers. Workers in this system are also highly interchangeable so that they usually get a thorough knowledge of the whole plant. There is more mutual dependence and closer supervision, especially in such work situations where output can largely be influenced by the operator (e.g. plant E). Work systems of type II can be found in parts of plant B and in plants D–F.

Type III is represented by an authoritatively supervised work flow combining several highly specialized and repetitive work performances. Each of them is strictly defined. There is also a strict division between supervisory and control functions of the superiors and the regulated work of the subordinates. Co-operation between these groups is largely limited to predetermined work relations leaving little margin for initiative. A typical example of such situations is the work group located along a conveyor belt with a fixed speed. This type of work system is found in plant G. Jobs are also highly interchangeable, but, facing a work load designed for experienced workers, some of them fear the initial loss of experience due to job rotation. Quite different from the situation in work systems of types I or II, such rotation does provide very similar experience while the work load, especially the time pressure, is the same everywhere.

Finally type IV, a work system based upon single work places for skilled workers, can be distinguished. Individual tasks are changing according to plant requirements. This system still maintains important traits of a craft tradition and we find it in the repair and maintenance shops of each plant. In some places special 'plant craftsmen' are assigned to deal with emergency cases in any particular aggregate.

While types III and IV can be found in most industrial branches according to the prevailing share of individual, serial or mass production, types I and II are a characteristic of technologically developed chemical plants.

The individual perception of a given work situation was tested for

each worker by asking questions on qualification, work rules, distribution of supervision, awareness of mutual dependence between colleagues and superiors, advantages and disadvantages of the individual
job, opportunity of social contacts during work hours, awareness of the
individual work load and its changes over the years and requests for
changes in the work-situation. The reactions show significant differences
between the investigated plants and permit some conclusions concerning
the influence of work systems on workers' attitudes.

It was found that training within the plant generally was realized as
training on the job by supervisors (23 % of all cases), colleagues (51 %)
or both of them (14%). In 11 % of all cases workers maintained
that they had received no training whatsoever on the actual job they
did. This percentage was greatest in plants F (26%), G (20%) and B
(17%). In the latter plant this relatively high share is due to the
fact that a group of maintenance craftsmen was included in the interviews.

An awareness of a special qualification needed for the actual job was
found among 52% of all workers interviewed. It was highest in
plants C (82%), D (70%) and A (65%), about average in plants
B (56%), E (48%) and F (44%)and very low in plant G (16%). In
plant B again we find differences according to the location of the
respective work place in a work system of type I (polymerization), II
(granulation) or IV (maintenance and repair).

The knowledge of general work rules is an important indicator of the
awareness of a functional integration of the actual job into a larger
work system. As can be seen from table 5 we get the remarkable result
that in plant G 57% denied the existence of work rules; rather they
hinted at immediate orders by superiors. Written work instructions
ranked highest in plants A–E (between 61% and 92% of the interviewed workers). A greater consciousness of accident prevention
rules could only be found in plant F (42%), producing dangerous
chemicals. The percentage of workers listing general works regulations as
well as combinations of the major types of general work rules was very
low. We may conclude that the awareness of objective work rules covers
the area of immediate action of the worker. It shows in plants A–F that
the worker is not entirely guided by orders from superiors but is observing objectified rules representing the 'technological logic' of the respective work system.

This conclusion is fostered by the fact that within the technologically
highly developed plants a new system of supervising functions has developed, giving each person of particular knowledge and experience a
certain order-giving authority. Table 6 shows that in plants A, C and D
more than half of the workers receive orders from more than one person.

Table 5. *Knowledge of general work rules (percentage figures)*

	All plants	A	B	C	D	E	F	G
1. Accident prevention	10	0	7	2	13	3	42	1
2. Written work instruction	62	80	67	71	61	92	32	18
3. General work regulations	4	3	5	0	4	0	2	17
4. Accident prevention and written work instruction	5	4	4	9	11	0	10	0
5. Accident prevention and general work regulations	1	0	1	5	2	0	3	0
6. Written work instruction and general work regulations	2	3	3	0	2	0	0	6
7. Accident prevention, written work instruction and general work regulations	1	3	0	2	0	0	1	1
8. Existence of work rules denied	15	7	13	11	7	5	10	57
Total	100	100	100	100	100	100	100	100

Table 6. *Distribution of order-giving functions (percentage figures)*

	All plants	A	B	C	D	E	F	G
1. Nobody	4	1	1	0	5	7	6	10
2. One person	59	35	64	41	43	68	65	85
3. Several persons	37	64	35	59	52	25	29	5
Total	100	100	100	100	100	100	100	100

Plant B drops down to 35% due to the already mentioned mix of work systems. In plants E and F a single relationship between supervisor and subordinates prevails, while in plant G multiple relationships are exceptional.

The awareness of a mutual dependence between persons occupied in the respective plant is generally low with the exception of plant C, where only 25% state that there is no person able to influence their own work and only 23% cent state that they have no influence upon other people's work. Within the other plants these percentages rank from 41% to 64% (first statement) and from 36% to 72% (second statement). Plant G has the highest share of workers denying a closer mutual dependence between their own work and the performances of others in the plant. This attitude may reflect the strict dependence of each worker upon an exactly predetermined work flow, it may also reflect a rather low attachment to the job and little knowledge of its implications.

Thirty-one per cent of the interviewed workers do not find particular advantages in their job. This figure is lowest in plants A (10%) and B (17%) and highest in plant G (60%). Among the advantages material factors (pay, working time etc.) prevail with an average of 47% against immaterial factors (17%) such as greater responsibility, interesting job, etc. Thirty-three per cent of all workers would like to get a different job (20% in plant A, 48% in plant F).

Concerning the relative awareness of the work load and its changes, we find only in plants C and E that the majority of interviewed workers list items they do not like about their work. This seems to be the result of a particular stress in the respective work situation which leads to overcharge. Generally, among the main factors perceived as particular burdens, physical factors still prevail (exception: plant A). Social factors (human relations) appear to be of minor importance. A quarter of all workers does not perceive any particular burden. In 26% of all cases we find statements hinting at an increase in work load since starting the particular job. Thirty-seven per cent of all responses indicate a decline in work load. Here the reduction of physical stress is the major factor. It obviously results from both increasing mechanization or automation and more personal experience on the job.

Requests for changes in the work-situation were made by 28% of the workers during their interviews. The percentage was highest in plants G and C. The majority, however, did not want any changes (53%) and 19% thought they were impossible. Major improvements were anticipated from technological improvements (25% of all workers).

It has been maintained by critics of modern work conditions that increased mechanization and automation would lead to social isolation of workers. In this respect it is interesting to note that only 7% of all interviewed workers would like to have more social contacts during work, while 88% think that contacts are sufficient and 5% do not want any contacts.

We can now interpret our findings with regard to general work situations prevailing in the investigated plants. As already pointed out, one major thesis describes the position of workers in modern production processes as 'alienated'. Robert Blauner has listed the 'elements' of such a personal alienation experience: 'Alienation exists when workers are unable to control their immediate work process, to develop a sense of purpose and function which connects their jobs to the over-all organization of production, to belong to integrated industrial communities, and when they fail to become involved in the activity of work as a mode of personal self-expression.'[1] As this paper is concerned with the immediate work-situation the aspect of social integration will not be considered but

[1] Robert Blauner, *Alienation and Freedom* (Chicago and London, 1964), p. 15.

Table 7.   *Relative awareness of work load (percentage figures)*

	All plants	A	B	C	D	E	F	G
Is there something, you do not like about your work?								
1. Yes	44	24	36	69	48	65	45	31
2. No	56	76	64	31	52	35	55	69
Total	100	100	100	100	100	100	100	100
Main perceived burden								
1. Physical factors	38	19	34	24	53	41	44	54
2. Psychical factors	17	23	19	16	14	17	14	11
3. Social factors (colleagues, superiors)	4	3	7	9	2	1	4	5
4. Shift work	7	8	4	27	5	12	1	0
5. Combinations	9	4	6	13	14	6	17	5
6. Nothing	25	43	30	11	12	23	20	25
Total	100	100	100	100	100	100	100	100

Table 8.   *Requests for changes in work situation (percentage figures)*

	All plants	A	B	C	D	E	F	G
1. Yes	28	29	24	36	25	21	30	38
2. Impossible	19	14	11	18	16	27	26	21
3. No	53	57	65	46	59	52	44	41
Total	100	100	100	100	100	100	100	100

Blauner's scheme shall otherwise be followed. While he himself has based his findings upon data from an opinion survey carried out in 1947 including 78 chemical workers, our own data seem fit for checking his hypotheses by taking account of the diversity of work situations in the chemical industry at the same time.

1. Control over the immediate work process can objectively be found in work systems of types I, II and IV. Type I enables workers to check the determining data of the work process and to make at least minor adjustments. They can move freely, do not work under time pressure and have a considerable margin for shaping their own work performance according to situational changes. Workers involved in type II still have major control functions though the different performances are linked together more neatly, leaving less margin for personal initiative. Type IV offers immediate work control, but strictly limited to the execution of a highly specialized task. In all these types we find a high degree of individual responsibility for accurate work performance. Especially in types I and

II (plants A–F) material losses through individual errors can be very substantial. Work control, however, is limited by the logic of technological processes and equipment, which has to be respected by all means.

Considering workers' reactions we can find from our data that 48% of all workers investigated do feel independent from any personal influence upon their work performance. They are, however, fully aware of the urge to pay strict attention to operating instructions. On the other hand, only 19% find it impossible to alter the work situation, while 28% make suggestions in this direction. In all plants work discipline is more maintained through situational, that is objectified, necessity than through personal and subjective pressure. If we maintain that work always involves task oriented and therefore disciplined behaviour, we can conclude that within these limits workers acting in work systems of types I, II and IV have a considerable span of control over their performance. Especially since, within the highly automated plants, work processes most of the time pass off without urging the worker for immediate and constant action, though he can still check fully the results of those stages of the work process which fall into his work area.

2. A sense of purpose and function with regard to the work situation is usually the result of training and experience. Though the general skill-level in the investigated plants is rather high, systematic training on the job and with respect to its larger context within the work-flow still seems to be unsystematic. Best conditions in this regard are offered in plants A and B. Thus, it is left to individual experience to get a general picture of the plant and the individual function within the work flow. Such an experience, however, is strongly fostered in plants A–F through the widespread application of job rotation. Still, a more systematic training would certainly develop the workers' capacity for perceiving theoretical implications. Many of them feel frustrated when they see chemical formulae and blue-print lay-out schemes. However, the fact that 52% of all workers consider special experience as decisive for their personal job, the percentage being highest in the technologically most advanced plants, shows that the majority of male workers have developed at least some degree of job-consciousness and a perception of relevant functional requirements. There is almost no feeling of social isolation and workers are aware of the need for co-operation which is rather indirect, however, in work systems of types I and II.

3. Personal self-expression through work is a psychological phenomenon difficult to observe by means of a sociological investigation. It is not only dependent upon situational opportunity but also upon relevant personality traits obtained during the early socialization process. The need

for identifying oneself with one's job is quite different among different social sub-cultures. An indirect means for getting data on personal self-experience is the measurement of job satisfaction. In our study 67% of all interviewed workers did not want to do another job. Perhaps the reasons for this attitude are quite complex, with material factors (high wage, job security etc.) prevailing. On the other hand at least 17% of the workers (26% in plant A) have explicitly named immaterial advantages of their actual job.

Facing these results we can conclude that 'alienation' in Blauner's sense of the term certainly is not a structural component of most workers' attitudes in the investigated chemical plants. At least in plants A–F work systems offer a substantial range for personal control, for understanding the purpose of the respective work processes and even for personal self-expression. The degree in which these opportunities are realized largely depends upon practices of management, that is upon components of the *social* structure of the plant, and upon personality traits. Not everyone is fit for working in an automated chemical plant and not everyone considers a special type of work as decisively important for his self-realization. Married women with children, especially, often show different goal orientations, and even many male chemical workers in our investigation point out that their goal in life was to build their own house. The concept of alienation when used without discrimination for the evaluation of work-situations can even be misleading, as it may superimpose measures prevailing in a certain sub-culture upon persons who do not accept the values underlying these measures.

THE SOCIAL FRAMEWORK: RELATIVE DEPRIVATION VERSUS SHARE IN OPPORTUNITIES

Though work systems resulting from technological advancements in work procedures fundamentally shape work-situations, an intervening factor of equal importance is the system of social relations by which different social roles are assigned to different groups of employees. The Marxian thesis that actual class-situations are conditioned by the state of development of productive forces but are definitely realized through production relationships still contains a fundamental truth. It would be shortsighted to describe and analyse the social position of workers only with regard to their status within the technological production process and to the functional content of their work. It is of at least equal importance to analyse their relative positions within the plant's social structure which in this paper is perceived as a social tension field. One of its main features is the unequal distribution of power and authority among the different ranks of the employees. A statement to be found very often in sociological literature maintains that the workers, perceived as members of the working class, are *the* underprivileged group in industry with no share in order-giving authority, decision-making and norm-setting power and no social opportunity to change this status. All this would lead to a diminution of life chances, to a total dependence on those owning and managing the firm. Therefore, their situation should be described as one of relative deprivation and their social relations within the enterprise would be structured accordingly. We shall now try to test the accuracy of this thesis with regard to chemical workers by using our research findings.

The worker and order-giving authorities

The formal social structure in all investigated plants has a common feature: the explicit existence of a hierarchy of social positions according to the different share of order-giving authority. Its realization appears to be most perfect in plants E–G. In contrast to the ideal convergence between hierarchical status and actual function we find, quite often, in plants A–D situations in which ascribed order-giving authority is competitive with the achieved functional competence to regulate the work process. In other words, the quality of work performance depends rather upon relevant competence and knowledge than upon 'order-giving'. The latter is widely reduced to maintaining a general discipline expressed in written works regulations and to guide immediate action in emergency situations. Many workers are quite aware of this situation. In their view the men who 'count' are the competent experts while foremen are often criticized, especially in plant B, for not knowing much more than the worker about the work process. In highly automated or mechanized chemical plants we can notice a trend towards the complementing of personal authority by functional authority based upon expert knowledge. Accordingly, the worker is not so much exposed to the order-giving of 'his' superior but to the advice, help and functional demands of those persons competent in the particular issue. The superior himself is not so much recognized through his official status but through his own functional contribution to rational and effective work relations. This trend does not lead to a general diminution of authority. It narrows, however, the margin for arbitrariness and gives the process of 'order-giving' a greater rationality. The more orders are based upon rational arguments the more they provoke an attitude of consent instead of obedience. Gradually the supervisor ceases to be a symbol of compulsion and starts becoming a symbol of equity based upon the rationality of the work process.

The interviews conducted in the different plants show some typical demands of workers upon their superiors. Generally a superior is evaluated

Table 9. *Confidential persons (percentage figures)*

	All plants	A	B	C	D	E	F	G
Confidential persons in personal matters								
1. Superiors	36	64	35	27	41	28	39	21
2. Colleagues	11	6	11	9	5	13	8	21
3. Personnel officer	2	1	3	0	0	5	0	1
4. Works counsellor	7	7	6	9	11	7	8	1
5. Nobody	21	11	28	19	7	20	19	39
6. Not wanted	14	3	12	11	25	18	18	13
7. Combinations	9	8	5	25	11	9	8	4
Total	100	100	100	100	100	100	100	100
Confidential persons in technical matters								
1. Superiors	69	89	60	52	70	59	69	69
2. Colleagues	11	3	15	16	5	12	9	20
3. Works counsellor	1	0	0	5	2	2	1	1
4. Nobody	8	1	17	4	4	10	9	10
5. Not wanted	4	0	6	0	14	7	5	0
6. Combinations	7	7	2	23	5	10	7	0
Total	100	100	100	100	100	100	100	100

by his workers according to his sense of social justice, his willingness to understand the worker's point of view and to appreciate his efforts. Seventy-five per cent of the investigated workers rank these factors highest, while 25 % put technical competence and guidance in the first place (plant A 33 %, plant E 32 %). Higher management also is judged according to its measures in the field of personnel and social policy (49 %), economic success ranking second (27 %) and technical competence (5 %) at the third place. Obviously the majority of the workers evaluate the plant authorities not so much on objective criteria but rather on the ground of their attitudes towards the workers. The relatively high share of workers (19 %) who have no opinion on the decisive qualities of higher management also hints at the great social distance still existing in the investigated plants.

A good indicator of the actual attitude of workers towards persons of higher authority seem to be questions on *confidential persons in personal and technical matters* (table 9). Thirty-six per cent of all interviewed workers stated that they had opportunities within the plant to talk about confidential personal problems. The percentage was highest in plant A (64 %) and lowest in plant G (21 %). Eleven per cent considered one or more colleagues as confidential persons in personal matters. Personnel

Table 10.   *Recognition of workers' opinions (percentage figures)*

	All plants	A	B	C	D	E	F	G
1. Yes	40	56	48	33	46	41	20	36
2. Partly	32	32	34	47	40	35	25	18
3. No	26	8	14	20	14	24	55	39
4. No opinion	2	4	4	0	0	0	0	7
Total	100	100	100	100	100	100	100	100

officers or works counsellors are only listed by a small minority. It is interesting that 21 % list nobody and 14 % do not want any confidential talk within the plant. Thus a substantial part of the workers (35 %) do not discuss personal difficulties at work. Technical difficulties are mainly discussed with superiors (69 %), in 11 % of all cases also with colleagues.

The general picture obtained from these data shows that the position of superiors as confidential persons in technical matters is particularly strong. A substantial number of workers also discuss personal difficulties with them, for example financial problems or sickness in the family. Therefore, we cannot conclude that social distance between workers and immediate superiors in the investigated plants is particularly high. Though workers usually address their foremen with the impersonal German 'Sie' instead of the more intimate 'Du' they are often members of the same trade union (organized for the whole industry) and even sometimes make joint outings or take a drink together after a shift. The higher technical staff, however, especially the university graduates, do not usually share these common leisure-time activities.

Authority within a plant is significantly shaped by communication procedures. If there is substantial two-way communication, workers might feel less exposed to arbitrary orders. Therefore the interviewed workers were asked whether they felt that a worker's opinion was recognized by his superiors in the respective plant. The results (see table 10) show that 40 % of all workers answered 'yes', while 32 % felt only partly recognized. However, we find substantial differences between the plants. While plants A, B, D and E show a rather good average, plants C, G and especially F have quite a portion of workers being rather sceptical on this point or even reacting negatively (plant F: 55 %). Combined with other indices this leads to the conclusion that in plant F substantial tensions between workers and the authority system are latent.

Table 11. *Improvement of workers' recognition (percentage figures)*

	All plants	A	B	C	D	E	F	G
How can workers get more recognition?								
1. Through activity of works council	19	19	20	16	2	28	19	16
2. Through activity of trade union	4	5	1	4	2	6	4	2
3. Through pressure upon superiors	21	24	12	24	17	20	25	30
4. Through workers' solidarity	14	22	10	11	12	6	21	13
5. Nothing	15	15	25	18	7	16	15	3
6. No opinion	21	9	13	20	53	24	12	34
7. Person is gang leader (not interviewed)	6	6	19	7	7	0	4	2
Total	100	100	100	100	100	100	100	100

The workers' share in decision-making and norm setting

The status of workers within the social tension field of the plant is fundamentally defined by their exclusion from management. They share this condition, however, with most of the white-collar employees. In the Western German chemical industry, in each plant the members of a 'works council', constituted by law and elected by all workers, represent workers' interests towards management and co-determine in some important personnel and social affairs. Thus, for example, no new payment system can be introduced without the consent of the works council. In case of dismissals it has to be asked for approval. In enterprises organized as corporations representatives of the workers are also members of the board of directors. This does not guarantee general co-determination of workers in the chemical industry, and their actual share in making technical or economic decisions is almost nil. It guarantees, however, substantial rights concerning the regulation of personnel and social problems. Though there are legal provisions valid for the whole industry, much depends upon the skill and experience of the individual works councillor. In plants A–D we found rather active works councils while in plants E–G they seemed to show little initiative.

It is interesting that among interviewed workers there existed quite diverse opinions about means of improving workers' recognition and influence within the plant. As all questions in the interviews were put open-ended, the answers to the respective question had to be sorted according to most common features. The results (table 11) show that 21 % hoped for improvements through direct influence upon superiors,

19 % through greater activity of the works council and 14 % through general strengthening of workers' solidarity. Only 4 % expressly thought of the trade union in this context, while 21 % had no opinion and 15 % thought that achieved recognition was sufficient. This result shows that obviously many workers are work-place minded. Work place and plant are the centres of their working life. Trade unions, which normally act at an inter-plant level, are too far off for most interviewed workers. A substantial number seem to have thought little about the problem of the greater influence of workers and quite a few do not even consider this a very urgent affair. This general picture is underlined by workers' attitudes towards the co-determination issue,[1] at the moment quite an issue in Western Germany. Twenty-six per cent had no opinion on this matter, 30 % thought of co-determination only as a work-place-centred issue, 30 % thought of the whole plant as an object of co-determination, while only 14 % included the whole branch of industry.

It can be concluded from these observations that workers' rights for presenting their interests before management were fully granted in the investigated plants. The majority of the interviewed workers only showed concern about issues directly related to their firm. There is even a strong minority which takes a rather passive attitude towards the problem of the workers' share in decision-making. The general feeling prevails that there are means of expressing one's opinions and reasonable claims within the plant and that it is not their function to run business or to give orders.

The workers' share in social opportunities

The social framework of the investigated plants offers to workers a definite and recognized position and even respect for their vital interests. This position, however, offers little personal prestige and almost no share in authority, workers' representatives excepted. The individual worker thus faces the fact that there are quite a few people in the plant who seemingly are better off in this respect and that he has almost no social contact with these groups during work hours. Especially in big plants workers said that they never met any members of higher management. Their knowledge about office work was only derived from members of the larger family or from neighbours being occupied as white-collar workers in lower positions.

It is of decisive importance for the interpretation of this situation by the workers whether they feel able to share social opportunities through the chances for promotion, for getting greater job security and for participating in the advantages of economic and technological progress.

[1] Trade unions claim an extension of the Co-determination Law valid within the coal and steel producing industries, to all big corporations.

Concerning chances for promotion, the objective situation in the investigated chemical plants is characterized by a strict hierarchy of levels of education. The top stratum is constituted of university graduates, mainly in chemistry. Their jobs are closed to non-academics. As it is extremely difficult for an adult to start studying while working, almost the only chance to enter this group is by proceeding to university straight from secondary school. The big corporations offer scholarships for children of employees with outstanding school records. There were a few workers who intended sending their sons to university but these are exceptional cases. In Western Germany students with working-class parents only form 4–5 % of all students at universities.

The usual channel of promotion within the plant open to non-academics has its starting point in an industrial or commercial apprenticeship within the firm. In the chemical industry the industrial apprenticeship usually provides training for laboratory and maintenance work. Operator work within the plant is usually not done by such persons, but by workers either entering the firm as unskilled labourers or as persons having interrupted their career as artisans, skilled or semi-skilled workers of other industries or as small farmers etc., mainly from financial reasons (in the chemical industry wages and job security are well above average). We therefore face the fact that up to now plant operators in the investigated enterprises of the Western German chemical industry are usually only marginally incorporated in the institutionalized training system of the firms. There are, however, cases in which young operators get a chance to start an apprenticeship in a firm offering opportunities for them to become assistant chemists. These persons usually never return to the plant unless they prepare themselves for a career as a master. In some plants the masters are mostly taken from this group (plants C and D). Operators who have not completed an apprenticeship can qualify themselves through length of service experience and reliability. A few additional training courses are offered in big firms. Workers may get a chance to advance in skill grade, eventually becoming gang leader or assistant foreman. In smaller plants they might even finally become a foreman, but this usually involves successfully completing a course for superiors during leisure-time and lasting at least about three years. The chances for advancing in skill grade are rather substantial for male workers, the chances for becoming gang leader are fairly good for young workers staying a longer period in the same plant. Becoming foreman is an exception for a worker from the floor.

Workers' statements in their interviews give us an opportunity to check the subjective perception of this situation (see table 12). General chances for promotion of workers are considered good by 24 % and fair

Table 12.   *Chances for promotion (percentage figures)*

	All plants	A	B	C	D	E	F	G
General chances								
1. Good	24	54	39	9	45	14	0	5
2. Fair	22	29	19	36	26	26	1	28
3. Not good	29	11	22	49	14	40	33	34
4. None	21	3	13	4	7	16	66	28
5. Undecided	4	3	7	2	8	4	0	5
Total	100	100	100	100	100	100	100	100
Personal chances								
1. No chance	33	13	25	51	26	47	47	30
2. Will be promoted	22	39	38	22	29	5	10	13
3. Content without promotion	20	27	23	16	26	18	5	26
4. Too old	15	15	7	11	12	20	22	15
5. Other plans	10	6	7	0	7	10	16	16
Total	100	100	100	100	100	100	100	100

by 22 % of all respondents. The share is highest in plants A, B and D, about average in plants C and E, rather low in plant G and almost nil in plant F. This particular plant is in a difficult market position, the diminishing orders causing a gradual reduction in personnel.

The perception of *personal* chances for promotion generally shows greater scepticism. Only 22 % of all interviewed workers expressed the opinion that they would advance within their firm, the percentage being highest again in the newly founded plants A and B. One third of the workers saw no chances, most of them working in plants C, E and F. It is significant that 15 % of the workers consider themselves as too old for promotion while 10 % pursue other plans, for example, eventually leaving the plant. Twenty per cent do not reflect upon chances for promotion; they say that they are content with the position they have achieved. It may be guessed that among this group the share of persons in higher skill grades and in positions with some authority (gang leader) is relatively high.

These results hint at a rather realistic evaluation of promotion opportunities by the workers. Differences in attitudes reflect both different situations in the investigated plants and personal factors. Those plants being in rapid expansion (A and B) give more reason for optimistic views than stagnating plants (E and F). In plant C we find the highest percentage of workers in wage groups 3 and 4 (see chart 4), there is, therefore, little margin for further promotion. Among personal factors age and date of entrance into the plant are of great importance, as correlational analyses have shown. The older a person and the longer his service with the firm, the lower the level of promotion expectations. We may conclude that social mobility within the plants also includes those workers who are young, ambitious and willing to make considerable efforts in additional training. With growing age chances rapidly diminish. The individual horizon of promotion and its realization is usually limited to jobs either as a more skilled operator or as a supervisor, in which case the worker can achieve the status of a salaried employee. Among younger workers there are some cases in which a qualification for laboratory work was possible.

Attitudes of quite a few workers towards labour turnover suggest that there is a widespread notion that an important achievement is the fact that one is able to leave small-scale industry or a craft and to get stable employment within a prospering firm granting job security and substantial fringe benefits. This notion might serve as a substitute for small chances of promotion. Therefore, an important aspect of social opportunities concerns the relative security of work place, achieved qualification standard, wage rate and achieved social status within the firm in general. As the chemical industry still enjoys substantial economic growth, employment security of its workers is rather high. Even in those cases where a reduction of production or a reduction of employment, due to automation, takes place, management tries to re-occupy workers concerned in other departments. For example, in plant E the number of work places decreased from 260 to 138 from 1956 to 1965 while, due to rationalization, production increased by 35%. Within this period, however, only 14 workers of this plant were dismissed by the firm due to labour shortage.

The practice of intra-plant or intra-firm labour turnover in order to avoid lay-offs generally guarantees a relatively stable employment and the maintenance of achieved wage rates and social status (seniority rights with regard to fringe benefits). It is much more difficult to maintain achieved qualification. If production processes change substantially, re-training appears to be unavoidable unless the worker gets less complicated tasks. In plant F, intra-plant labour turnover sometimes resulted in substantial reduction of earnings, as there is a high wage differential between work places according to differences in accident proneness. In cases where automation led to a reduction in highly dangerous jobs, their former holders had either to accept a lower income or to quit the firm.

The general picture obtained in this study shows rather high job security and substantial advantages for persons with longer periods of service in the plant. Each plant provides pension schemes and plants A–D offered some kind of profit sharing or general annual benefits. Due

Table 13. *Anticipated results of technological progress (percentage figures)*

	All plants	A	B	C	D	E	F	G
1. Mainly positive results	59	77	75	47	66	53	41	57
2. Mainly negative results	8	4	5	9	0	12	16	10
3. Undecided	29	18	17	38	29	32	43	26
4. No major changes	1	0	1	4	0	0	0	0
5. No opinion	3	1	2	2	5	3	0	7
Total	100	100	100	100	100	100	100	100

to almost constant changes in technology a high degree of willingness to adapt to new work procedures was asked from the workers. As most of them had acquired their skill while working on the job, their occupational training having taken place outside the industry, the problem of opposing skill-dilution, so important among craft-conscious workers, did not occur. Workers in the investigated plants also seem to be less workplace conscious, as their jobs often change within the whole plant. Instead they are more conscious of their individual pay rates.

The feelings towards individual security are reflected in the workers' responses to the question whether they believe in financial aid from the firm in cases of undeserved need. Sixty-eight per cent of all interviewed workers responded affirmatively, 17% were in doubt and only 13% denied the firm's willingness to aid, the percentage of this latter group being highest in plants F (28%), C (20%), D (17%) and G (16%).

Another important dimension of social opportunity is the future prospects for workers within the secular process of technological advancements. Though its long-term results cannot be foreseen the general feeling of workers towards such changes constantly influencing concrete work situations and their style of life indicates attitudes of participation, indifference or protest. Those who feel that technological progress will be advantageous to workers get a strong basis for a more optimistic view of their own situation which might lead to a greater willingness to adapt oneself to new tasks. On the contrary, if positive results of technological changes are questioned a more pessimistic view of one's own situation ought to prevail, leading to attitudes of resistance to or retreat from situational pressures.

The attitudes of interviewed workers towards the opportunities brought about by technological advancements (see table 13) are preponderantly positive (59%), the share being highest in those plants with the greatest rate of automation. While 29% of the workers were undecided about the possible outcome of technological progress, only 8%

showed a pessimistic attitude, being strongest in plants E–G, but even there not exceeding a share of 16 % of all respondents. We may conclude, therefore, that the majority of workers in our study showed willingness to accept technological advancements.

Concerning the factors bringing about these changes, 30 % of the interviewed workers thought of processes immanent in the socio-economic system, especially world-wide competition. Twenty-three per cent listed expert groups, especially technicians, as giving the main impulse. Sixteen per cent spoke of economic élites. Other factors listed were 'those on the top' (2 %), politicians (6 %), institutions like universities (5 %), decisions of single persons (1 %), other groups (2 %) and combinations of factors (11 %). Only 4 % articulated no opinion on the issue. This gives the picture of a rather reasonable view on the part of most workers. Though they are usually unable to describe relationships between observed phenomena accurately, they have a general realistic notion.

The results of our research show that under different aspects a considerable part of the interviewed workers was aware of sharing social opportunities, though quite a few of them knew that this share was limited. These limitations, however, were not only perceived as being immanent in a given social system of relationships. They were also found in personal factors such as age, lack of higher education, etc. There were quite a few older workers who stated that they had little or no opportunities to alter their conditions of life, but that younger workers would enjoy many more opportunities than they themselves had ever found in former times.

A final proof of this interpretation is given by workers' responses to the question whether they had achieved the goals they were striving for in life or whether they believed this would still be possible (see table 14). Twenty-six per cent stated that they had achieved their goals, 51 % thought it probable that they would reach their goals. Only 18 % gave negative answers and 5 % meant that it was useless to aim at something special in life. As has been noted, most workers (with the exception of female workers) thought of life goals in terms of building their own house. This seems to be a common symbol of achievement, and great personal sacrifices are made to share in it. All this hints at a great urge among workers to participate as fully as possible in the general life chances offered by modern society, made obvious through common status symbols. There were only very few workers who opposed this general trend by denying the universality of these symbols and the channels for achievement offered within the firm and within society. More widespread is an attitude which is aware of a personal failure and limits set for personal success. But this situation is rarely interpreted in terms of a doubt in general achievement symbols.

Table 14. *Achievement of personal life goals (percentage figures)*

	All plants	A	B	C	D	E	F	G
1. Goals are achieved	26	11	22	36	29	39	21	30
2. Goals are not achieved	8	8	7	2	12	9	10	10
3. Goals will be achieved	51	63	54	40	47	40	58	48
4. Goals will not be achieved	10	10	13	20	10	8	5	7
5. No use in setting oneself goals	5	8	4	2	2	4	6	5
Total	100	100	100	100	100	100	100	100

THE INTERACTION PATTERNS: SOLIDARITY VERSUS PRIVATIZATION

A still widespread thesis maintains that the working class is a social universe with common characteristics deriving from similar situations and chances both in work and private life. This situational similarity would create common patterns of conscience and attitudes, thus providing a strong platform for the growth of class solidarity. In this research significant differences between both work situations and social opportunities in the different investigated plants were found. Even within the plants themselves we find characteristic differences between subgroups of workers due to different positions in the work system, to different status within the social framework and to personality traits (age, former occupation, living place, etc.). Thus, we might presume that even within one industry a plurality of self-interpretations of the working class and of societal images exists.[1] Under these circumstances the notion of solidarity as a common interaction pattern of the working class needs to be reconsidered.

Solidarity can be defined as an attitude of mutual aid and concerted action based upon common interests and goals derived from similar situational challenges. With regard to workers, we may then distinguish between work-place situation, situation within the larger social context of the firm, and situation in private and public life outside the plant. Our research data only enables us to make some statements concerning solidarity caused by similar work-place situations.

As is shown by table 15, only 24% of the interviewed workers said that they were working alone. But the group of workers who have personal friends among their colleagues is also rather small (21%). The majority of workers has no contact with colleagues outside the

---

[1] This assumption has already been proved by H. Popitz, H. P. Bahrdt, E. A. Jüres and H. Kesting in: *Das Gesellschaftsbild des Arbeiters* (Tübingen, 1957), where they distinguish six different types of societal images which they found among workers in one steel mill.

Table 15.   *Social contacts with colleagues (percentages-figures)*

	All plants	A	B	C	D	E	F	G
Contracts during work								
1. Works always alone	24	34	25	2	2	33	14	39
2. Work always with others	74	62	75	98	94	64	85	61
3. Work partly with others	2	4	0	0	4	3	1	0
Total	100	100	100	100	100	100	100	100
Friends in the plant								
1. Yes	21	35	16	29	21	21	14	12
2. No	79	65	84	71	79	79	86	88
Total	100	100	100	100	100	100	100	100
Contacts outside the plant								
1. No	55	24	40	68	55	66	66	69
2. Yes, group contacts	18	45	29	5	20	7	8	5
3. Yes, individual contacts	22	9	30	18	18	27	25	26
4. Yes, partly group, partly individual contacts	5	22	1	9	7	0	1	0
Total	100	100	100	100	100	100	100	100

plant (53 %). It appears that leisure-time relations among workers are highest in the technologically most advanced plants A and B. Group activities outside the plant are only named by 23 % of the interviewed workers. These results show clearly the tendency of workers to limit their social contacts with colleagues to work-place relations. Sometimes this might quite unwillingly be a result of long distance commuting (7 % of the workers spend more than one hour daily on their journey to and from work). We can also note that female workers obviously showed a greater reserve towards closer contacts with colleagues.

The tendency to separate work life from private life is also shown by the fact that only 6 % of the interviewed workers said they would discuss problems of work within their families. Seventy-five per cent stated that this was rarely or never the case.

Though we may conclude that there is certainly a tendency towards growing plurality of life spheres with specific patterns of social contacts, enabling the workers to get 'privatized', at least at home,[1] this must not necessarily diminish their readiness for collective action in issues of vital interest to the workers. As already mentioned, 14 % of the interviewed workers would welcome greater solidarity of the workers as a

[1] In her study *Industriearbeiterprivat* (Stuttgart 1966), R. Wald states that the predominant leisure activities among chemical workers in one plant, located in the Ruhr valley, were family centred.

means of improving their recognition in the plant. There is certainly a rather substantial potential for solidarity as far as plant problems are concerned. On the other hand attitudes of workers towards their life chances and their style of life are either definitely individualized or influenced by goals no longer typical for workers alone. This can be seen for example by looking at plans for holidays, hobbies and even educational practices.

It seems as if workers' solidarity can no longer be regarded as a fundamental attitude shaping the whole style of life. It is rather centred around individual work-situations and dependent upon the degree of common interest of workers in a particular plant. Large areas of social activity, however, are no longer based upon solidarity but rather upon individual pursuit of private goals. This does not hinder workers from also entering into relationships with each other in private life. But these relationships are mainly private in their nature and are not directed towards concerted action to improve the conditions of the working class as was still the case in the late twenties when workers were not only organized successfully within the plants but also in their roles as consumers, as students in evening schools, as sportsmen, etc.

AMBIGUITIES IN THE SOCIAL SITUATION OF CHEMICAL WORKERS

Several authors on working-class problems are inclined to relate structural changes to general social influences upon private and public life while they maintain a relative stableness of workplace relations. Thus, in his study on French workers Serge Mallet points out: 'dans la production elle-même, les traits fondamentaux qui distinguent la classe ouvrière des autres couches de la population semblent . . . inchangés.'[1] Based upon our research findings, we doubt the validity of this statement as far as West German chemical workers are concerned. On the contrary, we found an inherent dynamic in the intra-plant position of workers due to constant changes in technology and its implications both upon social relations and workers' attitudes. Besides, we also found the trend towards growing heterogeneity of inter-plant positions of workers due to a great diversification of work systems and social structures of the respective plants. Thus the first thesis concerning structural changes in the investigated parts of the German working class can be formulated: *Constant technological and social changes and a heterogeneity of work-situations have deeply affected the consistency of the working class, promoting individualistic responses to situational pressures instead of concerted action.*

In the case of the investigated chemical workers the challenges in-

[1] S. Mallet, *La Nouvelle Classe ouvrière* (Paris, 1963), p. 9.

herent in work-situations do not uniformly lead towards alienation, relative deprivation or militant solidarity. There is some margin for an individual pursuit of private goals. These do not appear as privatized modes of specific working-class goals such as preserving traditional skill and traditional ways of life being distinct from those of other social groups. Instead, workers want to participate in the achievements of modern industrial society as equal citizens in all social situations. This point has also been stressed by Alain Touraine, stating that 'the working class is "new" to the extent that its action no longer rests on the defence of the job and the craft as factors of production, but on a conflictual participation in the values of economic development'.[1] This leads on to the second thesis: *In pursuing their privatized goals the workers adapt the ubiquitous values of modern society in which they want to participate as fully as possible.*

Though in the chemical industry underlying trends in the work system, especially in the technologically most advanced plants, enable workers to take an individualistic and rather favourable self-interpretation of their role in production, they are still handicapped by certain aspects of the social framework of the respective plants. Within this structure they usually share an inferior position, inferior not so much under economic aspects or with regard to authoritarian management. The inferiority is rather established by the social distance between workers and salaried employees, especially the higher grades of management, and by their exclusion from promotion channels leading out of the particular atmosphere of a given plant. In the chemical industry workers are plant-bound and production-bound to a relatively high degree. This adds to their relative social seclusion which, on the other hand, often creates an amazing degree of innocence concerning their actual contribution to plant economy on the side of salaried employees occupied outside the production units. Usually, workers only participate fully in the social tension field of their plants and the firm in which these are incorporated through their official elected representatives (workers' councillors). A third thesis can now be advanced: *Workers' urge to overcome an inferior social status through shared opportunities in the firm is handicapped by their relatively isolated position within the social structure of the enterprise, no longer corresponding with their functional contribution within highly developed work systems.*

Social distinctions between white-collar and blue-collar employees and between 'order-giving' and 'order-taking' personnel become increasingly doubtful at least in automated chemical plants. In these most advanced work-situations workers not only get emancipated from their

[1] A. Touraine, 'Management and the working class in Western Europe', *Daedalus*, vol. 93 (1964), p. 332.

traditional solidaric ways of behaviour reflecting their alienated work-situation and their status of relative deprivation, they also get emancipated from an antiquated system of status symbols which fixed their inferior status for many decades. This process of emancipation offers new opportunities for self-identification and social participation. It is, however, endangered by both the inertia of established formal relations in the enterprise and corresponding role expectations of persons concerned. The quest of privileged groups for preserving an antiquated status is one of the strongest means for re-establishing frontiers between workers and 'those on the top', aided by employees 'submissive to management'.

Concluding our interpretation of the workers' situation in chemical plants, we find some fundamental ambiguities between both highly developed and conservative work systems on the one hand, and between both more and less advanced social structures, especially its authority components, on the other hand, resulting in more 'solidaric' or more 'privatized' attitudes. One explanation of these ambiguities may be found in the last thesis: *The trend towards replacing the traditional 'proletarian' type of the worker by another, being 'emancipated' from traditional class consciousness, does not lead to the dissolution of working-class properties as long as they are needed for group identification and as demarcation from other groups challenging this identification without offering full acceptance in their own group.*

The underlying social process is self-enforcing. It seems as if at least some of the working-class patterns still to be observed among chemical workers are indicating rather reactive attitudes than active quests for a specific working-class culture.

8

SOCIAL STRATIFICATION IN
POLISH CITIES

WŁODZIMIERZ WESOŁOWSKI AND
KAZIMIERZ SŁOMCZYŃSKI[1]

The results of an empirical study of social stratification in three Polish
cities are discussed in the present paper. The survey was conducted in
Łódź (750,000 inhabitants), Szczecin (300,000) and Koszalin (50,000).
A total of 2,681 questionnaires were run: 1,000 in Łódź, 1,051 in
Szczecin and 630 in Koszalin. Married men, aged 24 to 60, were
randomly sampled from lists of voters in Łódź and from population
registers in Szczecin and Koszalin. In choosing married men as the
object of their study the present authors were guided by two considerations. For one, the family is assumed to be a 'stratification unit' in the
sense that all members of a family have the same status, usually determined by the status of the husband. For the other, the purpose of the
study was to trace a variety of factors which affect the standard of living
of the family.

The survey was conducted in Szczecin and Koszalin in the summer of
1964, and Łódź in the autumn of 1965. The following groups of
phenomena were studied: income, education, housing conditions,
cultural life, leisure, social intercourse, social background of marriage
partners, vertical and horizontal social mobility, and the visualization of
social differentiation. Eighty per cent of the questions were the same in
the Łódz questionnaire and in the questionnaire used in both Szczecin
and Koszalin. Otherwise, the Łódź questionnaire gave a more detailed
treatment to cultural life, whereas in the other questionnaire more
emphasis was put on the visualization of social differentiation.

The present paper deals with only some of the data obtained and
with the results of the first statistical treatment of these data. It is hoped
that even this fragmentary presentation may convey an idea of the
range of problems involved in the study.

[1] The authors wish to express their gratitude to Dr Tadeusz Miller of Łódź University and
Dr Michał Pohoski of Warsaw University for their advice and consultations on questions of
statistics.

A NOTE ON THEORY

The authors were aware of the theoretical issues involved in their approach to the collection of data as well as their processing and discussion in this report.

From among the various theoretical approaches to social stratification two 'pure' types can be isolated. They can be seen as 'ideal types' in Max Weber's sense.[1] The two 'pure' approaches can be defined in the following way: (1) Stratification is conceived as a system of social relations. Strata (or classes) are held to be variously interrelated with each other, and certain regularities can be discovered in these interrelations. A system of stratification is hence viewed as a cluster of interdependent economic, political and other social relations. (2) The other approach identifies stratification with the unequal distribution of goods (or values) in society. The goods involved are the economic goods (income, property, etc.) as well as non-material values (education, prestige, etc.). We must, therefore, speak of values rather than of goods in this context. By 'values' are meant here all kinds of things desired by men in a given culture, being in scarcity and distributed unevenly among the population, e.g. income, education, power, and social prestige.[2]

The latter approach underlines certain regularities in the distribution of values in society. A person sharing in one value tends to share in certain other values too. For example, there is a high correlation between income and education. Whereas the former approach considers clusters of relations between different strata, the latter considers clusters of values at different levels of stratification.

These two 'pure' theoretical approaches refer each to one aspect of social stratification. They in fact complement each other. The obvious corollary is that the distribution of values may not be considered in isolation from social relations, and, conversely, social relations cannot be considered in separation from value distribution, even though each of the two spheres of social life may be autonomous to some extent. Generally speaking, the participation of groups and individuals in social values is largely determined by the system of social relations, which may either exclude certain groups from sharing in a given value, or monopolize a value for one group, or limit a group's share in a value.

There may be also a reversed causation. Social relations are frequently determined by the distribution of values. For example, the possession of

[1] By stratification are meant here the phenomena discussed by other authors under the heading 'social classes' as well as under the heading 'social strata'.

[2] The term 'value', or 'stratificational value' is used here to denote what in stratification theory is usually called 'attribute of social status'. 'Attributes' and 'values' as understood here are evidently the same phenomena looked upon from different angles.

capital (also a value) enables certain persons to enter into definite economic relations with other people. The formation of definite relations under the influence of a particular distribution of values is fairly widespread in social life. For instance, education may account for membership in a definite social milieu, and property may account for self-identification with the 'propertied classes'. Economic exploitation, social isolation, feelings of enmity or solidarity, evidently refer to different spheres of social relations.

The links between the sphere of social relations and the sphere of value distribution were given consideration by many authors of social class theories in the past (e.g. K. Marx, M. Weber). The same can be said of contemporary sociologists. The two 'pure' types of approach are merely theoretical constructs. They should be viewed as two extremes between which we may place any of the actual sociological theories of social stratification.[1]

In empirical investigations, so numerous today, we find the second approach predominates. Actual studies of social stratification tend to concentrate on the distribution of values. This may be due to technical factors: it is relatively easy to operationalize research on stratification conceived as the distribution of values, whereas it is much more difficult to develop a programme of research on stratification conceived as a system of social relations.[2]

The present study of stratification likewise concentrates on the distribution of values rather than on systems of social relations. As in other countries, considerations of time and techniques were behind this predilection. The authors hope to be able to embark soon upon a project which combines the study of social relations with research on value

---

[1] A good example of a theory which combines the two approaches is that by G. Lenski, *Power and Privilege. A Theory of Social Stratification* (New York, 1966). G. Lenski conceives of the stratification system as a distributive system of society. At the same time he pays considerable attention to power relations as a determining factor of the processes of distribution.

[2] The authors feel tempted to discuss the place to be assigned to prestige stratification in the division of approaches outlined above into two extreme types.

Social prestige expresses a person's sense of superiority or inferiority in relation to another person. This is why the prestige stratification can be conceived as belonging to the first type rather than to the second. On the other hand, it must be admitted that in most cases prestige is conceived as a value desired by man, just as he desires a house or a car. The investigators are usually interested in the correlation between prestige and share in other values, such as income, education or power. The economic, political and kindred relations associated with the given distribution of values are little explored by these investigators. It is thus felt that studies of prestige stratification as we know them today should be included rather in the group described as investigation of the distribution of values.

In the case of 'power stratification', there seems to be a need for the integration of both aspects: that of value distribution and that of social relations. Power—in one aspect—is a peculiar 'value' which one 'possesses' or 'holds', but it can 'materialize' only in one's relations with other people. Thus, all theories of classes which emphasize the unequal distribution of power seem to be related to the first approach, rather than to the second.

distribution, with due consideration to the actual economic and political relations in the country.

The emphasis in the present investigation rests on the relative share of social groups in such objective values as income, education, and skills. Indeed, there is much to be said for the contention that the distribution of vocational skills, income, and formal education are the determining factors of social stratification in the cities of the socialist countries, that is to say, among the employees of the socialized sectors of the economy.

At the same time several other values were included in this survey. We shall call them 'cultural values' and 'technical values'. By the first we mean such values as reading of books and newspapers, television viewing, theatre going, and by the second, housing conditions, household gadgets and other durable goods (i.e. the products of technical civilization).

These different stratificational values can be looked upon as belonging to different 'tiers'.[1]

In industrial societies, the first tier (also the most fundamental tier for the whole system of stratification) is that of the unequal distribution of income, skills, education and power. This tier is crucial in that it determines the second tier, i.e. the tier of the consumption of cultural and technical values. But there are also some other factors involved in this process. A person's interest in, for instance, serious reading matter is co-determined by the habits he has acquired when reared by his parents, by his social environment, by his aspirations, and by other factors. These factors usually reflect the stratificational position of the parents. With this we have arrived at the working hypothesis that there may be a certain inconsistency between a person's share in the values of the first tier and his share in the values of the second tier (especially such cultural values as reading and theatre attendance). Such incongruence may occur especially within groups that have benefited by economic promotion but have made little progress in 'cultural consumption' (i.e. are lagging behind groups with lower incomes). The present investigation was designed to supply data bearing on this point. In particular, it was assumed that congruence of the groups' participation in 'first-tier' values and in 'second-tier' values would indicate a distinct strata

---

[1] The idea of causal and structural relationships between groups of stratificational variables is quite common in contemporary sociology, though it is formulated in different ways. It goes sometimes along with the multidimensional concept of stratification. Cf., e.g., H. Gerth and W. C. Mills, *Character and Social Structure* (New York, 1953); M. M. Gordon, *Social Class in American Sociology* (Durham, N.C., 1958); L. Broom, 'Social differentiation and stratification', in R. K. Merton, L. Broom and L. S. Cottrell (eds.), *Sociology Today* (New York, 1959).

Evidently, we prefer to speak of 'tiers' rather than of 'stratificational variables' and 'associated variables', or stratification itself and 'correlates of stratification' (cf. M. Gordon, *op. cit.*, L. Broom, *op. cit.*).

structuralization of the society, whereas the absence of such a congruence would have to be accounted for by the presence of some 'de-stratifying' factors. By strata structuralization is meant here the process of shaping and reshaping the stratification system in a changing society.[1]

Strata structuralization reveals still a third tier, that of differentiation in group consciousness. It is commonly known that a group's share in some values as contrasted with the share of other groups in the same values is a source of attitudes towards these groups or the entire socio-economic system and may also generate feelings of animosity towards, or conflict with, another group. But this process depends also on other factors, such as political or economic ideologies, or the historically determined national awareness of a people. It seems, therefore, essential to investigate the visualization of value distribution by members of different social groups. The formation of social opinions and social attitudes in members of groups among which values are unequally distributed could be called 'the crystallization of social consciousness'. Thus the third tier of the stratification system is that of the crystallization of social consciousness.[2]

A study of stratification systems and processes should, therefore, embrace the investigation of (1) the synchronization of group participation in values within the first and second tiers, (2) the synchronization of group participation in values between these tiers as well as the pertinent interdependence of the second tier, (3) the relative weight of the factors within the first and second tiers which affect the visualization of social differentiation (e.g., third tier).

The extent to which there occurs a congruence in the participation in values of two tiers and in the respective crystallization of consciousness can be called 'the general degree of strata structuralization' in a society.

The socialist society does not emerge in a 'blank'. On the contrary, it has to cope with an extensive capitalist heritage. Accordingly, the stratification system of the socialist society does not begin with a random distribution of values in society, nor with a distribution dictated exclusively by the principles of socialist distribution of values. What

---

[1] Some processes of de-stratification and re-stratification occurring in present-day Poland under the impact of the social revolution and industrialization are discussed by W. Wesołowski in his article 'Les notions de strates et de class dans la société socialistes', *Sociologie du travail*, no. 2, 1967. The same paper explains why the authors find it more expedient to speak of strata rather than of classes (in the Marxist sense) when analysing the stratification of the urban population in the socialist countries.

[2] The focus of this approach is on the group's 'consistency of status' rather than on the consistency of the individual's status. In this respect the authors follow the approach of L. Broom rather than that of G. Lenski. (Cf. L. Broom, *op. cit.*; G. Lenski, 'Status crystallization: A non-vertical dimension of social status', *American Sociological Review*, no. 4 (1954)).

Above, the term 'crystallization' is borrowed from G. Lenski, but it is given a different meaning.

actually takes place are processes of re-stratification. In particular, the following issues should be attended to in a stratification study of socialist society:

(1) Which segments (strata, or classes) of the old structure disappear completely, and which new ones are born?

(2) What is the new distribution of values among groups which have survived? What changes have occurred in the hierarchy of groups in terms of their relative share in values?

(3) Over what range does the participation of the extreme groups in important stratification values spread?

(4) What is the role of the following three factors in the processes of stratification: (a) factors inherited from the capitalist system (e.g. private enterprise in retail trade, or handicrafts); (b) factors introduced by the economic and other social mechanisms of the socialist society (e.g. the principle 'to each according to his work'); (c) factors present in all kinds of industrial societies (e.g. advanced technology).

Two phenomena seem to deserve special attention: (1) the absolute range of differentiation along the given dimension of stratification, i.e. discrepancy in value participation of the two extreme groups in the whole hierarchy; (2) the degree of congruence in value participation within a group.

The systems of social stratification in the socialist countries may differ in both respects, and so we can speak of stronger and weaker strata structuralization of society. By the weaker type is meant a society with a relatively narrow range of differentiation and with a low congruence in value participation. By the stronger type is meant a society in which the range of social differences is wider and congruence in the participation of groups in different values is higher. (The two types may differ accordingly in the degree of crystallization of strata consciousness.)

There is still another general characteristic of the stratification system: the pattern of interrelations between stratificational values. Otherwise kindred societies may differ in this respect. And so, patterns of cultural consumption or patterns of social intercourse may be more strongly affected by income in one socialist society, and more strongly by education in another.

Naturally, we must have a suitable frame of reference in order to be able to assess a structuralization as either weak or strong. Such a framework is given in the stratification systems of other, either existing or past, societies. As far as present-day Poland is concerned, one could adopt as a frame of reference: any other socialist society, a contemporary capitalist society, or Poland's society as it existed in an earlier period. At the present stage of their study the authors do not intend to make systematic comparisons. At the same time they feel obliged to give the reader some historical clues for a better understanding of the findings. In view of the different level of economic development of Eastern and Western European societies in the past the present findings could be misunderstood by the western reader without such an historical background.

SOME HISTORICAL AND METHODOLOGICAL NOTES

The studied population was divided into the following groups:
- (i) professionals (in Polish usage: intelligentsia);
- (ii) office employees of middle and lower rank;
- (iii) semi-professional workers with secondary vocational education (in Polish usage: technicians);
- (iv) intermediate group between manual and non-manual workers (comprising salesmen, conductors, drivers, post-office clerks);
- (v) foremen;
- (vi) artisans (both self-employed and employed in co-operatives);
- (vii) skilled workers;
- (viii) semi-skilled workers;
- (ix) unskilled workers.

This classification is much more detailed than the division—usually applied by investigators—into manual workers and non-manual workers which in Poland corresponds to the customary division of society into the working class and the very broadly conceived 'intelligentsia stratum'.

It was assumed that the dichotomic division loses its validity for research purposes with the development of the industrial socialist society.

By adopting the more detailed classification the authors have been able to ascertain (1) if there are such socio-occupational categories which, though belonging to the broadly conceived manual category, share in one or another value to a higher degree than certain groups traditionally assigned to the non-manual workers; and (2) whether there have been any internal shifts among the non-manual workers in general and the manual workers in general.

The distinctions between non-manual (white-collar) and manual (blue-collar) workers were very pronounced in Poland between the two world wars, just as in any other economically less developed country of Eastern Europe. The average monthly income of a white-collar worker was 211 zlotys and that of a blue-collar worker only 77 zlotys. There was a strong differentiation between these groups in education and participation in cultural values. The vast majority of the manual workers were without complete elementary education, whereas the 'intelligentsia' distinguished themselves by their completed secondary, or even higher, education. General secondary education and a satisfactory income enabled the white-collar workers to read good books, frequent the theatre and read literary magazines, having also considerable influence on housing conditions.

These two basic groups differed sharply in their social prestige. Manual work was considered as inferior to any kind of 'brain work', and the manual workers were pushed down the social ladder by their low income, and low cultural standards.

Obviously, there were also low-grade clerks, on the one hand, and groups of 'working-class aristocracy', on the other, but these intermediate groups were not so numerous and hence of little effect on social stratification as a whole. In addition, all white-collar workers, irrespective of their relative placing (and income), strove to adapt in their way of life to the highest echelons of the 'intelligentsia', whereas members of the 'working-class aristocracy' tended to emphasize their ties with the working class. This served to make the basic distinction into working class (all manual workers) and 'intelligentsia' (all non-manual workers) even more pronounced.

Very much has been changed in this set-up by the post-war social revolution and industrialization of the country. Generally speaking, social distinctions between non-manual and manual workers have greatly diminished. The share of these two categories in many values has tended to converge. There have also been shifts in the internal occupational system of each of these two categories. As in other industrial societies, the number of skilled workers has greatly increased, and many new groups of lower-rank white-collar workers have appeared, including such intermediate groups as shop-assistants, post-office clerks, transport workers. In place of the 'old middle class' (the self-employed artisans and petty traders), whose numbers have been very much reduced, there have appeared the numerous employees of state-owned trade and services (called in the West 'the new middle classes').

In their vast majority, the inhabitants of cities are employees of state-owned industries, the administration, and the entire network of public utility institutions. These people all have the same relationship to the means of production and derive their income from the same source. Thus they are all in the same 'market situation', using here M. Weber's phrase.

But it is precisely this situation which makes an inquiry into the other stratificational values so urgent. The present authors have attempted to provide some of the answers to the questions posed by such an inquiry.

EMPIRICAL FINDINGS

Each of the three cities in which the present survey was conducted has distinctive features of its own. Their common feature is that they function as administrative capitals of regions (voivodships).

With 730,000 inhabitants, Łódź is the biggest of the three cities, and it is also the most heavily industrialized. Being a centre of the Polish textile and garment industry, it is a working-class city in every sense of the word. Since 1945, the metallurgic, electrical and leather industries have been developed there. Several academic schools were founded in the city, among them the University, the Technical University, and the Medical School. This has resulted in a marked increase of professionals in the city. None the less, Łódź has retained its character of a predominantly industrial city.

Szczecin with its 300,000 inhabitants is a port and industrial city. Since the war the port of Szczecin has been developed into the biggest port on the Baltic (in terms of cargo volume). A steel mill and several metallurgic plants were built. Severely damaged during the war, Szczecin has been completely rebuilt since.

Koszalin is the smallest of the three cities (50,000 inhabitants). It lacks major industries, being chiefly an administrative centre (voivodship capital).

With all these distinctions, the three cities cannot differ very much in the distribution of the stratificational values; they lie in a country with a uniform economic and political system and a historically determined culture. The peculiarities of each of the three cities, however, can be assumed to account for some specific deviations in the distribution of stratificational values. The first statistical analysis of the data was therefore made separately for each of the three cities.

These peculiarities are reflected in the occupational structure of the population above all (see table 1), but there are no significant shifts in the principal distribution trends and in the interrelations between the stratificational values. And so, the hierarchy of socio-occupational groups—as referred to the distribution of values—is roughly the same in the three cities. The correlations between pairs of variables (e.g. education and reading, or income and reading) reveal the same regularities in the three cities.

Consequently, the data from the three cities were processed jointly as long as there were no significant deviations. This enabled the authors not only to reduce the number of tables but also to subject the correlational data to factor analysis.

At the present stage of data processing the authors are unable to deal systematically with the degree of congruence in the value participation

Table 1.   *Socio-occupational groups in 3 cities*

Socio-occupational groups	Cities			Total
	Łódź	Szczecin	Koszalin	
White collar	24·2	33·4	44·6	32·6
Professionals	9·1	12·3	12·8	11·2
Technicians	5·8	9·7	10·9	8·6
Office employees	9·3	11·4	20·9	12·8
Intermediate groups	27·6	22·6	14·9	22·6
Intermediate group	12·2	12·3	8·4	11·4
Craftsmen	7·5	6·5	4·4	6·3
Foremen	7·9	3·8	2·1	4·9
Blue collar	44·2	35·5	27·3	36·8
Skilled workers	29·3	21·3	13·3	22·5
Semi-skilled workers	5·9	8·0	5·6	6·6
Unskilled workers	9·0	6·2	8·4	7·7
Others	4·0	8·5	13·2	8·0
$N=$ 100%	1000	1051	630	2681

of different groups. They must restrict themselves to ranking socio-occupational groups in terms of their participation in a number of selected values, as well as to the range of value participation of extreme groups, that is, the groups which have the largest and the smallest share in the given value. Moreover, they have tried to establish the relationships between participations in certain values.

(i) Classification of occupations

Attention must be paid in the first place to the classification of occupations, if only because any such classification is bound to be more or less arbitrary in view of the lack of universally accepted criteria of occupational grouping. Moreover, there is the difficulty of designating specific local (national) categories when writing in a foreign language and for the foreign reader.

The category of professionals ('intelligentsia') comprises chiefly those professions which require higher education, i.e. doctors, lawyers, engineers and scientists. The category comprises also the managers of big organizations (industrial, political, social and administrative), artists, writers, actors, journalists and teachers, irrespective of their formal education. In Polish society this category has always been regarded as the highest echelon of white-collar workers.

The category of office workers comprises middle- and lower-rank administrative workers of industrial enterprises and all kinds of public institutions (industrial, cultural, administrative etc.).

The category of technicians comprises chiefly employees of various industries with completed technical secondary education (i.e. graduates of the metallurgical, electrical, and mechanical 'technicums'), and also accountants (graduates of secondary vocational schools). In the same category were located a dozen or so technicians who acquired their qualifications at factory courses rather than in the 'technicums'. This category could also be called 'semi-professional workers'.

All industrial workers in charge of work teams of one kind or another were classified as foremen.

The 'intermediate category' comprises the borderline occupations between the manual and non-manual workers, e.g. shop-assistants, telephone operators, postmen, bus drivers, railwaymen, etc. There is a growing consensus among Polish sociologists that such a category is necessary for empirical investigations. Otherwise the researcher is forced to include these workers either in some white-collar or some blue-collar category.

Owners of private artisan shops were classified as artisans as well as artisans employed in co-operatives. In the same group were included owners of small retail shops.

With regard to the three groups of workers (skilled, semi-skilled and unskilled), the respondents were assigned to one of them on the basis of their own statement in Szczecin and Koszalin and on the basis of very complex criteria laid down by the regional council of trade unions in Łódź. In either case much 'liberalism' was shown, and this has resulted in a relatively high percentage of workers in the skilled group. The 'others' comprise servicemen and policemen (irrespective of rank), and also janitors, travelling salesmen, etc.

Two of these groups, the artisans and the 'others', are omittedi n the present considerations on account of their heterogeneity. In the artisan group there are private merchants as well as employees of co-operatives whose situation is not much different from that of industrial workers. The exclusion of this group is also due to the authors' concentration on the social stratification of employees of the socialized sector of the economy, that is, on the occupational groups which are typical of socialist society. As revealed by our statistical analysis, the artisans were in all respects close to the foremen.

For the sake of uniformity the persons belonging to the two omitted socio-occupational categories were excluded in all analyses, i.e. also those based on other stratificational variables (education and income).

The socio-occupational classification employed in the present study is based on two criteria: formal education and kind and level of skills required for the given job, the latter being not always dependent on education. It was therefore decided to approach both membership in a socio-occupational group and education as independent variables. This is, incidentally, the prevailing practice among investigators of social stratification. The undeniably growing role of formal education in industrial societies, especially in the process of selecting people for jobs, and the likewise growing role of education in the cultural differentiation of the population has induced some investigators in this country to raise the question whether formal education should not be considered the most important stratification value and hence the occupation omitted as a variable in research on stratification. The present study may be expected to yield an answer to this question.

(ii) The Basic Stratificational Variables: Occupation, Education, Income

The interrelations between these three basic variables of stratification are given in tables 2–6.

The educational group hierarchy is exactly the same as the income-per-capita hierarchy. The three groups of white-collar workers (professionals, technicians and office workers) are at the top, and the labourers are at the bottom, whereas both foremen and the intermediate group are in the middle of the hierarchy.

Somewhat different is the monthly earnings hierarchy. Foremen are above office workers, and the intermediate group is below the skilled labourers. This order reflects the relative rise of monthly earnings of foremen and skilled labourers in the industrialized socialist society. In inter-war Poland, medium and lower-grade office workers (i.e. those comprised by our group of office workers) had higher earnings not only than foremen but even higher than most technicians. The intermediate group also had higher earnings than the skilled labourers.

These shifts could be recorded precisely because the authors replaced the dichotomic division (manual and non-manual workers) by a more discrete classification of socio-occupational groups. It should be noted, nevertheless, that both the income-per-capita and educational hierarchies are quite similar to those of the inter-war period.

The wage and income differential is much narrower than it used to be in the inter-war period: an 'average' professional earns only twice as much as an 'average' unskilled worker. This relative levelling out of earnings is much more pronounced in Poland than in any other European socialist country. This accounts for a peculiar feature of the stratification system in present-day Poland. In such a situation there is a greater likelihood that other factors than income (e.g. education) have a strong influence on social stratification.

Table 2. *Monthly earnings in socio-professional groups (3 cities)*

io-occupational groups	Monthly earnings (zlotys) Up to 1000 (%)	1001–2000 (%)	2001–3000 (%)	3001–4000 (%)	4001–5000 (%)	above 5000 (%)	Arithmetic mean x	Standard deviation σ	Coefficient of variation V	N = 100%
fessionals	—	10·0	37·6	32·6	14·0	5·8	3177	1064	0·34	300
hnicians	0·4	20·2	59·8	15·0	3·1	1·3	2531	776	0·31	228
eman	—	26·0	59·6	11·4	3·0	—	2416	699	0·29	131
ice employees	0·6	37·0	48·7	9·6	4·1	—	2286	776	0·34	345
lled workers	1·2	51·3	42·5	4·3	0·7	—	2019	631	0·31	602
ermediate group	2·6	62·6	29·2	4·6	1·0	—	1884	642	0·34	304
ii-skilled workers	4·5	62·5	32·4	0·6	—	—	1802	510	0·28	177
skilled workers	6·2	66·9	25·5	1·4	—	—	1755	513	0·29	209

$p < 0.001$ $T = 0.18$ $T' = 0.19$

T = standardized value of Tschuprow's T eliminating dependency of this coefficient on the number of rows and columns in the contingency table.

Table 3. *Income per capita in socio-professional groups (3 cities)*

o-occupational groups	Income per capita (zlotys) up to 400 (%)	401–600 (%)	601–800 (%)	801–1000 (%)	1001–1500 (%)	above 1500 (%)	Arith-metic mean x	Standard devia-tion σ	Coeffic-ient of variation V	Wage earners per family (mean) x	N = 100%
essionals	0·3	5·6	11·0	20·4	37·4	25·3	1236	446	0·36	1·73 1·8 1·7	300
nicians	2·6	9·3	15·5	26·6	33·2	12·8	1052	408	0·39	1·89 1·9 1·8	228
e employees	3·5	12·9	21·9	25·0	27·1	9·6	969	410	0·42	1·87 1·9 1·8	345
men	0·7	12·2	20·6	31·4	25·2	9·9	947	344	0·36	1·76 1·9 1·6	131
mediate group	8·2	22·0	21·6	24·9	18·3	5·0	824	365	0·44	1·80 2·0 1·6	304
d workers	6·8	21·0	26·4	23·9	17·7	4·2	791	343	0·43	1·76 2·0 1·8	602
-skilled workers	7·9	24·3	26·6	23·1	14·1	4·0	789	342	0·43	1·88 2·2 1·7	177
illed workers	14·4	24·0	29·9	20·2	10·1	1·4	733	291	0·40	1·96 2·2 1·7	209

$p < 0.001$ $T = 0.18$ $T' = 0.19$

Arithmetic mean and standard deviation was calculated in relation to nine categories of income per apita; midpoints of class intervals were following: 250, 350, 450, 550, 700, 900, 1250, 1750, 2250. n column 10, centre: mean for all three cities; on the left: mean for Łódź; on the right: mean for zczecin + Koscalin.

Table 4. *Occupation and education (3 cities)*

	Levels of education								
Socio-occupational groups	Complete + uncomplete higher	Complete secondary	Incomplete secondary	Complete elementary	Incomplete elementary	Mean score x	Standard deviation σ	Coefficient of variation V	N 100
Professionals	81·6	15·0	2·7	0·7	—	5·5	0·89	0·16	30
Technicians	11·4	72·8	12·3	3·5	—	3·9	0·64	0·16	22
Office employees	12·8	53·3	22·0	11·6	0·3	3·7	0·94	0·25	34
Foremen	2·3	16·1	36·6	35·1	9·9	2·7	0·99	0·37	13
Intermediate group	1·6	9·2	23·4	50·0	15·8	2·3	0·92	0·40	30
Skilled workers	0·5	5·0	31·0	42·7	20·8	2·2	0·85	0·39	59
Semi-skilled workers	—	1·7	10·3	48·9	39·1	1·7	0·71	0·42	17
Unskilled workers	0·5	3·5	7·1	31·8	57·1	1·7	0·82	0·48	19

$$p < 0\cdot001 \quad T = 0\cdot47 \quad T' = 0\cdot54$$

Scores: incomplete elementary 1, complete elementary 2,
incomplete secondary 3, complete secondary 4,
incomplete higher 5, incomplete higher 6.

Table 5. *Education and monthly earnings (3 cities)*

	Monthly earnings								
Education	up to 1000 (%)	1001–2000 (%)	2001–3000 (%)	3001–4000 (%)	4001–5000 (%)	above 5000 (%)	Arithmetic mean	Standard deviation σ	Coefficient of variation	N 10
Complete higher	—	8·3	29·7	38·5	16·6	7·0	3343	1151	0·34	2
Incomplete higher	1·0	22·0	48·0	22·0	7·0	—	2625	826	0·31	1
Complete secondary	0·6	24·5	58·1	11·6	4·4	0·8	2428	790	0·33	4
Incomplete secondary	1·1	43·6	47·5	6·9	0·9	—	2134	658	0·31	4
Complete elementary	1·9	56·4	37·5	3·7	0·5	—	1954	603	0·31	6
Incomplete elementary	4·7	69·2	25·1	0·5	0·5	—	1755	520	0·30	3

$$p < 0\cdot001 \quad T = 0\cdot25 \quad T' = 0\cdot25$$

Obviously, average earnings are bound to obscure the real differential. It must be noted therefore that minimum monthly earnings have
been set in Poland at 900 zlotys, which means that those few respondents
who were classified in this study below 1,000 zlotys earn in fact close on
1,000 zlotys. (This was the reason for taking 1,000 zlotys as the midpoint
of the class interval 'up to 1,000 zl.'.) The monthly earnings of some
professionals approach 7,000 zlotys (as declared by the respondents). It
will be further noted that some professionals—principally engineers

Table 6. *Occupation, education and monthly earning (3 cities)*

Education	Socio-occupational groups	Monthly earnings (zlotys)				Arithmetic mean of earnings	$N = 100\%$	Level of significance and T coefficient for occupation and earnings when education held constant
		up to 2000 (%)	2001–3000 (%)	3001–4000 (%)	above 4000 (%)			
Complete and incomplete higher	Professionals	9·0	33·1	35·2	22·7	3283	245	$p < 0.01$
	Technicians	11·5	46·2	42·3	—	2808	26	$T = 0.16$
	Office employees	29·5	36·4	22·4	11·4	2659	44	
Complete secondary	Professionals	11·5	57·2	24·4	6·9	2789	45	
	Technicians	18·2	64·2	11·5	6·1	2573	166	$p < 0.02$
	Office employees	29·9	55·0	10·3	4·8	2391	184	$T = 0.12$
	Intermediate group	39·3	46·5	7·1	7·1	2321	28	
	Skilled workers	33·4	56·6	6·7	3·3	2267	30	
Incomplete secondary	Foremen	16·7	58·3	20·8	4·2	2625	48	
	Technicians	42·9	46·4	10·7	—	2179	28	
	Skilled workers	42·1	52·0	5·4	0·5	2141	185	$p < 0.001$
	Office employees	49·4	48·0	1·3	1·3	2047	75	$T = 0.16$
	Intermediate group	60·5	29·6	9·9	—	2028	78	
	Semi-skilled and unskilled workers	62·5	37·5	—	—	1828	32	
Complete elementary	Foremen	36·2	57·4	6·4	—	2202	47	
	Skilled workers	55·3	39·5	4·3	0·9	2002	253	$p < 0.001$
	Intermediate group	67·3	29·3	2·7	0·7	1921	150	$T = 0.13$
	Semi-skilled and unskilled workers	69·6	29·6	0·8	—	1855	148	
Incomplete elementary	Skilled workers	66·6	31·0	1·6	0·8	1857	129	
	Semi-skilled and unskilled workers	77·8	22·2	—	—	1691	190	$p < 0.001$
	Intermediate group	81·4	18·6	—	—	1646	48	$T = 0.20$

and factory managers—receive quite considerable bonuses every three
months for meeting production targets (up to 100 % of their basic
salaries). Their real income is therefore much higher than the average
calculated from their ordinary salaries. On the other hand, the groups at
the lower end of the hierarchy also have higher incomes on account of
odd jobs done by skilled workers outside their workshop (especially
carpenters, painters, blacksmiths, electricians, etc.). Thus the figures
obtained from the questionnaire should be viewed as rough approxima-
tions of reality. The respondents on the whole tended to under-estimate
their real incomes. No attempt was made to probe into the additional
earnings in view of the customary reticence of people on this subject.
Parenthetically speaking, the money earned from odd jobs is often
expended without the earner being able to tell (in retrospect) how much
he had earned over a specific period.

In view of the strong relationship between occupation and education it was necessary to check whether the socio-occupational group is an independent variable differentiating the earnings of the population under investigation. As can be seen from table 6, this is indeed so. The average earnings of people with the same education are differentiated according to their occupations, from which it follows that job affects earnings independently of education. The job must therefore be regarded as a stratificational variable. At the same time Tschuprow's T coefficients of contingency between education and earnings, on the one hand, and between socio-occupational group and earnings, on the other, show (tables 2 and 5) that the former pair of factors is slightly more strongly interrelated than the latter pair.[1]

An interesting feature of our findings is that the average number of employees per family is very similar in all socio-occupational groups (table 3, col. 10). Only working-class families are slightly above the average. This shows that a common pattern of 'income accumulation' is gaining ground throughout Polish society.

The respective difference between professionals and labourers is more pronounced in Łódź than in Szczecin and Koszalin, which may be due to the fact that in Łódź there is an old tradition for wives to work as spinners, and this tradition may persevere in view of the relatively low wages of textile workers (when compared with other industries).

The standard deviations and coefficients of variation calculated for earnings and income per capita in different socio-occupational groups show that in absolute figures there is a greater discrepancy (i.e. a wider inner differential) within the 'higher' than within the 'lower' group, but when relativized to the values of means, these discrepancies of earnings and income are practically of the same magnitude.

(iii) Housing Conditions and Durables

Among the more important aspects of the standard of living are the housing conditions: the technical and sanitary conditions of the home and the number of inhabitants per room. The daily routine of life depends also on the extent to which the family is provided with household gadgets and other durable goods (refrigerator, washing machine, vacuum cleaner, TV set, car, etc.).

The housing conditions and the durables in a home have been used for quite some time as indicators of social status. They were usually incorporated into the 'socio-economic indices' of social status. The present authors recorded and examined these data, too, because they fit into the value distribution concept of stratification.

[1] On corrected T (T') consult: H. M. Blalock, *Social Statistics* (New York, 1960), pp. 229–30.

The standard of housing seems particularly important in Poland in view of the extensive destruction of housing in Polish towns and cities during the Second World War (Szczecin was a heavily tried city in that respect) and the housing policy of the government since the war. The present proportion of people per room in different social groups is the outcome of several successive tendencies in the government's housing policy which varied in its emphasis on egalitarian principles.

The distribution of gadgets appears to be important for somewhat different reasons. Most of these gadgets appeared on the Polish market only 10 to 15 years ago, and their present distribution is not only an indicator of the affluence and cultural advancement of certain social groups but also of their readiness to adopt the new culture patterns in everyday life.

The number of people per room and the technical and sanitary standard of housing were strongly differentiated in Poland before the war.[1] Since 1945 the government has been pursuing a policy of reducing contrasts. Right after the war upper-class and middle-class people used to be deprived of some of their spacious housing with a view to meeting the housing needs of other people in the damaged and overcrowded cities. In the following years the government's policy was to assign flats in newly built residential areas on the basis of fixed norms as regards the number of people per room (or, strictly speaking, per square metre of housing), and little distinction was made between families in terms of either occupation, education or income. The low rents made the modern, well-equipped flats accessible to everyone, even those with lowest income. This was a largely 'egalitarian' policy. Since 1960 there has been a rapid growth of co-operative housing, and this marked the onset of a new differentiation (within certain limits) of housing conditions, the differentiating factor being the financial resources of the family.

The present housing conditions of different categories of the population are reflected by the figures in tables 7–10.

The average number of people per room ranges from 1·1 to 1·8 in the different subgroups which emerged from the distinction between socio-occupational groups, educational status, monthly earnings and income per capita. The differences are relatively small, especially when compared with those of the inter-war period. There is more differentiation in Łódź, the old working-class centre, than in Szczecin or Koszalin, the two cities in north-western Poland where the influx of the Polish population in 1945 made the widespread application of egalitarian principles much easier than in the relatively little damaged old working-class centre.

[1] Cf., e.g., W. Wesołowski, 'Changes in the class structure in Poland', in J. Szczepański (ed.), *Empirical Sociology in Poland* (Warsaw, 1966).

Table 7.   *Occupation and Housing Conditions (3 cities)*

Socio-occupational groups	Persons per room				Persons per room (mean) x	Per cent of apartments in new houses	Per cent of apartments with		N
	1 or less (%)	1·5 (%)	2 (%)	3 and more (%)			plumbing, flush toilet	bathroom, gas, central heating	
Professionals	58·0	26·4	11·4	2·6	1·2 1·3 1·1 1·3	40·6	84·4	51·3	3
Technicians	41·4	30·1	13·2	12·6	1·6 1·3 1·4	22·8	66·7	26·3	2
Office employees	36·8	33·9	16·5	9·8	1·7 1·3 1·6	22·8	68·1	29·3	9
Foremen	31·2	28·6	18·1	10·7	1·7 1·4 1·6	17·4	47·7	20·4	
Intermediate group	30·0	25·9	28·9	14·2	1·9 1·4	15·7	51·6	16·1	
Skilled workers	22·5	26·3	25·0	23·6	1·7 2·1 1·5 1·8	12·6	40·1	13·8	
Semi-skilled and unskilled workers	24·4	22·7	29·9	21·5	2·4 1·5	8·8	33·7	8·8	
	$p < 0.001$ $T = 0.14$ $T' = 0.17$					$p < 0.001$ $T = 0.25$ $T' = 0.39$	$p < 0.001$ $T = 0.26$ $T' = 0.41$	$p < 0.001$ $T = 0.21$ $T' = 0.33$	

Mean calculated from original data on the total number of persons and rooms in each socio-occupational group.
In column 5: centre, mean for all three cities; on the left, mean for Łódź; on the right, mean for Szczecin + Koszalin.

Table 8.   *Education and Housing Conditions (3 cities)*

Education	Persons per room				Persons per room (mean) x	Per cent of apartments in new houses	Per cent of apartments with		
	1 or less (%)	1·5 (%)	2 (%)	3 and more (%)			plumbing, flush toilet	bathroom, gas, central heating	
Complete and incomplete higher	57·6	29·4	9·6	3·4	1·20	42·7	82·7	50·4	
Complete secondary	42·3	30·1	18·1	9·5	1·37	26·1	68·1	32·1	
Incomplete secondary	30·5	29·6	24·3	15·6	1·54	15·2	50·2	15·6	
Complete elementary	22·7	26·4	28·7	22·8	1·69	15·1	42·0	12·8	
Incomplete elementary	21·1	23·5	34·3	21·1	1·80	8·1	33·9	9·1	
	$p < 0.001$ $T = 0.17$ $T' = 0.18$					$p < 0.001$ $T = 0.28$ $T' = 0.39$	$p < 0.001$ $T = 0.33$ $T' = 0.46$	$p < 0.001$ $T = 0.34$ $T' = 0.48$	

Table 9.   *Monthly earnings and housing conditions (3 cities)*

Monthly earnings (zlotys)	Persons per room 1 or less (%)	1·5 (%)	2 (%)	3 or more (%)	Persons per room (mean) x	Per cent of apartments in new houses	plumbing, flush toilet	bathroom, gas, central heating	N = 100%
o 2000	27·5	22·5	29·9	20·1	1·69	10·6	41·8	13·6	1011
2001–3000	34·7	31·4	21·0	12·9	1·48	18·2	57·4	22·4	932
3001–4000	51·1	30·4	12·6	5·9	1·25	34·4	77·2	45·9	221
ver 4000	58·5	24·5	12·8	4·2	1·18	37·3	85·1	56·4	94

$p < 0.001$ $T = 0.13$ $T' = 0.14$ $p < 0.001$ $p < 0.001$ $p < 0.001$
$T = 0.21$ $T = 0.26$ $T = 0.28$
$T' = 0.30$ $T' = 0.37$ $T' = 0.39$

Table 10.   *Income per capita and housing conditions*

Income per capita (zlotys)	Persons per room 1 or less (%)	1·5 (%)	2 (%)	3 and more (%)	Persons per room (mean) x	Per cent of apartments in new houses	plumbing, flush toilet	bathroom, gas, central heating	N = 100%
o to 400	17·9	24·0	43·4	12·4	1·8	9·3	50·4	13·2	129
1–600	19·3	35·1	28·7	15·6	1·7	12·5	51·6	14·6	384
1–800	21·1	28·7	28·3	20·5	1·7	16·7	50·2	19·7	502
1–1000	30·9	28·8	20·8	18·0	1·5	17·9	50·5	20·4	549
01–1500	46·1	24·6	17·3	10·8	1·3	23·5	57·3	29·6	520
ove 1500	64·2	15·4	12·9	6·0	1·1	34·3	67·2	34·3	201

$p < 0.001$ $T = 0.17$ $T' = 0.19$ $p < 0.001$ $p < 0.001$ $p < 0.001$
$T = 0.11$ $T = 0.06$ $T = 0.10$
$T' = 0.16$ $T' = 0.09$ $T' = 0.16$

The other major element of the housing conditions is the technical and sanitary standard of housing. Tables 7–10 also list the percentage of flats in apartment houses built since 1945 (which are as a rule equipped with all modern facilities) as well as the plumbing and central heating facilities regardless of the date of construction. Here the differentiation between socio-occupational groups, educational groups and earning groups is much more pronounced than in the previous instance (cf. the differences in the percentages and in the T coefficients at the bottom of tables 7, 8 and 9). As evidenced in table 7, the professionals and other white-collar groups enjoy better housing conditions than the foremen and the intermediate group, and the three labourer groups have even

Table 11. *Occupation, education, income per capita and housing conditions (3 cities)*

Education	Socio-occupational groups	Income per capita (zlotys)	
		to 1000	over 1000
		Per cent of apartments with less than 1·5 persons per room	
Complete secondary	Professionals	82·6	86·3
	Office employees	70·9	76·5
	Technicians	63·8	70·4
	Intermediate group	48·3	60·0
Complete elementary	Skilled workers and foremen	40·4	51·7
	Semi-skilled and unskilled workers	32·0	38·1

worse housing conditions. It will be noticed that office workers, whose average earnings and incomes are lower than those of the technicians, have a slightly higher percentage of housing with plumbing, gas, bathroom and other facilities. This is being attributed to higher cultural aspirations of the office workers. The intermediate group likewise surpasses the skilled workers in this respect, though the latter have higher earnings. Here again we come upon the influence of subjective needs and aspirations on housing.

Somewhat surprising are the distributions in Table 10. They reveal that the sanitary standard of housing is much less differentiated by income per capita than by other variables (occupation, education, earnings). Nevertheless, income per capita does equally differentiate the number of persons per room (housing density). These phenomena call for further analysis. At any rate, they seem to indicate that housing conditions are by no means more strongly differentiated by the financial resources of the families than by other stratificational variables.

The differences in magnitudes of the T coefficients suggest that education is a more effective determinant of the sanitary standard of housing than is membership in socio-occupational group or earning group.

Because of the existing relations between education, occupation and earnings, it was necessary to check whether housing density is independently affected by each of these variables. It was discovered that this is indeed so. The same analysis was made for occupation, education, income per capita and housing density. By way of example, in table 11 is shown the distribution relative to education, occupation, income per capita and housing density.

Table 12. *Housing conditions: A synthetic hierarchy of socio-occupational groups (Łódź)*

Socio-occupational groups	Mean of standard scores z'	Standard deviation $\sigma_{z'}$	Mean score of evaluation scale
Professionals	398	38	2·99
Office employees	361	40	2·40
Technicians	354	41	2·98
Foremen	348	40	2·42
Intermediate group	343	43	2·27
Skilled workers	338	43	2·17
Semi-skilled workers	336	35	1·95
Unskilled workers	334	33	1·97

In an attempt to develop a hierarchy of socio-occupational groups with synthetic reference to several aspects of the housing conditions the authors applied a measure called 'standard score' (z) (for the time being in relation to the Łódź population).[1]

The resultant ranking of groups is the following: professionals, office workers, technicians, foremen, intermediate group, skilled workers, semi-skilled workers and unskilled workers.

The standard score makes it possible to transform measurable characteristics stated in natural units into a standardized measure expressed in numbers and hence amenable to such arithmetic operations as addition. For example, housing density and possession of bathroom are stated in entirely different natural units, but the standard score enables us to treat them jointly.

Our standard score of 'housing conditions' comprises: (*a*) housing density, or number of persons per room, and (*b*) the availability of the following facilities; plumbing, flush toilet, bathroom, gas, and central heating.

The hierarchy of socio-occupational groups was determined in the following way: (1) aggregate 'z' for each person was calculated, (2) mean 'z' for all respondents in the given socio-occupational category was calculated. Moreover, the standard deviation from 'z' was calculated in order to establish the degree of homogeneity of housing conditions within each group.

The measure 'z' is usually employed to express the aggregate values of measurable characteristics over a continuum. For the purposes of this data treatment, 'z' has been adjusted so as to measure also dichotomized

[1] Cf. G. A. Ferguson, *Statistical Analysis in Psychology and Education* (New York, 1959), pp. 213–14.

characteristics (has a bathroom—has no bathroom, etc.), distinguishing between those facilities which are more common among the given population (lower 'z'), and those which are rare (higher 'z'). As a result, a respondent got a higher score for, e.g., a bathroom than for plumbing.[1]

The hierarchy of socio-occupational groups as determined by the synthetic measure is shown in table 12. The standard deviation of 'z' shows that there is less homogeneity in the middle categories than in the extreme groups of the hierarchy. This means that there is a greater inner differentiation of housing conditions in the middle groups.

Besides the average values of standardized units, table 12 contains the score of self-ratings of housing conditions by the respondents. In response to the question 'How do you assess your housing conditions?', the respondent was given the choice between the following answers: very good, fairly good, fairly poor, very poor. (No 'medium' rating was allowed in view of the respondents' tendency—revealed in earlier

---

[1] The values assigned to unmeasurable two-valued variables (having or not having plumbing, gas, bathroom, etc.) were based on the frequency of appearance of the given property in the population. Usually the values assigned to such two-valued variables are chosen arbitrarily by the researcher. The modified measure 'z' (standard score) made it possible to find a more 'objective' scale of values. This measure was suggested by Dr T. Miller, who holds the Chair of Statistics at Łódź University.

In order to find the value of 'z' for unmeasurable two-valued variables ('having' or 'not having'), the normal distribution N (o·1) was used. This distribution was dichotomized at different points and then the arithmetic mean values of variables (mathematical expectations) were considered for cases situated on both sides of the ultimate value dichotomizing the distribution. For example: if the ultimate value was established for the value $x = 0$ (the division of the normal distribution N [o·1] in two equal parts), the mathematical expectation for $x > 0$ would amount to $+ 0·80$, and for $x < 0$ it would amount to $- 0·80$. In establishing the mathematical expectations, normal distribution N (o·1) tables were used.

Mathematical expectations were treated as the values of 'z' for unmeasurable two-valued variables. Thus, if 50% of the units in the investigated population had a definite property and the remaining 50% had no such property, each unit having this property was assigned a 'z' $= + 0·80$, and each 'no-having' unit, a 'z' $= - 0·80$. Another example: if 30% of the units in the investigated population had a definite property and the remaining 70% had no such property, each unit having this property was assigned a 'z' $= + 1·10$, and each 'non-having' unit, a 'z' $= - 0·50$. Vice versa: if 70% of units in the investigated population had a definite property and the remaining 30% had no such property, each unit having this property was assigned a 'z' $= +0·50$, and each 'non-having' unit, a'z' $= - 1·10$.

In order to avoid negative values, the well-known formula was adopted: $z' = 50 + 10z$. Thus, if 30% of the units in the investigated population had a definite property and the remaining 70% had no such property, each unit having this property was assigned a $z' = 50 + 10(+ 1·10) = 61$, and each non-having unit was assigned $z' = 50 + 10(- 0·50) = 45$.

In this study the following assignments were made, according to the percentage of having and non-having units. Central heating: 64 for having ($\approx$ 20%) and 46 for not having ($\approx$ 80%); bathroom: 63 for having ($\approx$ 25%) and 46 for not having ($\approx$ 75%); toilet: 60 for having ($\approx$ 40%) and 43 for not having ($\approx$ 60%); gas: 59 for having ($\approx$ 45%) and 43 for not having ($\approx$ 55%); sewage: 57 for having ($\approx$ 60%) and 40 for not having ($\approx$ 40%); plumbing: 57 for having ($\approx$ 60%) and 40 for not having ($\approx$ 40%).

Table 13. *Occupation and durables (3 cities)*

Socio-occupational group		Percentage of those who own a			
	TV set	Washing machine	Vacuum cleaner	Refrigerator	$N = 100\%$
Professionals	60·0	87·3	71·3	43·3	300
Technicians	61·4	78·9	52·5	22·8	228
Office employees	52·2	82·3	49·3	20·6	345
Foremen	63·8	81·5	38·5	17·7	131
Intermediate group	47·4	69·2	29·3	13·8	304
Skilled workers	49·3	72·0	24·8	9·1	602
Semi-skilled workers	42·3	65·0	22·1	6·7	177
Unskilled workers	37·0	60·6	9·6	3·7	209

Polish sociological surveys—to 'medium' ratings over a wide range of issues. The excessive percentage of such ratings would make the whole question irrelevant.)

The mean scores listed under column 3 represent the respondents' self-ratings ranked from 4 to 1. A comparison of these mean scores with the group hierarchy obtained from objective data reveals a parallelism of objective conditions and subjective evaluations and suggests that different socio-occupational groups employ quite similar standards in assessing their housing conditions. This is particularly striking in the case of the professionals, whom one might expect to assess their housing conditions less favourably in view of their higher aspirations. The absence of such a tendency among the professionals could be interpreted as evidence of a democratization of this group involving a renunciation of privileges (at least as far as housing is concerned).

The distribution of some durable goods among the socio-occupational groups is shown in table 13 (which lists four durables: TV set, refrigerator, vacuum cleaner, washing machine). For Polish conditions the most expensive of them is the TV set and the least expensive is the vacuum cleaner. And yet the former is evidently more uniformly distributed over the socio-occupational groups than the latter. The TV set is owned by 60 % of professionals and 37 % of unskilled workers. The vacuum cleaner is owned by 71·3 % of professions and 9·6 % of unskilled workers. This demonstrates the influence of culture patterns on spending. It could be hypothesized that technical goods associated with entertainment are more readily assimilated by working-class families than goods designed to assist the woman in her household work and capable of modifying the pattern of family life. This hypothesis is not confuted by the fairly wide distribution of the washing machine in working-class households. The washing machine seems to perform a radically different function in white collar and in blue-collar families. In the former, the machine is used for small-scale laundry, whereas the big pieces go to a public laundry, anyway. In working-class homes, however, the washing machine is used to save money on laundry in general, at the expense of the women, of course.

Our data seem to suggest, especially as far as the distribution of TV sets and vacuum cleaners is concerned, that the possession of durable goods in general is affected by other factors than income. This is not to mean that there is no influence of income whatsoever. The data shown in table 14 illustrate the relationships of refrigerator to occupation and income per capita. Table 15 shows the differentiating influence of both education and occupation on the presence (possession) of the four basic durables.

The standard score was also used as a synthetic measure for determining the hierarchy of socio-occupational groups in terms of the possession of several durable goods. The possession (or absence) of a washing machine, refrigerator, vacuum cleaner, TV set, record-player, camera, motorcycle (or scooter), car and telephone were taken into account.[1] The hierarchy obtained in this way for Łódź is the same as the hierarchy in terms of housing conditions (cf. table 16).

The standard scores for durable goods in Szczecin and Koszalin has not yet been calculated, but the distribution of these goods in these two cities suggest that the hierarchy of socio-economic groups is the same in all three cities.

(iv) Cultural consumption

The questionnaires used in this survey contained various questions referring to what is in Poland called 'cultural consumption', in other words, the absorption by the people of such cultural values as theatre performances, films, television, books, newspapers, etc. The sociologist is naturally concerned with both the quantitative and qualitative aspect of cultural consumption: with how many books are read, but also what books are read (e.g. novels or thrillers).

As pointed out at the beginning of this paper, cultural consumption (in terms of both quantity and quality) was an important differentiating factor in inter-war Poland. Ever since 1945 this clear distinction between the respective ways of life of the professional and the labourer has been diminishing under the impact of various governmental schemes for promoting culture among the less educated classes (the 'dissemination of culture'). The results of this survey are a measure of the success (or failure) of these schemes.

Our data on cultural consumption are apt to be burdened by error

[1] The procedure was the same as described in the preceding footnote.

Table 14. *Occupation, income per capita and refrigerators (3 cities)*

Socio-occupational groups	Income per capita	
	to 1000	over 1000
	Percentage of those who own a refrigerator	
Professionals	31·9	57·5
Technicians	24·2	25·0
Office employees	16·8	25·2
Intermediate group	17·1	24·3
Foremen	11·8	22·6
Skilled workers	8·7	16·3
Semi-skilled workers	6·8	12·5
Unskilled workers	2·9	12·5

Table 15. *Income per capita (601–1000 zl.), occupation, education, socio-occupational groups and durables (3 cities)*

Education	Socio-occupational groups	Percentage of those who own a				$N =$ 100%
		TV set	washing machine	vacuum cleaner	refrigerator	
Complete and incomplete secondary	Technicians	62·7	79·5	45·8	20·5	83
	Office employees	60·1	79·0	45·4	18·0	128
	Foremen	61·3	87·1	38·7	16·2	31
	Intermediate group	64·9	70·6	36·9	14·0	54
	Skilled workers	42·2	70·7	23·9	8·2	109
Complete and incomplete elementary	Foremen	60·2	80·5	31·6	8·3	36
	Intermediate group	54·1	70·2	27·7	13·2	83
	Skilled workers	44·0	71·2	20·1	8·4	191
	Semi-skilled workers	41·5	63·7	19·4	6·5	77
	Unskilled workers	40·3	63·1	14·7	3·2	95

caused by the respondents' apparent tendency to overestimate their participation in cultural values. There are reasons to believe that this tendency is more pronounced among the professionals and in the inter- mediate group comprising those who aspire to the professionals' way of life. On the other hand, the aforementioned promotion of culture among the working class appears to have produced similar effects among the labourers. In an attempt to eliminate the influence of this bias in at least book owning, our interviewers had been instructed to assess the actual number of books in the respondents' homes. Otherwise it was decided to treat the respondents' answers as indicative of their aspira- tions, if not of the actual state of cultural consumption.

Table 16. *Durables: A synthetic hierarchy of
socio-occupational groups (Łódź)*

Socio-occupational groups	Mean of standard scores z'	Standard deviation $\sigma_{z'}$
Professionals	539	40
Technicians	515	28
Office employees	507	35
Foremen	504	22
Intermediate group	491	29
Skilled workers	490	23
Semi-skilled workers	490	33
Unskilled workers	481	24

Our discussion shall be restricted to the data obtained in response to questions concerning: the number of books owned by the respondent and the number of books, novels and magazines read by him. The questions concerning book owning was included in both the Łódź and the Szczecin and Koszalin versions of the questionnaire. The questions concerning reading were included only in the Łódź questionnaire.

Book reading in Poland implies above all reading of Polish and the world's classics, i.e. books of considerable aesthetic and moral value. (By classics are meant also such contemporary authors as Hemingway, Camus, and Sholokhov.) The term newspaper reading is used here to denote the reading of magazines and political and literary weeklies (Przekrój, Panorama, Świat, Polityka, Kultura), i.e. newspapers which represent mass culture of medium and high standard.

In tables 17 to 19 are shown the percentages of certain answers (usually the two extremes) as chosen by the respondents from the alternatives printed in the questionnaire.

As can be seen from the percentage distributions in table 17, the socio-occupational groups are ranked by cultural consumption quite similarly as by housing conditions and the possession of durables. Thus there is a marked parallelism in the consumption of the goods of technical civilization and the consumption of cultural values (whether actual or aspired).

The three groups of white-collar workers (professionals, technicians and office workers) are at the top of the hierarchy. The professionals rank highest in all three spheres of cultural consumption, whereas there is a reshuffle of technicians and office workers as regards book reading and newspaper reading. The middle of the hierarchy is occupied by foremen and the intermediate group. The three groups of manual workers are at the bottom.

Table 17.   *Occupation and Reading (Łódź)*

ocio-occupational group	Per cent of those who have no books at home	Per cent of those who have more than 50 books	Per cent of those who within 2 months did not read any books	Per cent of those who within 2 months read at least 3 books	Per cent of those who do not read weeklies	Per cent of those who read weeklies regularly	$N =$ 100%
'rofessionals	14·3	83·7	20·9	41·8	3·3	91·2	91
Technicians	15·5	65·5	29·3	32·8	12·1	69·0	58
)ffice employees	24·8	50·6	30·1	37·6	19·4	62·4	93
'oremen	34·2	31·7	59·5	21·5	30·4	30·0	79
ntermediate group	54·2	17·2	59·8	13·1	41·8	37·0	122
killed workers	51·2	20·1	62·5	17·4	44·7	35·8	293
emi-skilled workers	62·6	15·3	59·3	20·3	67·8	23·9	59
Jnskilled workers	66·7	8·9	77·8	10·0	68·9	21·1	90
	$p < 0.001$ $T = 0.22$ $T' = 0.30$		$p < 0.001$ $T = 0.18$ $T' = 0.22$		$p < 0.001$ $T = 0.24$ $T' = 0.32$		

In columns 3 and 6 we find a considerable difference between office workers and foremen, which may be viewed as the 'threshold' between clearly white-collar and the remaining groups. (The percentage of those who failed to read even one book in the past two months was 30 among office workers and nearly 60 among foremen, and the respective difference in regular newspaper reading was 62·4 and 30.) Reading habits appear to be singularly resistant to change. At any rate, office workers have much stronger reading aspirations than foremen.

In the educational hierarchy, a distinct threshold occurs between primary education and primary vocational education, on the one hand, and incomplete secondary education on the other (cf. table 18), which can be taken to mean that the very frequenting of a secondary school (even for a limited period) is instrumental in developing reading habits, or at least, that attending schools above primary level contributes to the adoption of the personality pattern of a 'reading person'. There is also a clear distinction between incomplete secondary and complete secondary education.

In fact, education has proved to be a somewhat stronger differentiating factor than occupation and monthly earnings with regard to all three spheres of cultural consumption. This can be seen from the T coefficients at the bottom of tables 17–19.

Along each of the three dimensions (occupations, education and earnings), newspaper reading was found to differentiate the population more strongly than book reading and the number of books at home. Thus newspaper reading can best serve as a simple indicator of cultural stratification—a result which runs counter to our expectations.

Table 18.   *Education and Reading (Łódź)*

Education	Per cent of those who		Per cent of those who within 2 months		Per cent of those who		N = 100%
	have no books at home	have more than 50 books	did not read any books	read at least 3 books	do not read weeklies	read weeklies regularly	
Complete and Incomplete higher	7·8	77·0	17·7	46·7	—	83·3	90
Complete secondary	22·7	59·7	30·0	33·6	13·6	69·3	140
Incomplete secondary	33·4	33·9	40·1	31·9	26·6	55·0	207
Complete elementary	55·8	18·7	62·0	16·6	46·0	33·5	337
Incomplete elementary	66·0	9·6	84·1	2·7	68·8	16·7	221

$p < 0.001$ $T = 0.26$ $T' = 0.31$ $p < 0.001$ $T = 0.24$ $T' = 0.26$ $p < 0.001$ $T = 0.30$ $T' = 0.36$

Table 19.   *Monthly earning and reading (Łódź)*

Monthly earnings (zlotys)	Per cent of those who		Per cent of those who within 2 months		Per cent of those who		N = 100%
	have no books at home	have more than 50 books	did not read any books	read at least 3 books	do not read weeklies	read weeklies regularly	
to 2000	53·7	18·5	62·1	18·3	51·6	32·9	471
2001–3000	36·7	37·8	46·9	25·6	25·9	53·1	305
3001–4000	19·7	74·3	36·4	25·8	16·7	62·1	66
over 4000	10·0	77·5	27·5	35·0	2·5	87·5	40

$p < 0.001$ $T = 0.22$ $T' = 0.26$ $p < 0.001$ $T = 0.19$ $T' = 0.21$ $p < 0.001$ $T = 0.26$ $T' = 0.31$

In view of the relatively smaller differentiating effect of monthly earnings, the authors decided to include income per capita in their advanced statistical analysis. From among the three cultural factors (number of books owned, the reading of books, and the reading of newspapers), the 'private library' was chosen as the most reliable indicator in view of the interviewer's capability of checking the number of books owned by the respondent. As is shown in tables 20 to 22, the private library proved to be independently differentiated by education, occupation, and income per capita. As can be seen from the T co-efficients at the foot of the tables, occupation is a stronger differentiating factor in the higher education groups than in the lower education groups as well as in the higher income groups than in the lower income groups.

Table 20.   *Occupation, education and books (3 cities)*

Socio-occupational groups	Education			p and T for education and books when occupation is held constant
	Complete secondary	Incomplete secondary	Complete elementary	
	Per cent of those who own more than 50 books			
Professionals	58·1	x	x	$p < 0.001$ $T = 0.30$
Office employees	65·2	40·8	20·0	$p < 0.001$ $T = 0.38$
Technicians	50·0	35·7	x	$p < 0.01$ $T = 0.29$
Intermediate group	38·0	26·4	13·6	$p < 0.001$ $T = 0.37$
Foremen	33·3	29·6	19·6	$p < 0.05$ $T = 0.32$
Skilled worker	30·3	23·5	15·8	$p < 0.001$ $T = 0.24$
Semi-skilled and unskilled worker	x	15·4	1·6	$p < 0.001$ $T = 0.45$
p and T for occupation and books when education is held constant	$0 < 0.001$ $T = 0.28$	$p < 0.01$ $T = 0.26$	$p < 0.001$ $T = 0.22$	

x = percentage not computed because group N was smaller than 30 (applies to all tables).

Table 21.   *Occupation, income per capita and books (3 cities)*

Socio-occupational groups	Income per capita (zlotys)			p and T for income and books when occupation is held constant
	to 600	601–1000	over 1000	
	Per cent of those who own more than 50 books			
Professionals	x	71·3	79·9	$p < 0.05$ $T = 0.27$
Office employees	37·5	54·7	66·0	$p < 0.05$ $T = 0.30$
Technicians	x	51·5	54·8	$p < 0.02$ $T = 0.31$
Foremen	23·5	26·5	37·0	$p < 0.05$ $T = 0.23$
Intermediate group	15·7	20·7	21·3	$p < 0.10$ $T = 0.18$
Skilled workers	11·4	16·6	27·9	$p < 0.10$ $T = 0.21$
Semi-skilled and unskilled workers	3·6	10·9	14·3	$p < 0.05$ $T = 0.22$
p and T for occupation and books when income is held constant	$p < 0.01$ $T = 0.23$	$p < 0.001$ $T = 0.27$	$p < 0.02$ $T = 0.26$	

(v) *Psychological aspects of social differentiation*

In the section devoted to the psychological aspects of social differentiation the questionnaires used in Szczecin and Koszalin contained three
sets of questions concerning: (1) the respondent's assessment of his own
social status, (2) the respondent's awareness of class and strata distinctions in society, and (3) the respondent's self-identification with a

Table 22.   *Occupation, education, income per capita and books at home (3 cities)*

Education	Socio-occupational groups	Income per capita (zlotys)		p and T for income and books when education and occupation are held constant	
		to 1000	over 1000		
		Per cent of those who own more than 50 books			
	Professionals	63·6	77·7	$p < 0·10$	$T = 0·22$
Complete	Office employees	58·9	76·5	$p < 0·10$	$T = 0·15$
secondary	Technicians	48·1	51·9	$p < 0·10$	$T = 0·11$
Complete	Skilled workers and foremen	13·2	28·8	$p < 0·10$	$T = 0·19$
elementary	Intermediate group	12·5	16·6	$p < 0·10$	$T = 0·18$
	Semi-skilled and unskilled workers	7·8	9·5	$p < 0·10$	$T = 0·16$

class or stratum. We shall discuss in this paper some of the questions within set (2).

The first question opening the whole battery was: 'Do you think that the inhabitants of the city fall into distinct social groups, strata or classes?' The alternative replies were: 'yes, quite distinctly', 'yes, but not so clearly', 'no, can't tell'. The second question was 'If so, what are these distinctions? (You may name more than one distinction, indicating the character of each.)'

By using three different terms in the first question (groups, strata, classes) it was hoped to provide more room for positive replies. For example, the connotations of the term 'class' are in Poland such that only the working class and the farmers' class, and possibly the 'intelligentsia', may come to mind. It was further hoped that the answers would reveal different views on the structuralization of society. The authors assumed that not many respondents would name social groups completely unrelated to strata or classes, and that even then their replies would be of some value, for instance by showing that other than stratificational distinctions were perceived more clearly in one city than in another city.

The results of the questionnaire indicate that most respondents had in mind stratificational distinctions when answering that question. The answers varied greatly in their concrete formulations but it has been possible to classify them into several types. The most numerous were those answers in which traditional class distinctions (between the working class and the 'intelligentsia') (the latter term subsuming professionals, technicians, and office worker) were listed, or else those stating (in more or less vague terms) distinctions along such stratificational

Table 23. *Occupation and psychological aspects of social differentiation*

				Percentage of those who				
Socio-occupational groups	State the existence of		state a smaller differentiation now	postulate differences in income[1]		claim to ascribe equal prestige to all occupations	believe that other people ascribe different prestige	N = 100 %
	class and strata distinctions	animosity between class and strata		small	great			
	1	2	3	4	5	6	7	
rofessionals	82·3	32·1	93·9	50·7	44·9	63·1	74·7	209
ffice employees	82·1	25·3	91·7	63·9	29·3	62·7	70·6	252
echnicians	77·2	36·5	91·8	60·6	34·1	60·6	61·7	170
itermediate group	66·5	30·8	81·3	66·5	28·0	60·4	70·4	182
remen	64·2	30·5	94·3	71·7	20·8	71·7	62·2	53
illed workers	77·6	31·0	92·2	71·4	18·8	64·3	65·2	308
emi-skilled and iskilled workers	71·7	31·2	76·9	70·5	16 9	56·1	67·1	237

[1] The third possible answer was: 'none'

dimensions as occupation, education (sometimes more generally: 'culturedness'), standard of living, power, and prestige. One more distinction was named in any appreciable number of answers (15 %), namely the regional or ethnic distinction between those who came to the city in 1945 'from beyond the Bug river', and those 'from Poznan region', and also between 'Poles' and 'Ukrainians'. The regional-ethnic distinction, however, was nearly always accompanied by a stratificational distinction.

As can be seen from table 23, the awareness of social distinctions is universal (col. 1), whereas the view that there are animosities between classes and strata is much less widespread (col. 2). Further, the view is very widespread that social distinctions are less conspicuous now than they used to be in the inter-war period (col. 3). The predominant opinion among all groups (though not uniformly) is that the wage differential should not be so great. People of different occupations are frequently assigned equal prestige (col. 7). These answers suggest that egalitarian ideals have won the upper hand among the city inhabitants in Poland.

There is a distinct discrepancy in the prestige evaluations of the respondents themselves and the views ascribed by them to other people (cf. columns 6 and 7). A majority of our respondents believe that city inhabitants assess the prestige of different occupations differently, whereas they themselves claim to ascribe equal prestige to all occupations. This discrepancy will require further studies, but it may be due to a certain dissonance in the systems of value in the current historical period. No positive correlation between such discrepant prestige evaluations and membership in civic or political organizations was discovered, contrary to expectations.

Additional evidence was obtained from a further question put to those respondents who had declared to ascribe equal prestige to all occupations ('egalitarianists'). They were presented with a list of twenty occupations and asked to assess the prestige of each (five scores: very high, high, average, low, very low). By far the most 'egalitarianists' differentiated these occupations in terms of prestige, in defiance of their earlier declaration. Their 'egalitarianism' seemed to extend to the general ideological principle that each job is of equal value, but stopped short of actual occupational differentiation.[1]

As far as other aspects of social awareness are concerned, interesting differences between socio-occupational groups were obtained. The highest percentage of the answer 'Society in Poland falls into classes and strata' (see under col. 1) was chosen by the white-collar groups and the lowest percentage by the labourer groups. The percentages of answers concerning 'dislike' did not reveal any clear-cut linear differences between the groups.

This tendency seems even more striking if we consider that manual labourers are by no means those who have the largest share in material values, education, cultural values, housing, etc. Sociologists have usually suggested that the lower groups within a stratification system tend to view the system as more steeply stratified than the upper groups. The findings of this survey suggest that the social revolution in Poland has resulted in radical shifts in the psychological plane.

In contrast, the views concerning occupational differences in income coincided with the investigators' expectations. Among the better-off professionals 44·9 % stated that income differences should be great, and the percentage of this answer declines as we pass from group to group, reaching a mere 16·9 % in the group of semi-skilled and unskilled workers.

The opinions on income differentiation are most strongly correlated with levels of earnings. Among those earning below 2,000 zlotys per

---

[1] Differentiated evaluations of occupations were revealed in earlier studies of occupation prestige in Poland (cf. A. Sarapata and W. Wesołowski, 'The evaluation of occupations by Warsaw inhabitants', *American Journal of Sociology* (May 1961), pp. 581–91). Furthermore, a high consistency of differentiated occupation ratings (in terms of prestige) among both urban and rural population in Poland was recently demonstrated by Michał Pohoski (using, among others, Gutman's scale). In a country like Poland, where the system of values is subject to rapid change and quite discordant standards exist side by side, various aspects of the people's social awareness, revealed in different contexts, in both overt and verbal behaviour, should be subjected to a thorough analysis.

Table 24. *Monthly earnings and psychological aspects of social differentiation (Szczecin + Koszalin)*

	Percentage of those who							
	state the existence of		State a smaller differentiation now	postulate differences in income		claim to ascribe equal prestige to all occupations	believe that other people ascribe different prestige	N =
Monthly earnings (zlotys)	class and strata distinctions	animosity between class and strata		small	great			100%
	1	2	3	4	5	6	7	
to 2000	71·9	31·5	81·3	68·0	22·8	61·0	66·8	552
2001–3000	77·5	29·0	89·3	62·0	26·9	62·0	68·0	642
3001–4000	84·0	30·4	93·7	55·1	35·1	35·4	69·7	158
over 4000	77·6	46·3	88·9	29·6	61·1	59·2	74·1	54

Table 25. *Education and psychological aspects of social differentiation (Szczecin + Koszalin)*

	Percentage of those who							
	state the existence of		state a smaller differentiation	postulate differences in income		claim to ascribe equal prestige to all occupations	believe that other people ascribe different prestige	N =
Education	class and strata distinctions	animosity between class and strata		small	great			100%
	1	2	3	4	5	6	7	
complete and incomplete higher	84·5	32·5	91·0	54·1	46·3	60·8	73·2	240
complete secondary	80·5	34·4	92·7	61·0	32·9	63·1	68·3	352
incomplete secondary	74·5	31·1	88·7	73·6	21·6	64·6	67·1	264
complete elementary	72·1	29·5	85·0	69·7	19·1	61·8	66·6	357
incomplete elementary	67·7	30·3	75·3	65·1	22·2	57·7	65·7	198

Table 26.   *Education, occupation, monthly earnings*
and postulates of differences in income

Education	Socio-occupational groups	Monthly earnings (zlotys)		
		to 2000	2001 3000	over 3000
		Percentage of those who postulate great differences in income		
Complete and	Professionals	x	41·3	46·4
incomplete higher	Office employees	x	36·4	46·7
	Technicians	x	30·0	45·4
Complete	Professionals	x	52·9	55·5
secondary	Technicians	26·4	32·9	52·6
	Office employees	21·6	32·9	50·0
Incomplete	Intermediate group	30·0	35·3	x
secondary	Foremen	x	27·3	33·3
Complete	Intermediate group	29·7	34·5	x
elementary	Foremen	x	30·0	40·0
	Skilled workers	18·7	20·0	x
	Semi-skilled and unskilled workers	7·7	26·5	x
Incomplete	Skilled workers	16·1	25·0	x
elementary	Semi-skilled and unskilled workers	27·2	3·4	x

month only 22·8% expressed the view that there should be a great income differentiation. Among those earning more than 4,000 zlotys this percentage rose to 61·1.

Nevertheless, education and occupation are independently differentiating factors in relation to the opinions on that subject, as follows from table 26. But there is one important exception. Among manual workers the regularities are somewhat obscure; there is no clear positive relationship between level of education and 'elitarian' opinions on income differentiation between the occupations.

The studied population was somewhat more clearly differentiated by the answers to the question discussed above than by the answers to the remaining aforementioned questions concerning psychological aspects of social differentiation, and this is why the authors decided to discuss the former in more detail. It must be recalled, however, that the most striking finding was the absence of clearly antagonistic attitudes and views among the socio-occupational, educational and earning groups as revealed in the answers to the question concerning 'animosity' or 'dislike' between groups. This may be due to the fact that the labourers, whose participation in values is still the lowest of all the socio-occupational groups, have in fact benefited more than any other group from the social revolution in the country. This alone must have reduced their dislike of the better-off groups. The better-off groups, and especially the professionals, on the other hand, have had their participation in such values as income clearly reduced, but this has not caused them to dislike the workers. Generally speaking, the reduction of differences in income has brought the socio-occupational groups closer together, also contributing to a decline in mutual animosity.

CONCLUSIONS

The data presented in this paper deal with the following questions:

(1) The hierarchy of socio-occupational groups as determined by the groups' participation in values. The degree of this participation was determined either by the average level of value participation within the group (e.g. mean earnings, or mean score of education of all respondents in the given group), or by the percentage of those members of the given group who share in the given value (e.g. the percentage of respondents in a given group who possess a refrigerator or read books).

(2) The scale of difference between the two extreme groups in the hierarchy of groups; in other words, the range of inequalities.

(3) The extent to which the four basic stratificational variables (occupation, education, earnings, and income per capita) determine a group's participation in the values of the second tier (e.g. housing conditions and cultural activities).

(4) Some of the psychological aspects of social differentiation, and, specifically, the crystallization of strata consciousness as affected by the unequal distribution of first-tier and second tier values.

Whether we take as an indicator average education, or the synthetic measure of housing conditions, or the synthetic measure of durables in possession of the respondents, or the reading of books or newspapers, or the number of books in what we call the private library—the hierarchy of socio-occupational groups is roughly the same in all instances. The only marked deviation occurs when we consider socio-occupational groups in terms of earnings.

The highest participation in all values is revealed by the professionals, who are followed by the two other groups of white-collar workers. Then come the foremen and the intermediate group. At the lower end of this hierarchy are the three groups of blue-collar workers.

There is nothing extraordinary in this order, for white-collar workers are everywhere better off than blue-collar workers. There is, however, an exception: it is the group hierarchy as determined by earnings. Here foremen are ahead of office employees and skilled workers are above the intermediate group. These shifts are a *signum temporis*, an indicator of the system we live in. But they have no parallel in the participation in other values, especially the values of spiritual culture. There are evidently some obstacles to the foremen's and skilled workers' promotion in what might be broadly called culture absorption. A possible explanation of the nature of these obstacles might be sought in the sphere of personality, as shaped by the cultural class-heritage. It is a well grounded sociological assertion that the people from the lower strata have lower cultural aspirations as a result of their rearing, influenced, in turn, by the life conditions of their parents.

The overall hierarchy of socio-occupational groups is rather traditional, but there are some significant shifts in comparison with the situation between the two world wars. There is first of all the striking reversal in the order of office employees and technicians. In inter-war Poland the technicians were below office employees, and now the order is reversed. The same is probably the case in all the other socialist countries, and possibly also in advanced industrial societies in general.

There are less conspicuous changes around the middle and at the bottom of the hierarchy. But although no reversals were noted among the middle and bottom groups, there have been some important shifts between foremen, the intermediate group and the skilled workers. In comparison with the inter-war period there is first of all a marked improvement in the relative position of the skilled workers, who were much worse off than the foremen and the members of the intermediate group before the last war. To-day, all three groups are in nearly the same situation in numerous instances. This bears out the relative improvement in the position of the skilled workers.

Another thing to be noted in our hierarchies is the discrepancy in the scale of differences for different values. Though the respective figures do not lend themselves to direct comparisons (e.g. we cannot compare mean earnings with the percentage of those who read at least two books), we are entitled to some common-sense observations. And so, we find that the scale of earnings is not large. The differences in education are still rather great because there is a high percentage of workers without full elementary education. As for housing conditions, several elements must be taken into consideration. Differences in housing density have been markedly reduced, but the differences in the technical standard of housing are still quite pronounced.

Reading habits are a fairly strong differentiating factor. On the whole, the differentiation in the absorption of cultural values appears to be more resistant to change than in the absorption of other values. Special significance should be attributed to what might be called a distinct reading threshold between the manual and non-manual groups. Here the burden of the past seems to be the heaviest.

The following relationships were discovered in the groups' participation in various values:

(1) Education and occupation are independently related to earnings.

(2) Occupation, education, and income per capita are independently related to housing conditions, possession of durables, and possession of books. Thus the three basic values are stratifying variables which independently differentiate the groups' participation in the values of the second tier. The most distinct relationships are associated with education and occupation as the independent variables, but the differences in the strength of the relationships (measured by Tschuprow's T coefficient) are not very great.

Finally, in the visualization of social distinctions, as revealed by our respondents, there were no crystallizations of strata consciousness comparable with the objective distribution of values. In other words, members of groups which differ markedly in the participation in various values did not reveal equally marked differences in their visualization of social distinctions. This phenomenon can be ascribed, no doubt, to the social revolution accomplished in Poland and the social transformations which took place in the past twenty years.

9

SOCIAL STRATIFICATION
IN AUSTRALIA

LEONARD BROOM, F. LANCASTER JONES AND
JERZY ZUBRZYCKI

INTRODUCTION

The existence of an Australian stratification system has not been readily acknowledged by historians or other trained observers in any important sense, and just as all men are reputed to be born free and equal 'in the bright glow and warm presence of the American Dream',[1] so Australians have been said to assume the existence of 'fair and reasonable standards for everyone'—an assumption institutionalized in 1907 by the Arbitration Court with the introduction of a national basic wage.[2] However, social reality presents a rather more complicated picture than such idealized accounts suggest.

In the penal settlements out of which early Australia grew, the major social division was between the 'emancipists' (or ex-convicts) and the 'exclusives' (free-born landowners, officials and officers of the garrison), breeding what one author describes as 'the stultifying hostility' between the two groups.[3] But the gold rushes of the 1850s, which attracted large numbers of immigrants with varied occupational and social origins, quickly made this division largely irrelevant, introduced in its place new social distinctions, and saw the consolidation of a distinctive working-class movement. The historical documentation of this movement in the form of trade unionism and its subsequent extension into radical politics is a major theme of an influential school of Australian historiography, represented by such writers as V. G. Childe, H. V. Evatt, Robin Gollan,

---

[1] W. Lloyd Warner, *Social Class in America* (New York, 1960), p. 3.
[2] See W. K. Hancock in *Cambridge History of the British Empire*, vol. 7, p. 510. For recent summaries of the literature on stratification in Australia see A. F. Davies and S. Encel, 'Class and status', in Davies and Encel (eds.), *Australian Society: A Sociological Introduction* (Melbourne, 1965); and Kurt B. Mayer, 'Social stratification in two equalitarian societies: Australia and the United States', *Social Research*, vol. 31, no. 4 (Winter 1964), pp. 435–65.
[3] R. M. Crawford, 'The Australian national character', *Journal of World History*, vol. II, no. 3 (1955), p. 707.

Russel Ward, and Brian Fitzpatrick.[1] Indeed in many respects their historical writings provide an important key to the understanding of Australia's political and social history.

Yet the idea of an egalitarian paradise characterized by a wide working-class base set against a small aristocracy of independent men represents an oversimplified model of Australian society, even in the late nineteenth century. There is abundant evidence in the writings of contemporary observers (such as E. J. Brady, R. E. N. Twopeny, Francis Adams, T. A. Coghlan, and Albert Métin[2]) that any analysis of Australian society in the latter half of the nineteenth century must take into account a much greater variety of social groups, not all of them based exclusively on economic factors. For example, none of the above writers doubted the existence of effective middle or intermediate class groups, and although they were usually less easily identified and tended not to display the militant solidarity of the working-class movement, the middle-class nature of bodies in the temperance movement, the philanthropic and mutual improvement associations was readily apparent.[3] Moreover, such groups constantly recruited new members and were thus an important medium of social mobility.

It was not until after the Second World War that the assumptions underlying the radical interpretation of Australian society received an empirical test. As in the United States a decade or more earlier, the necessary data on social stratification did not exist for the total society. Consequently those interested in the study of stratification were obliged to concentrate upon social units amenable to analysis by available

[1] V. G. Childe, *How Labour Governs: a Study of Workers' Representation in Australia*, London 1923; H. V. Evatt, *Australian Labor Leader: the Study of W. A. Holman and the Labor Movement* (Sydney, 1940); Robin Gollan, *Radical and Working Class Politics: a Study of Eastern Australia, 1850–1910* (Melbourne, 1960); Russel Ward, *The Australian Legend* (Melbourne, 1958); Brian Fitzpatrick, *The Australian Commonwealth* (Melbourne, 1956).

[2] E. J. Brady, 'The clerk and the capitalist', *The Centennial Magazine*, vol. 3, no. 2 (September 1890), pp. 93–6; R. E. N. Twopeny, *Town Life in Australia* (London, 1883), esp. pp. 104–12; Francis Adams, *The Australians—a Social Sketch* (London, 1893); T. A. Coghlan, *Wealth and Progress of New South Wales, 1894* (Sydney, 1896), p. 531; Albert Métin, *Le Socialisme Sans Doctrines*, Paris 1901. As the Government Statistician in New South Wales (1886–1905) Coghlan was responsible for an annual survey *Wealth and Progress of New South Wales* which included, amongst other data, employment statistics. In his analysis of the 1891 census Coghlan showed that in the total male workforce of 382,000 there were two relatively large groups of 'employers' (53,000) and 'persons working on their own account' (58,000) who could not be rightly classified with the 'working class'. The latter presumably included 245,000 'wage-earners'. The French scholar Métin visited Australia in 1899 to observe at first hand the conditions which he later described as 'Le paradis des ouvriers'. He also found lack of any doctrinal basis in the emerging Labour parties.

[3] J. D. Bollen, 'The temperance movement and the Liberal party in New South Wales politics, 1900–1904', *Journal of Religious History*, 1 (1960–1), 160–82; Allan Barcan, 'The development of the Australian middle class', *Past and Present*, 1954–55, pp. 67, 73; and N. B. Nairn, 'The political mastery of Sir Henry Parkes: New South Wales politics', *Journal of the Royal Historical Society*, vol. 53, Part 1 (March 1967), p. 39.

methods, and the local community was the obvious choice. The first survey to throw light on people's ideas about social stratification in Australia was carried out in 1949–50 by the Department of Psychology in the University of Melbourne as part of an international UNESCO project on communities and social tension.[1] Interviews were conducted with a small sample of adults and school children in Melbourne and a Victorian country town, and among other things findings on the behavioural characteristics of the sample, such as place of residence, political preference and occupational aspirations, were related to subjective class identification. Interestingly enough, this pioneering study employed a deliberately open question on class identification ('A society is made up of groups of people. To what part of society do you belong?'), but most respondents interpreted this as a question about social class and gave replies that revealed broad uniformities in class terminology. The most frequent response in this study, as in others since, was 'middle class' or 'working class'.[2] However, similarities in class terminology masked some differences in the way respondents saw the different classes in society (their class schemes), an area of stratification research studied in detail more recently by Davies.[3]

The wide recognition of social stratification as a fact of social life has similarly been demonstrated by national surveys of occupational prestige and voting behaviour. Congalton's study[4] of the social grading of occupations conducted in six State capitals in 1963 (and preceded by local surveys in Sydney and Perth[5]) revealed a hierarchical grading of occupations broadly consistent with degree of skill, amount of education and, to a lesser degree, level of earnings. Alford,[6] in his analysis of the results of five Gallup Polls conducted between 1955 and 1961, also found consistent relationships between voting and social class defined variously in terms of education, income, subjective social class, or trade union membership conjointly with occupation.

[1] O. A. Oeser and S. B. Hammond (eds.), *Social Structure and Personality in a City* and O. A. Oeser and F. E. Emery (eds.), *Social Structure and Personality in a Rural Community* (London, 1954). There are of course some interesting, but rather slender, data reported for Australia in William Buchanan and Hadley Cantril, *How Nations See Each Other: A Study in Public Opinion* (Urbana, 1953).

[2] Oeser and Hammond, *op. cit.* p. 265.

[3] A. F. Davies, *Images of Class: An Australian Study* (Sydney, 1967).

[4] Athol A. Congalton, *Occupational Status in Australia* (Sydney, 1963). For a methodological assessment of Congalton's work see John D. Allingham, 'On the measurement of occupational prestige', *The Australian and New Zealand Journal of Sociology*, vol. 1, no. 1 (1965) and Congalton's rejoinder, 'Methodology of research into occupational prestige: Reply to Allingham', *The Australian and New Zealand Journal of Sociology*, vol. 1, no. 2 (1965).

[5] See R. A. Taft, 'Social grading of occupations in Australia', *British Journal of Sociology*, vol. 4, no. 2, 1953; A. A. Congalton, *Social Standing of Occupations in Sydney*, Sydney 1962.

[6] Robert R. Alford, *Party and Society: the Anglo-American Democracies* (Chicago, 1963), pp. 105–6.

Apart from these studies empirical research into social stratification in Australia is meagre in the extreme. There is, for example, no work which attempts a delineation of the Australian system of stratification, no general or indeed local studies comparable to those which exist for the United States or Great Britain. The concept of social class in its various connotations has been employed by sociologists, educationists, psychologists and political scientists as a correlate of a particular kind of behaviour they were studying.[1] But while such studies have led to a gradual accumulation of relevant evidence, there has been no parallel effort directed to theorizing about the structure and functions of social stratification in Australia. Yet, as noted above, class explanations of Australian society have been readily put forward by both participants and observers.

The present paper reports the preliminary results of a nationwide survey designed to provide a first approximation to delineating the social stratification of Australia. We do not at this point set out to give a fully articulated theoretical statement, since to do so would necessitate general statements about other aspects of Australia's social structure, the evidence for which has yet to be accumulated. When the results of this study, and other interdependent projects, have been fully analysed, it will be possible to move closer towards that goal.

The present survey was designed so that for the first time in Australia nationwide data permitting detailed analysis of the inter-relationships among the major components of the stratification system could be assembled. In an attempt to identify major social strata and to locate the position of individual Australians in them, we sought information on five measures of social rank. Two of these were subjective measures of rank position (subjective social class identification and interviewer's assessment of the respondent's 'economic class'), and three were objec-

---

[1] While this paper does not attempt to summarize the publications in all these fields the following items are relevant to the discussion of our findings: A. Barcan, 'Education and Catholic social status', *Australian Quarterly*, vol. 34 (March 1962), pp. 47–61; G. W. Bassett, 'The occupational background of teachers', *Australian Journal of Education*, vol. 2 (1958), pp. 79–90; Creighton Burns, *Parties and People* (Melbourne, 1961); A. F. Davies, 'The child's discovery of social class', *The Australian and New Zealand Journal of Sociology*, vol. 1, no. 1 (1965), pp. 21–37; and *Images of Class: an Australian Study* (Sydney, 1967); S. B. Hammond, 'Stratification in an Australian city', in G. E. Swanson *et al. Readings in Social Psychology* (New York, 1952); A. F. Davies, 'Concepts of social class', *Australian Journal of Politics and History*, vol. 2, no. 1 (1956), pp. 84–93; N. F. Dufty, 'Relationship between paternal occupation and occupational choice', *International Journal of Comparative Sociology*, vol. 2, no. 1 (1961), pp. 81–7; W. C. Radford, *School-leavers in Australia 1959–60* (Melbourne, 1962); S. Encel, 'The political élite in Australia', *Political Studies*, vol. 9, no. 1 (1961), pp. 16–36; R. Taft, 'The social grading of occupations in Australia', *British Journal of Sociology*, vol. 4 (June 1953), pp. 181–7; H. Y. Tien, *Social Mobility and Controlled Fertility* (1965); Leonard Broom and Richard J. Hill, 'Opinion polls and social rank in Australia: methods and first findings', *The Australian and New Zealand Journal of Sociology*, vol. 1, no. 2 (Oct. 1965), pp. 97–106.

tive attributes of the respondent: income, occupation, and education. Thus we are in a position to ask not simply how the respondent sees himself and is seen by others in the stratification system, but also to what extent these subjective evaluations are a function of widely used objective criteria of social ranking. In addition to these data information was also obtained on demographic characteristics, residential mobility, career and generational mobility, political affiliation, religion, ethnic origin, and life style correlates. The present paper, however, is limited to a consideration of our findings on the five measures of social rank, and aims at a first statement of the social stratification of Australia's population through an examination of the interrelationships among them.

THE SAMPLE

The data reported in this paper were obtained in a national survey (February–May 1965) of Australia's adult male workforce. The interviews were conducted by the Roy Morgan Research Centre Pty Ltd (Australian Gallup Poll) for the Department of Sociology at the Australian National University. Some supplementary interviews were conducted by the Department in rural areas of New South Wales, Victoria and Western Australia.[1] The sample, which was drawn by the Australian Gallup Poll, used a two-stage probability design, the first stage of which involved selecting 23 of the 122 Federal Electoral Districts into which Australia (excluding the Northern Territory) is divided. Within each electorate ten names, representing ten starting addresses, were selected from the Electoral Roll, and interviewers were instructed to call at the starting address and at every adjoining dwelling until ten interviews with a male worker twenty-one years of age or older (or his wife) had been conducted. Only one interview was conducted in any one dwelling, and 1,925 interviews were completed in the 2,319 'eligible' dwellings contacted, giving an overall response rate of 83 %. The main causes of non-response were refusals (10 % of the total contacted), and insufficient English among recent immigrants (4 %).

The only control in selecting our sample, apart from age and workforce status, was geographical location according to State of residence and metropolitan/urban/rural location within States. Compared with the distribution of the adult male workforce at the 1961 Census, the geographical representativeness of the sample was good: 56·2 % of respondents lived in metropolitan areas, 27·0 % in other urban areas, and 16·8 % in rural areas. The metropolitan percentage differs hardly at all from the census percentage (56·8 %), but there was a slight over-

---

[1] We are indebted to Professor J. Nalson, then of the University of Western Australia, for assistance in interviewing in rural Western Australia.

representation of 'other urban' (a census percentage of 24·3 %) balanced by some under-representation in rural areas. So far as States were concerned, Victoria was slightly under-represented (26·1 % compared with a 1961 Census figure of 28·5 %), but no other State differed from the census by more than 1 %. The mean deviation for the six States and the Australian Capital Territory was 0·9 %.

A final statement concerning the representativeness of our sample must await the publication of the 1966 Census results. However, preliminary comparisons with the 1961 Census suggest that some under-representation occurred among younger workers (under 30 years of age), the foreign-born (both through inability to speak English and the use of Electoral Rolls as an initial sampling frame), and the lower occupational grades, where young workers and the foreign-born tend to be over-represented. No corrections of our data have yet been attempted, but when the 1966 Census data become available and more precise estimates of the degree of bias can be made, some form of weighting may be considered. However, while any bias may affect the extent to which our present findings can be generalized to the Australian population, it is unlikely to have any marked effect on the internal analysis attempted in this paper.

SUBJECTIVE SOCIAL CLASS

Although Australia is widely regarded as an equalitarian society, the present survey, like others before it, found that most Australians are not only familiar with the terminology of social class but use the concept of class in their descriptions of Australia's social structure. Thus 81 % of our sample thought there were social classes in Australia, 12 % though there were not, and 7 % were uncertain. Moreover, when each person was asked to place himself in a social class, 80 % of the sample used terms like upper, middle, working, or lower class.

Mindful of the work of Richard Centers[1] and others on the sensitivity of class responses to the form of the inquiry, we structured our social class question so that the respondent was given both an open and forced-choice question on his subjective class identification. The precise wording of our questions was as follows:

11a Some people say there are social classes in this   ARE
     country. Do you think there *are*—or are *not*—   ARE NOT
     social classes in Australia?   UNCERTAIN

11b Why do you think that?

---

[1] Richard Centers, *The Psychology of Social Classes* (Princeton, 1949); see also Richard F. Hamilton, 'Reply to Tucker', *American Sociological Review*, vol. 31, no. 6 (December 1966), p. 856.

11c (If there are social classes) to which class would
      you say you belong?

11d Here (HAND *YELLOW* CARD) are the   UPPER   Go to 12
      names some people use for social classes. MIDDLE   Ask *e*
      If you *had* to say which of *those* social LOWER
      classes you belong to, what would you   WORKING
      say?   OTHER   Go to 12
                                               NO ANSWER

11e If *MIDDLE*: Would you say you're in the   UPPER MIDDLE
      upper middle, or *lower* middle?   MIDDLE
      CIRCLE 1 IF ANSWER IS "JUST MIDDLE"   LOWER MIDDLE.

Thus, after introducing the subject of the existence of social classes in
Australia, we gave the respondent an opportunity to offer reasons for his
opinion. Then, if he thought there were social classes, or was uncertain,
he was asked to what class he belonged. If he thought there were not
social classes in Australia, then he was asked to class himself on the
supposition that there were. It is important to note that in Question 11c
no pressure was put on the respondent to class himself. Yet three out of
four of those who said there were not social classes in Australia in fact
gave a class identification in response to this question. This finding
suggests an interesting area for research into the emotional commitment
of respondents to their views of class phenomena, an area which cannot
be far investigated with the data at hand.

In Question 11d, however, some pressure towards response was
applied, for in addition the respondent was asked to use a fixed list of
class labels in identifying his own class position. Following Kahl and
Davis,[1] we also probed middle-class respondents as to whether they saw
themselves as upper middle, lower middle, or 'just middle'.

The responses to the open-ended question on class identification are
of particular interest when tabulated in relation to the closed ballot.
As table 1 shows, most repondents saw themselves as members of one of
two classes, the middle class or the working class. Looking across the
rows of table 1, we see that 806 persons (42 %) volunteered a middle-
class identification, and 647 persons (34 %) a working-class identification. The next largest group, 237 persons (12 %), consisted mainly of
those who declined to class themselves and a small number of persons
who gave an idiosyncratic response. Comparatively few respondents
volunteered class identifications of upper, upper middle, lower middle,
or lower, and some described themselves simply as 'average' or 'same
as most'.

[1] Joseph A. Kahl and James A. Davis, 'A comparison of indexes of socio-economic status',
American Sociological Review, vol. 20 (June 1955), p. 324.

Table 1. *Subjective social class identification: A comparison of responses to the open and closed questions (percentages)*

Subjective Social Class (open question)	Subjective Social Class (closed question)								
	Upper	Upper middle	Middle	Lower Middle	Work- ing	Lower	No reply	Total	N
Upper	67	17	17	—	—	—	—	101	6
Better, best people	0	36	36	0	18	—	9	99	11
Upper middle	6	89	6	0	—	—	—	101	18
Middle	0	17	52	18	10	2	0	99	806
Average	—	5	24	15	50	2	5	101	110
Lower middle	—	0	0	69	12	19	—	100	16
Working	0	2	3	2	89	3	0	99	647
Lower	—	0	2	4	45	49	—	100	55
Poorest, lowest	—	0	0	0	89	11	—	100	19
Other (inc. no answer)	1	8	25	8	41	1	16	100	237
Total	1	10	28	11	44	4	2	100	1925

The columns of table 1 give the distribution of combined responses to Questions 11*d* and 11*e*. It is interesting to note that the non-response rate dropped from 12 to 2 %, reflecting the slightly more insistent tone of the closed question. Sixteen per cent of those who did not reply (to Question 11*c*) persisted with their non-response but the remainder distributed themselves mainly into the middle and working classes. Again a two-class system emerges, with 49 % replying middle class and 44 % working class. After probing, a little over half of the middle class maintained a middle-class response, and the remainder split evenly between upper and lower middle. A small number of respondents put themselves into the lower class, but very few saw themselves as members of an upper class. Some of these 'upper' class responses were so anomalous as to suggest that this is virtually an empty category.[1]

How do the results of this survey compare with previous Australian studies and with studies in other countries? Comparisons are difficult to make, not only because different surveys have used different forms of enquiry, but also because a national survey must be expected to give different results from a community study. Any comparison of our results must therefore be with other national surveys, and with surveys which

---

[1] As Table 3 below shows, a number of 'upper class' respondents were in the lower occupational grades. Interestingly enough, most of the clearly anomalous replies came from persons living in small towns or rural areas, suggesting that the local frame of reference dominated their class identification. The two 'upper class' miners, for example, lived in small mining towns and may well have been located in the highest local stratum. One respondent appears to have given an 'upper class' response in protest against the question. However, the number of cases is small and we have accepted these responses as given without attempting to impose an artificial consistency upon them.

employed a similar form of enquiry. So far as Australia is concerned nationwide data on social class identification were provided by a Gallup Poll conducted in December 1961, which gave the following results:

Social Class	%
Upper	0·4
Upper middle	5·2
Middle	42·5
Lower middle	11·6
Working	37·0
Don't know	3·3
Total	100·0
N	1,652

Although the wording of the question asked in this poll was similar to our Question 11d, the fixed alternatives offered to respondents differed. The term 'lower class' was not used, but instead 'working class' appeared at the bottom of a list of differentiated 'middle classes'. This change probably accounts for the fact that this 1961 poll gave a lower working-class response than our 1965 survey (37 and 44 % respectively). There is certainly no evidence that the Australian population has become less middle class since 1961.[1]

Compared with other industrialized countries the middle-class component of the Australian population seems very high. In our study, for example, 'middle class' was the most popular class identification, and for every 100 middle-class respondents there were only 90 working-class respondents. But in both the United Kingdom and the United States, while essentially the same two-class system emerges, the relative size of the working class seems to be much higher. In a recent national survey in Britain working-class respondents outnumbered middle-class respondents by more than 2 to 1 (67 and 32 % respectively), and the 1964 Election Study conducted by the Survey Research Centre of the University of Michigan returned percentages of 56 % for working class but only 39 % for middle class.[2] These differences in subjective class

[1] Hamilton (loc. cit.) suggests that differences in class identifications among his sample and those reported by Tucker are due to a different choice of class labels. Tucker offered six classes, including lower middle, middle, and upper middle, and obtained a higher proportion of middle-class responses in selected occupational groups. See Charles Wright Tucker, Jr., 'On working-class identification', American Sociological Review, vol. 31, no. 6 (December 1966), pp. 585–6.

[2] The British figures are taken from Michael Kahan, David Butler, and Donald Stokes, 'On the analytical division of social class', British Journal of Sociology, vol. 17, no. 2 (June 1966), pp. 122–32. We are indebted to Mr Kahan for providing the American figures.

identification do not seem explicable in terms of differences in occupational structure between these three countries, or in terms of sample bias,[1] but more likely reflect real differences in the functions of and conceptions about social class in each of these three countries. The fact that Australia emerges as the most middle-class nation among the three considered would seem to cut across commonly offered views of Australian society. Whatever may have been the truth of the Australian legend which saw nineteenth- and early twentieth-century Australia as a working man's paradise free of the class distinctions of the old world, contemporary Australia is seen by its inhabitants as a predominantly middle-class society. It may well still be true that class differences and class consciousness are less important in Australia than in some other countries, but this is not a question on which our survey provides direct evidence. However, it is worth pointing out that a number of respondents, while agreeing that there were social classes in Australia, volunteered the qualification that class differences were less noticeable in Australia than elsewhere.

Industrial societies are stratified along multiple dimensions of social differentiation and not according to subjective social class alone. In contemporary Australia the most salient of these other dimensions are probably income, occupation, education, and ethnicity. In our sample, however, the number of persons of non-British stock is too small to sustain detailed stratification analysis, and we intend in subsequent reports to approach the question of ethnic stratification mainly through census data relating birthplace to occupation and education.

Granted that individuals can be located along several rank scales, a number of questions naturally arise, the most important of which are how far subjective class position can be seen as a function of a person's differential location along other scales, the extent to which the different scales reinforce one another, how consistent an individual's different statuses are, and what are the behavioural correlates of the major strata that can be identified. In this paper we concentrate our attention on the first two questions but indicate the lines along which our analysis will be extended into other areas.

Tables 2 through 4 show the subjective social class composition of categories of personal income, occupation, and education. For simpli-

---

[1] Such differences in occupational structure as do exist would tend if anything to *increase* the working-class proportion. See Mayer, *op. cit.* p. 450, and Abdelmegid M. Farrag, 'The occupational structure of the labour force: Patterns and trends in selected countries', *Population Studies*, vol. 18 (July 1964), pp. 17–34. Sample bias, on the other hand, towards under-representation among semi-skilled and unskilled workers would tend to increase the middle-class proportion. Although the proportion responding 'middle class' in our sample may require a downward revision when 1966 Census figures are available and a correction for bias is made, this proportion will undoubtedly still be high by comparison with the U.S.A. and the U.K.

city of presentation those who did not reply to the closed question on subjective social class or more than one of the objective measures of social stratification have been excluded, reducing the number of cases to 1,877.[1]

INCOME

To the surprise of experienced observers of the Australian scene, little resistance was met to the question on income. In fact, the non-response rate for income (1·8%) was slightly lower than for subjective social class. Respondents were asked to choose from six lettered categories ranging from less than $1,800 per annum to $5,000 or more.[2]

6a   Here (HAND *WHITE* CARD) are some *income groups*.   A
     Would you please say the letter at the end of   B
     the line which includes your (*husband's*) total   C
     income last year—that is, *before* any deductions.   D
     CIRCLE FIGURE AFTER LETTER NAMED.   E
                                                              F
                                                              Don't know

In determining these income categories, two considerations were uppermost. Firstly, only a limited number of categories could be used, to avoid confusing the respondents or suggesting that we were prying unduly into their private affairs. Secondly, it was essential that the categories selected covered as wide a range of incomes as possible but were still sufficiently narrow to measure meaningful gradations. Thus, we decided to use six categories of income, and took as our first category incomes of less than $1,800, which was about $200 above the Commonwealth basic wage for adult males in the six State capitals. Using a uniform class interval of $800, we derived six income categories ranging from less than $1,800 per annum to $5,000 or more. A general comparison can be made between the results of our survey and recent taxation figures.

These two sets of figures fit together well, the only noticeable discrepancies occurring in the three higher income categories. These small discrepancies will presumably be less apparent when figures closer to the year in which our survey was conducted are available.

---

[1] In order to keep our sample as large as possible, we estimated the income group of 31 respondents who had replied to all four other questions on social rank from the multiple regression equation between income, occupation and interviewer's assessment, and the education category of 7 respondents from the multiple regression equation between education, occupation, and interviewer's assessment. In no case, however, were estimations carried out for subjective social class or for respondents who had not replied to two or more of the questions on social rank. Information on occupation and interviewer's assessment was available for all respondents.

[2] The income question was asked in pounds, before the conversion to decimal currency.

Grade of actual income ($A)	Resident Male Taxpayer. Income Year 1963–64*	A.N.U. Survey 1965
1600–1799	5·8	5·9
1800–2599	39·1	39·1
2600–3399	28·3	24·9
3400–4999	17·7	18·4
5000 or more	9·2	11·7
Total	100·1	100·0
N	2,580,845	1,190

Source: Australia, Taxation Branch, *Taxation Statistics 1964–65*, pp. 23–4.

Table 2 suggests a close association between subjective social class identification and income level. The lowest income groups have the highest proportions of working-class members, and as income rises so the proportion of those identifying as middle or upper middle class rises. However, while this trend is quite marked, it is important to note that about one-sixth of those in the highest income group saw themselves as working or lower class, and just over a quarter of those in the lowest income group saw themselves as middle class. Computing a simple correlation between the two scales, we derive a coefficient of $+0·37$. Thus, differences in income at best explain only part of the variation in subjective class identification and other factors (including age and social mobility as well as those discussed below) obviously require investigation. However, it should be emphasized that although the size of this and other coefficients reported in this paper may seem rather low, in fact they compare closely with similar measures derived from national data for the United States and Great Britain.[1] The trends which emerge from tables presented here seem quite strongly marked, but because most respondents are concentrated in only a few cells frequencies in other cells are quite low, and the correlation tends to be dominated by the higher frequencies.

[1] For example, the correlation between income and occupation in the United States calculated from recent statistics was $+0·38$ (six categories of income and six grades of education were used with data taken from *Statistical Abstracts of the U.S.A., 1963* (Washington, D.C.), table 156); and between subjective social class and occupation in Great Britain $+0·50$ (data taken from Kahan, Butler and Stokes, *loc. cit.*). All correlations reported in this paper are Pearsonian product-moment coefficients, using scores of 1 to 6 for subjective social class, income and education, 1 to 16 for occupation, and 1 to 4 for interviewer's assessment.

Table 2.   *Subjective social class by grade of personal income (percentages)*

Subjective social class	Grade of personal income						Total
	$5,000 +	$4,200– 4,999	$3,400– 4,199	$2,600– 3,399	$1,800– 2,599	Less than $1,800	
Upper	0	—	0	1	1	—	0
Upper middle	32	21	14	7	5	3	11
Middle	41	43	34	34	19	17	29
Lower middle	8	16	18	12	10	8	11
Working	16	15	29	42	63	68	45
Lower	3	5	4	4	3	4	4
Total	100	100	99	100	101	100	100
N	212	122	233	471	727	112	1877

OCCUPATION

Incomes fall into a natural scale. Occupations, on the other hand, form a scale only to the extent that they are evaluated hierarchically in terms of prestige (or other criteria) by the members of a given society. In the present study an occupational scale could have been derived in a number of different ways; for example, by ranking occupations from high to low in terms of the median subjective social-class identification, income, or education of their occupants.[1] However, such a scale would not have been technically independent of these other factors, and would have prevented us from analysing the degree of fit between occupation and other measures of social rank. We therefore developed an independent occupational scale in a series of stages. The first stage, which involved grouping the 342 occupational titles used in the 1961 Census of Australia into 100 groups, has been reported elsewhere.[2] In the second stage, these 100 occupational groups were condensed into sixteen broad categories, the main criterion being that jobs so grouped involved the same skill or skill-type. Wherever possible, meaningful industrial distinctions were maintained. Finally, these sixteen categories were ordered to form a prestige hierarchy, using the 1947 and 1963 NORC studies[3] of occupational prestige in the United States and Congalton's findings for Australia.[4]

[1] This is the general procedure employed by the U.S. Bureau of Census. United States, Bureau of the Census, *Methodology and Scores of Socioeconomic Status* (Working Paper no. 15) (Washington, D.C., 1963), p. 4.
[2] Leonard Broom, F. Lancaster Jones, and Jerzy Zubrzycki, 'An occupational classification of the Australian workforce', *The Australian and New Zealand Journal of Sociology*, vol. 1, no. 2 (October 1965), Supplement.
[3] Reproduced in Thomas E. Lasswell, *Class and Stratum: An Introduction to Concepts and Research*, (Boston 1965), pp. 428–32.
[4] Congalton, *op. cit.*

Table 3. *Subjective social class by occupation (percentages)*

	Occupation	Subjective social class: Upper	Upper middle	Middle	Lower middle	Working	Lower	Total	N
I	1. Upper professional	2	28	48	13	8	1	100	100
I	2. Graziers, wheat and sheep farmers	—	27	46	14	10	3	100	63
I	3. Lower professional	—	23	36	19	20	3	101	70
II	4. Managerial	—	16	42	13	26	3	100	219
II	5. Self-employed shop proprietors	—	16	44	12	24	4	100	25
II	6. Other farmers	1	10	35	8	40	7	101	141
III	7. Clerical and related workers	1	15	37	14	27	6	100	226
III	8. Members of Armed Services and Police Force	—	21	26	—	42	11	100	19
IV	9. Craftsmen and foremen	—	5	22	12	57	4	100	422
V	10. Shop assistants	—	8	29	13	48	2	100	48
V	11. Operatives and process workers	1	5	19	6	65	4	100	178
V	12. Drivers	—	5	12	8	74	1	100	129
VI	13. Personal, domestic and other service workers	1	5	18	15	58	3	100	76
VI	14. Miners	11	—	11	—	72	6	100	18
VI	15. Farm and rural workers	—	6	19	6	67	3	101	36
VI	16. Labourers	1	2	14	8	72	3	100	107
	Total	0	11	29	11	45	4	100	1877

Table 3 shows the sixteen point occupational scale (Arabic numerals) and a shorter six-point scale (Roman numerals) designed for more general analysis. The scale can also be conveniently dichotomized between groups 8 and 9, to give a non-manual/manual split. In evaluating the scale, it should be emphasized that a major limiting factor was the decision to base our groups on the Australian census classification. In doing so we balanced the limitation that occupations as stated in national censuses may not uniformly report meaningful prestige gradations against the gain in generality and utility obtained by being compatible with the major source of national social statistics in Australia. The fact that the occupational scale, either in the long or short form, correlates better with our other measures of social rank than education (which like income forms a natural scale), suggests that it is a valid measuring instrument.

Looking again mainly at the upper middle class and working and lower class columns we find a fairly consistent trend. The percentage identifying as upper middle class is highest among upper professionals and lowest among miners and labourers. This percentage falls as we move down the occupational scale and the few reversals which do occur are not surprising, given the detail of this tabulation. Farmers see themselves as less middle class than clerical workers, and shop assistants as more middle class than craftsmen or operatives. However, the difference in class identification between clerical workers and shop assistants is very marked, with close to one half the latter identifying as working class compared with only one quarter of clerical workers. This marked difference, together with a relatively low prestige of shop assistants in Australia, would seem to support our low ranking of shop assistants compared with their position on some occupational scales.[1] Another interesting feature of the scale is that, apart from the very small and heterogeneous eighth group, those above craftsmen see themselves predominantly as middle class whereas those below and including craftsmen see themselves predominantly as working or lower class. Even so, however, fully 39 % of craftsmen and foremen put themselves into the middle class. This figure is very much higher than those reported in recent American and British studies,[2] and suggests that the absorption of skilled workers into the middle class may have proceeded more rapidly in Australia than in these other countries.[3] The overall relationship between subjective social class and occupation, as measured from the data of Table 3, is $+0\cdot36$, which is only slightly lower than that found between class and income. The use of the shorter, six-point occupational scale has virtually no effect on the magnitude of this correlation, the coefficient being $+0\cdot35$.

EDUCATION

In measuring differences in education we were confronted with the problem of how to divide an array that has natural breaks signifying levels of skill. Although it would have been more convenient statistically to collect educational data by single years of schooling, a gain in reliability and meaning was obtained by calling for responses in the functionally pertinent categories reported in table 4. The breaks in the

[1] An interesting finding reported by Oeser and Hammond (*op. cit.* pp. 279–80) is that whereas most working-class identifiers claimed both shop assistants and office workers as working class, most middle-class identifiers (81 %) saw office workers as middle class but fewer than half of them (45 %) included shop assistants in the middle class.

[2] Richard F. Hamilton, 'The marginal middle class: A reconsideration', *American Sociological Review*, vol. 31, no. 2 (April 1966), pp. 192–9; and Kahan, Butler and Stokes, *loc. cit.*

[3] For recent comparative material see Gavin Mackenzie, 'The economic dimensions of embourgoisement', *British Journal of Sociology*, vol. 18, no. 1 (March 1967), pp. 29–44; John H. Goldthorpe and David Lockwood, 'Affluence and the British class structure', *Sociological Review*, new series, vol. 4 (1963), pp. 133–63.

Table 4. *Subjective social class by education (percentages)*

	Education						
Subjective social class	Completed technical or university	Some technical or university	Completed secondary	Some secondary and trade certificate	Completed primary	Some primary	Total
Upper	2	3	0	0	0	—	0
Upper middle	32	12	18	7	6	5	11
Middle	43	49	34	28	21	13	29
Lower middle	12	12	13	12	10	4	11
Working	10	21	30	49	60	75	45
Lower	1	3	5	4	4	3	4
Total	100	100	100	100	101	100	100
N	169	81	212	869	428	118	1877

distribution are not statistical artefacts but are consequential for the allocation of manpower and *pari passu* financial rewards. Since our survey, a question on education has been asked for the first time in an Australian census (June 1966), and this will allow detailed comparison between our results and those of the census when these become available. The first point of interest about table 4 is that the majority of our sample (1081, or 58%) ceased education during or at the end of secondary schooling. Only about one in eight (13%) had begun or completed tertiary education, and more than one in four (29%) had no more than primary education. The concentration of respondents in our sample in the primary and secondary levels of education has considerable implications for the role of education as a stratifying variable in Australian society, and although table 4 suggests a close relationship between subjective social class and educational attainment, the small frequencies at higher educational levels means that the measured correlation ($+0.35$) between these two variables is not as high as might be expected. As the number of persons with tertiary education increases, the differentiating impact of education in Australia's stratification system will become increasingly marked.[1]

[1] The proportion of persons aged 17 to 22 proceeding to tertiary education doubled from 6% to 12% between 1947 and 1963, and is estimated to rise to 18% by 1975. *Tertiary Education in Australia: Report of the Committee on the Future of Tertiary Education in Australia* (Chairman, Sir Lesley Martin) (Melbourne: Government Printer, 1964–65), vol. I, p. 34.

Table 5.   *Subjective social class by interviewer's assessment of
economic classification (percentages)*

Subjective social class	Interviewer's assessment				Total
	Well-to-do	Better-off	Artisans, clerks, etc.	Lowest income	
Upper	3	1	0	1	0
Upper middle	50	19	4	4	11
Middle	37	42	23	10	29
Lower middle	6	14	11	8	11
Working	4	21	58	73	45
Lower	—	3	4	5	4
Total	100	100	100	101	100
N	70	586	1067	154	1877

INTERVIEWER'S ASSESSMENT

The fifth measure of social rank used in our survey was the interviewer's
assessment of the 'economic class' of the respondent, a standard item of
information provided by Australian Gallup Poll (A.G.P.) interviewers
based upon an evaluation of occupation, possession of telephone and
private motorcar, home, apparent education, and demeanour. We
modified these instructions and interviewers were told to consider income as well, a question not ordinarily asked by A.G.P. From one standpoint the decision to augment instructions was correct. This additional
objective criterion was congruent with those customarily used and probably improved the validity and reliability of this measure. However,
from one methodological viewpoint the decision was incorrect, in that
the interviewer's assessment was contaminated, but in a way not dis-
coverable, by the fact that he was instructed to combine consciously
indicators used as separate measures in our analysis. Therefore, in the
analysis of the interrelationships among our five measures of social rank
we cannot assume the technical independence of this measure.

Table 5 gives the subjective social-class composition of the four
economic classes into which respondents were grouped by the interviewers. Over half the sample (57%) were placed in one category
(artisans, clerks, etc.), and most of those in this category saw themselves
as working or lower class. Clearly the fit between subjective social class
and interviewer's assessment is quite good, with 90% of those in the
highest economic class seeing themselves as upper, upper middle, or
middle class, and 86% of those in the lowest group identifying as

lower middle, working, or lower class. But again the relatively small frequencies in the highest and lowest groups results in only a moderately strong correlation between the two series ($+0.43$).

INTERRELATIONSHIPS OF THE FIVE MEASURES

The preceding tables have been restricted to the relationship of subjective social class to four other measures of social rank—income, occupation, education, and interviewer's assessment of economic class. Obviously it would be both interesting and important to investigate the relationships among all these variables. This has been done, but for reasons of space we present only a summary table showing the degree of relationship between each pair of variables, but not the bivariate distributions from which they have been derived. In all cases the scales are the same as shown in tables 2 through 5: six-point scales for subjective social class, income, and education, a sixteen-point scale for occupation, and a four-point scale for interviewer's assessment.

A number of comments can be made about the simple correlations given in table 6. The first is that all are in the expected direction, and high social rank on one scale tends to be associated with high social rank on the others. All, moreover, are significantly different from zero at the 0.1% level of statistical significance. However, none can be described as strong, and only three of the ten approach or exceed 0.50. Nevertheless, as we have indicated above the magnitude of these coefficients compares closely with those obtained for other countries. Taking in turn subjective social class and interviewer's assessment as dependent variables, and income, occupation, and education as independent variables, it is interesting that whereas the respondent's self-assessment is about as strongly related to each of these three independent measures, the interviewer's assessment is more highly related to income and occupation than to education. Although the two subjective measures of social rank cannot be regarded as equivalent, interviewers and respondents seem to differ in their evaluation of the importance of the objective criteria of income, occupation, and education as determinants of social rank. Whether this simply means that interviewers were overly influenced by income (as our instructions may have suggested), or whether it reflects a differential weighting of these criteria when evaluating one's own class position than when estimating the class position of another person, it is difficult to say.

The pattern of intercorrelations of table 6 indicates that all five measures of social rank throw significant light on Australia's stratification system. Yet no single measure is sufficiently discriminating to warrant treatment as a criterion variable. It would in principle be open

Table 6. *Correlation coefficients between five measures of social rank*

Measure	Correlation coefficients				
	1	2	3	4	5
1. Subjective social class		0·37	0·36	0·35	0·43
2. Income			0·51	0·33	0·59
3. Occupation				0·41	0·49
4. Education					0·31
5. Interviewer's assessment					

to us to take subjective social class as the key measure, and to examine to what extent income, occupation, and education can be used to predict subjective class position. In fact the multiple correlation between subjective social class and these three objective measures was only $+0·46$. The regression coefficients[1] indicated that relative to their scales each of these three independent variables made about equal contribution to subjective social class position. This result is confirmed by the fact that a socio-economic status score calculated simply by summing the scores for each respondent on income, occupation (using the short six-point scale), and education yielded a simple correlation of $+0·46$ with subjective social class, a figure identical with the multiple correlation reported above. But a correlation of this magnitude, while higher than those recorded in the first row of Table 6, is hardly high enough to warrant our taking subjective social class as a criterion variable.

THE INDEX OF SOCIAL RANK

A more useful approach to the analysis of Australia's system of social stratification is to regard each of these five measures of social rank as contributing *some* information about a given individual's position in the national stratification system, and to treat them as a set of interdependent variables whose joint effect determines an individual's social rank position. The adoption of a multivariate model leads naturally to the application of factor analytic methods, and in this study the related but mathematically more direct method of principal components analysis has been applied to the correlation matrix shown in table 6. The nature

---

[1] The regression equation was x_1 (SSC) $= 1·57 + 0·18\, x_2$ (INC) $+ 0·05\, x_3$ (OCC) $+ 0·20\, x_4$ (ED). It is important to bear in mind the different 'shapes' of each distribution and the fact that the occupation scores range from 1 to 16 whereas the other scores range from only 1 to 6.

of our research problem and the construction of our measures led us to postulate a general factor, identified here as the Index of Social Rank. Consequently we are concerned only with the first principal component, which in this instance accounts for 54 % of the variance among the original five measures and has the following factor coefficients:

Primary variable	Index of Social Rank factor coefficients
Subjective social class	0·67
Income	0·78
Occupation	0·77
Education	0·63
Interviewer's assessment	0·79

These factor coefficients indicate the relative importance of each primary variable to the derived construct of social rank and by applying them to the original observations for each individual (expressed in standardized form) a new series of summary scores can be obtained. Since these scores for the Index of Social Rank are based on an empirically derived composite measure, they have much higher correlations with the primary measures of social rank, approximating the factor coefficients shown above. Thus, the Index of Social Rank correlates +0·67 with subjective social class, +0·78 with income, +0·77 with occupation, and so on. In short, the constructed Index of Social Rank provides a much more powerful measure of social rank position than any single primary measure.[1]

The logic of the above procedure owes much to the work of Hollingshead and his colleagues, and their Index of Social Position.[2] Some differences should, however, be noted. The first, and possibly most important, is that the Index of Social Position does not utilize subjective measures but is restricted to three objective measures—education, occupation, and area of residence. Two researchers then estimated the class position of each respondent in one of five social classes, and subsequently applied regression analysis to determine the relative weight of each of the three above measures in their estimate of class position. Estimated class could thus be used as a criterion variable in a way not

---

[1] A clear account of the method of principal components analysis can be found in C. A. Moser and Wolf Scott, *British Towns: A Statistical Study of their Social and Economic Differences* (London, 1961).

[2] August B. Hollingshead and Friedrich C. Redlich, *Social Class and Mental Illness* (New York, 1958), especially Appendix 2. Other composite measures of social class have been employed by Warner and his associates: W. Lloyd Warner, Marcia Meeker, and Kenneth Eells, *Social Class in America: A Manual of Procedure for the Measurement of Social Status* (New York 1949).

applicable to the present study. If we were to restrict our attention to objective measures only, then the results of our survey suggest that equal weight should be given to income, occupation and education, and that a simple socio-economic status score (with values ranging from a low of three to a high of eighteen points) should be constructed from six-point scales for each measure. In our study these individual socio-economic status scores correlate with scores on the Index of Social Rank at the level of +0·93, indicating a very close fit between the two series. Secondly, being concerned with a local rather than a national study, Hollingshead and his colleagues were dealing with a more determinate class structure, obtained higher correlations, and selected somewhat different measures. Area of residence is clearly inappropriate in a national study covering large cities, small towns and rural villages. Despite these differences, however, strong similarities between the two Indexes remain, in particular the general procedure of deriving by empirical multivariate techniques a composite measure of social rank position.

Following Hollingshead we have employed our Index of Social Rank to derive an initial stratification of Australian society. If meaningful social strata do exist, in the sense that certain patterns of scores and associated levels of social rank position occur more frequently than others, then it should be possible to determine what these major strata are by examining the distribution of individual scores on the Index of Social Rank. In the present study these scores ranged from 10 (low social rank) to 150 (high social rank),[1] and in order to derive an initial grouping they were successively dichotomized using the logic of analysis of variance. First, all 1877 individual scores were ranked from the highest to the lowest. A breakpoint in the array was then sought which would so dichotomize the series that the within-groups variance of the two groups would be at a minimum and the between-groups variance at a maximum. This breakpoint gave the first dichotomy, that is the 'best' two groups. This strategy was applied in turn to each of these two groups, to yield four groups, and again to these groups to yield eight groups.[2]

---

[1] In fact, since standardized observations are used to calculate component scores, their values range from low negative to high positive values with a mean of zero. To obtain an all-positive series for easier statistical manipulation this series was scaled to give the range reported in the paper.

[2] See F. Lancaster Jones, 'A social ranking of Melbourne suburbs', *The Australian and New Zealand Journal of Sociology*, vol. 3, no. 2 (October 1967), pp. 93–110. The method achieves what Hollingshead and Redlich (*op. cit.* pp. 392–3) set out to achieve by inspection of scale scores and consistency patterns. We have not at this point considered consistency patterns in determining strata but prefer to examine consistency, or lack of it, as a characteristic rather than as a determinant of social strata. It is possible, for example, that some strata are characterized by status inconsistency.

Current analysis is designed to test the sociological significance of these eight groups, or social strata, by examining the internal composition and status consistency of each strata,[1] their behavioural correlates, and the nature of the differences between strata. In this way we hope to be able to answer such questions as how many social strata are required to analyse meaningfully social stratification in Australia, and how 'real' they are in terms of their behavioural and attitudinal correlates.

[1] The general lines along which our analysis of status consistency will proceed has been indicated elsewhere. Leonard Broom, 'Social differentiation and stratification', in Robert K. Merton, Leonard Broom, and Leonard S. Cottrell, Jr., *Sociology Today: Problems and Prospects* (New York: Basic Books Inc., 1959). For further applications of this concept, see Elton F. Jackson, 'Status consistency and symptoms of stress', *American Sociological Review*, vol. 27 (August 1962), pp. 469–80; and Elton F. Jackson and Peter J. Burke, 'Status and symptoms of stress: Additive and interactive effects', *American Sociological Review*, vol. 30 (August 1965), pp. 556–64. Some methodological problems are discussed by Hubert M. Blalock, 'The identification problem and theory building: The case of status inconsistency', *American Sociological Review*, vol. 31 (February 1966), pp. 52–61; and Martin D. Hyman, 'Determining the effects of status inconsistency', *Public Opinion Quarterly*, vol. 30 (Spring 1966), pp. 120–9.

INDEX

Abel-Smith, B., 7, 8
Abrams, Mark, 11, 12
Adams, Francis, 213
Africa, 8
Alford, Robert R., 214
alienation, 19, 123, 124, 149, 156,
 159, 173, 174
Allardt, Erik, 10, 18 n.
Allingham, John D., 214 n.
American Dream, 212
Andrzejewski, Stanislaw, 39 n.
Aristotle, 20, 21, 48
Australia, 13, 118, 212–233

Bahrdt, H. P., 170 n.
Bailey, F. K., 82 n.
Balazs, E., 82 n., 88 n., 91 n.
Barber, B., 82 n., 96 n.
Barber, E. G., 82 n., 96 n.
Barcan, Allan, 213 n., 215 n.
Bassett, G. W., 215 n.
Beloff, M., 81 n., 82 n., 84 n.,
 85 n.
Bendix, R., 6, 62 n.
Berger, P., 4 n.
Beteille, A., 82 n.
Blalock, H. M., 190 n., 233 n.
Blauner, Robert, 156, 159
Bloch, Marc, 47, 99
Blum, J., 82 n., 85 n.
Blunt, E. A. H., 82 n.
Boas, F., 30
Bodde, D., 82 n.
Bollen, J. D., 213 n.
Booth, C., 133, 134
Bowley, J., 134
Brady, E. J., 213
Brazil, 47
Britain (incl. England, United King-
 dom), 3, 7, 8, 12, 13, 120, 140, 142,
 215, 220, 221 n., 223
Broom, L., 9, 12, 178 n., 179 n., 215 n.,
 224 n., 233 n.
Buchanan, William, 214 n.
Buckley, William, 6
bureaucracy, 26, 55, 87, 90
Burke, Peter J., 233 n.

Burns, Creighton, 215 n.
Butler, David, 220 n., 223 n., 226 n.

Camus, Albert, 200
Canada, 7, 118
Canetti, Elias, 31 n.
Cantril, Hadley, 214 n.
Cartwright, Dorwin, 32 n.
caste, 27, 40, 44, 46, 47, 51, 56, 62, 72,
 77, 92–5, 97
Centers, Richard, 217
Childe, V. G., 212, 213 n.
China, 11, 57, 76, 77, 82, 87, 88, 89, 90,
 91, 99
Clark, G., 82 n.
class, 1, 2, 4, 9, 11, 25–61, 62, 72, 75, 102,
 106, 130, 137–42, 145, 146, 170, 176,
 177, 180, 203, 204, 213, 214, 215, 217,
 220–31
class consciousness, 6, 28, 84, 127, 128 n.,
 149, 174
Coghlan, T. A., 213
Cohen, B. S., 95 n.
Congalton, Athol A., 214, 224
consumer behaviour, 133
Cottrell, L. S., 178 n., 233 n.
Coulborn, R., 82 n.
Crawford, R. M., 212 n.

D'Aeth, F. G., 133, 134
Dahl, Robert A., 50 n.
Dahrendorf, Ralf, 6, 14, 15, 16, 24, 28 n.,
 39 n.
Dandekar, V. M., 104 n.
Davies, A. F., 212 n., 214, 215 n.
Davis, James A., 55 n., 218 n.
Davis, Kingsley, 5, 6, 45 n., 62 n.
de Bary, W. T., 88 n.
deference, 1, 2, 12, 29, 63, 64, 65, 67, 68,
 69, 104–32
Deutsch, Karl W., 50 n.
division of labour, 2, 6, 11, 62, 94
Dore, R. P., 8
Dufty, N. F., 215 n.
Dumont, L., 82 n., 92 n.
Duncan, O. D., 3 n., 55 n.
Durkheim, Émile, 18, 19